Law & Science

A selected bibliography

Compiled by Morris L. Cohen, Naomi Ronen,
and Jan Stepan

Edited by Vivien B. Shelanski
and Marcel C. La Follette

The MIT Press

Cambridge, Massachusetts, and London, England

First MIT Press edition 1980

Printed and bound in the United States of America

This bibliography was prepared and produced under the auspices of
Science, Technology, & Human Values, a quarterly journal devoted to
discussion of the ethical and social dimensions of science and technology. Science, Technology, & Human Values is sponsored by the John
F. Kennedy School of Government at Harvard University, and the Program
in Science, Technology and Society at M.I.T., and is published by the
M I T Press.

Library of Congress Cataloging in Publication Data

Cohen, Morris L.   1927-
    Law & science

    Includes index.
    1. Science and law--Bibliography.
2. Technology and law--Bibliography. 3. Science
and state--Bibliography. 4. Technology and state
--Bibliography. I. Ronen, Naomi, joint author.
II. Stepan, Jan, joint author. III. Shelanski,
Vivien B. IV. La Follette, Marcel Chotkowski.
V. Title.
K487.S3A13   016.34409'5   79-26107
ISBN 0-262-03073-X

Contents

iv

Preface

In the last few decades, advances and changes in science and technology have increased the interaction between science and the law. Each new scientific or technological development brings its own potential for new effects on society and, hence, new hazards or benefits that must be managed. The scientific community has also been confronted with public and legal interest in the previously sacrosanct domain of research. This confrontation arises from the implementation of controls or monitoring bodies, administrative structures, and threatened restriction of topics or methods. At the same time, the law increasingly relies on scientists and engineers as expert witnesses or advisors to the judiciary, on scientific methods to obtain evidence, and on computer management of legal data systems. Each of these areas of interaction has resulted in its own literature "explosion" and it is remarkable, therefore, that so little bibliographic attention has been paid to the relations between law and science.

One early effort to draw attention to these issues was an April 1965 conference held under the joint auspices of Rockefeller University and the Walter E. Meyer Research Institute of Law. The proceedings of that conference were published in 1966 by Rockefeller University Press as Law and the Social Role of Science, edited by Harry W. Jones. That book included an extensive bibliography of published writings (through 1965) on various aspects of the interaction of law and science. The bibliography "Literature of the Law-Science Confrontation," compiled by Morris L. Cohen and Betty J. Warner, attempted to provide a manageable and selective bibliographic guide to a broad sample of the relevant research.

In 1975, a supplement covering the years 1965-75 was prepared for the Program on Public Conceptions of Science (Harvard University) by Morris L. Cohen and Jan Stepan, with the assistance of Sandra Rosenstock. That supplement followed the general outline and scope of the original bibliography but exhibited a somewhat greater degree of selectivity, as required by the proliferation of publications on the topic. The supplement was published in three installments in the Newsletter of the Program on Public Conceptions of Science: Numbers 12 (June 1975), 14 (January 1976), and 15 (April 1976).

In the years that have elapsed since the publication of the Law and the Social Role of Science bibliography and the 1965-75 supplement, the volume of writing on law and science has continued to accelerate. Probably more has been published since 1965 than in all the preceding years combined. Some topics, such as environmental law, have expanded tremendously, and many new areas of interest have arisen. Moreover, interaction between the legal system and the scientific world has become more frequent and more intense. The consequent increase in relevant publications clearly warrants a new and more current bibliographic record. Therefore, the publishers of the 1965-75 supplement have sponsored a major bibliographic revision that brings together, in a new bibliography, the most important references from the 1966 and 1975/76 publications and adds selected recent references, through the first quarter of 1978.

In an area so wide-ranging, loosely defined, and rapidly changing, it would be a Sisyphean task to compile a definitive bibliography. Due to the volume of the literature and the exigencies of publishing, this revision is even more selective than its predecessors. We must emphasize that this book is not intended as an exhaustive treatment of the subject; many worthy and useful publications have not been included and omission should not be construed as dismissal. In general, preference was given to materials such as indices, bibliographies, and review articles which could lead the reader to additional references. Short articles, and those focusing on tangential areas such as criminology, penology, and mining law, have generally been omitted. By and large, entries are confined to United States publications (periodical articles, books, monographs, and government documents), although these are occasionally supplemented by English-language materials from other jurisdictions. To facilitate location of additional publications, selective listings are provided from current periodicals, bibliographies issued as serials, and looseleaf services (the ingenious form of legal publication that brings together primary sources of law and explanatory text with frequent, often weekly, supplementation). Using these "Current Sources" sections, readers should be able to supplement this bibliography with new material as it appears.

Acknowledgments

The editors gratefully acknowledge the cooperation of the Rockefeller University Press (and, especially, Helene Jordan) in this effort to develop a new version of the Law-Science bibliography. With their permission, we are reprinting a revised version of Morris L. Cohen's essay on the historical background of the law-science relationship; the original essay appeared in Law and the Social Role of Science (1966). Preparation of the 1965-75 supplement was made possible by National Science Foundation Grant GPP 74-14718. Publication of this book is made possible by funds generated by a project co-sponsored in 1974-76 by the National Science Foundation and the National Endowment for the Humanities, under NSF Grant OSS 76-16404.

With remarkable cheerfulness, Betts Carlton typed the bibliography for publication, and we thank her for her help. Also, in a reversal of usual practice, the editors and publishers of this volume would like to thank the compilers, Morris L. Cohen, Jan Stepan, and Naomi Ronen, for their cooperation, good will, and dedicated effort. In record time and on schedule, they turned a hope and an idea into a completed manuscript.

> - Vivien B. Shelanski and Marcel C. La Follette
> August 1978

This Second Edition, with 1979 Supplement and revised Index, was greatly furthered by the encouragement and support of Larry Cohen, Science Editor at the M.I.T. Press, and has been produced under the sponsorship of the quarterly journal, Science, Technology, and Human Values. Kudos again to the compilers for development of the supplement. Susan Howe and Loretta Lynch ably produced and set this new edition.

> - M.C.L., November 1979

Essay

THE LITERATURE OF THE LAW-SCIENCE CONFRONTATION

By Morris L. Cohen
Librarian and Professor of Law
Harvard Law School

Scholarship has yet to produce a comprehensive historical or bibliographic study of the continuing relationship between law and science. Although a search of historical bibliographic sources reveals little evidence of anything resembling the prolific interdisciplinary literature that has been developing over the last thirty years, careful probing uncovers a variety of contacts and mutual concerns. These interactions were not always obvious to or recognized by the editors, indexers, and catalogers of the past. However, sufficient references are scattered here and there to indicate that many of the problems which mark the contemporary law-science confrontation have existed for some time.

David F. Cavers, in his introductory essay to the volume Law and the Social Role of Science, describes five categories[1] that provide a helpful framework for analyzing the law-science encounter: 1) Points at which the law, in discharging its traditional adjudicatory function, must draw on scientific knowledge to reach its decision; 2) Points at which scientific developments compel us to reexamine the adequacy of established legal doctrines; 3) Points at which scientific developments have created new hazards that have led the state to intervene, thereby creating new points of confrontation; 4) Points at which government, acting through the legal mechanisms of appropriation, executive order, and contract, must choose scientific objectives, ration scarce research resources, and seek to maximize the contributions of the scientific community; and 5) Points at which scientific developments bring us into new contacts with our neighbors on this planet, thus creating the need for new legal relationships. Following this outline, we can find examples in many literatures, from even ancient times, of encounters that fall within these categories.

---

[1]Harry W. Jones, ed., Law and the Social Role of Science (New York: The Rockefeller University Press, 1966), p. 6. These categories, with some change, also provided the organizational outline for the original bibliography, but have been substantially revised in the present version.

In the early history of adjudication, scientific knowledge and scientific experts were employed on occasion to assist the fact finders.[2] However, such encounters on the procedural side were far outnumbered by contacts arising from the law's continuing concern with medical science, mechanics, astronomy, agriculture, mathematics, and human behavior. An English lawyer of the 16th century, Henry Finch, in recommending a broad course of study for the prospective lawyer, noted that "the Sparks of all Sciences in the world are raked up in the ashes of the Law...."[3]

With respect to Professor Cavers' next category, the historical evidence is less substantial. Until recent times, governments have not often been involved in the allocation of scientific research resources; but, from the days of Ancient Greece and Rome, governments have responded (often unpleasantly) to the new research and teaching of scientists. From Anaxagoras in the Athens of the 5th century B.C. to Galileo in 17th-century Rome to John T. Scopes in Dayton, Tennessee, in 1925, we can trace a pattern of negative reactions.[4]

If we search widely in the relevant literature for references to contacts such as these, we find that most can be grouped into three areas: 1) the reaction of law and government, often under strong religious influence, to new and apparently subversive teachings of science; 2) the regulation of medical practice and related activities; and 3) the law's concern with the various branches of science and technology in the formulation and application of rules governing human activity and behavior. Before approaching the bibliographies of the current literature, let us first glance at the highlights of these three points of confrontation.

LAW VERSUS THE SCIENTIST

Only occasionally will classical literature produce a specific reference to cooperation between the worlds of law and science. One example is the popular version of Archimedes' famous dash from his bathtub to the

---

[2]Jewish Courts of Justice from ancient times employed physicians as expert witnesses with respect to the injuries sustained in certain criminal matters (Jewish Encyclopedia, Vol. 8; New York: Funk & Wagnalls Co., Inc., 1904, p. 409). In Roman law, specialized fact finders were sometimes employed for particularly esoteric matters and in Jewish law the Judges of the Sanhedrin were themselves required to possess knowledge of the general sciences (Codes of Maimonides, Book 14, the Book of Judges, translated by Abraham M. Hershman; New Haven, CT: Yale University Press, 1949, p. 7). Learned Hand, later a distinguished judge, wrote an interesting survey of the development of expert testimony, "Historical and Practical Considerations Regarding Expert Testimony," 15 Harvard Law Review 40-58 (1901).

[3]Henry Finch, Law, or a Discourse Thereof (London, 1678 edition), p. 6.

[4]Benjamin Farrington's Science and Politics in the Ancient World (London: Allen & Unwin, 1939) is perhaps the best study of this problem in the classical period. See also Hayward R. Alker, Mathematics and Politics (New York: The Macmillan Company, 1965).

streets of Syracuse, shouting "Eureka" while clothed only in the exuberance of his discovery of the first law of hydrostatics. It is said that the discovery stemmed from an experiment in forensic science performed at royal request. The scientist had, at the moment of that discovery, been considering an appropriate method of computing the proportion of gold in his King's crown. A goldsmith had been accused of fraudulently adulterating the gold content of the crown and King Heiro had sought Archimedes' help in establishing evidence of his guilt. Such was the rather tenuous law-science connection behind this famous incident.[5]

A far more frequent, and serious, type of encounter involves society's reaction to new scientific thinking that offends the religious authorities of the State. This conflict began with the persecution of one of the earliest Greek scientists, Anaxagoras, an Ionian who lived and taught in Athens in the 5th century B.C. He was the leading intellectual figure of his time and is generally considered to have been one of the earliest physicists and one of the founders of the scientific method; his work and writing in several sciences influenced later thought, and among his many students was the great Pericles. However, Anaxagoras' teaching concerning the heavenly bodies angered the religious authorities, and he became a convenient target for the political enemies of Pericles. Anaxagoras was tried for impiety and exiled. Although the various accounts of his legal difficulties differ in detail, several (including Plutarch's) indicate that his prosecution was based at least in part on religious opposition to his scientific investigation and teaching of astronomy. Sarton has said of him:

> He was certainly not the first victim in the incessant
> war between bigotry and science, but he is the first
> known one. We may not call him a martyr of science,
> because his sentence was simply of banishment, but he
> was the first man in history who was punished for think-
> ing freely, for following the dictates of his reason and
> conscience rather than the opinions of the community.[6]

In Science and Politics in the Ancient World, Benjamin Farrington describes the efforts of early science to assert itself against the obstacles of the religious establishment. Farrington saw in Aeschylus' great drama Prometheus Bound a symbolic presentation of "the political problem of adjusting contemporary institutions to meet the great upheaval of the old ways of life represented by the Ionian enlightenment."[7] Prometheus' impudence in stealing fire from the gods and giving it to men for their use is likened to

---

[5]E.T. Bell, Men of Mathematics (New York: Simon and Schuster, Inc., 1937), p. 29.

[6]George Sarton, A History of Science: Ancient Science Through the Golden Age of Greece (Cambridge, MA: Harvard University Press, 1952), p. 244. See also Daniel E. Gershenson and Daniel A. Greenberg, Anaxagoras and the Birth of Science (New York: Blaisdell, 1964), which includes accounts of the trial at pp. 346-348.

[7]Farrington, op. cit. (note 4), p. 69.

the efforts of the rationalists who sought to discover and teach the secrets of nature for human betterment against the will of the representatives of the gods on earth. The invocation of the law against the Ionian scientists paralleled Zeus' torment of Prometheus.

Andrew D. White, in History of the Warfare of Science with Theology in Christendom,[8] and John W. Draper, in History of the Conflict Between Religion and Science,[9] describe the continuing struggle for freedom of scientific inquiry. Anne Haight's bibliography of censored literature, Banned Books: Informal Notes on Some Books Banned for Various Reasons at Various Times and in Various Places, lists Roger Bacon (between Abelard and Dante) with the note:

> 1257 England: Bonaventura, General of the Franciscan order, suspicious of Bacon's supposed dealings in the black arts, interdicted his lectures at Oxford, and placed him under the superintendence of the order in Paris, where he remained for ten years under injunction not to write for publication.[10]

Bacon sought with his writing, teaching and inventions to revive experimental research and applied science. After a reprieve under Pope Clement IV, his work was again condemned in 1278 and he was imprisoned for fourteen years. Some may consider it unfair to tax the law with these ecclesiastical persecutions, but it is quite difficult to separate Church and State during these centuries.

Bacon foreshadowed the great Renaissance conflict between religion and law on one side and science on the other. The overthrow of the Ptolemaic view of a geocentric universe, which had become part of Church dogma, involved a long struggle. Many of the most illustrious names in the founding of modern science were involved--Kepler, Copernicus, Galileo, among others. Bruno, a contemporary of Galileo, died at the stake in 1600 for his imprudent philosophic and scientific views, including acceptance of the Copernican system of the universe. He allegedly retorted to his judges, "Perhaps it is with greater fear that you pass the sentence upon me than I receive it."[11] Despite Galileo's recantation of his scientific theories, his trial in 1633 was one of the most dramatic episodes of the long confrontation. Giorgio de Santillana's The Crime of Galileo[12] describes both the scientific and philosophic issues involved, as well as the underlying human and political conflict.

[8](New York: George Braziller, Inc., 1955); first published 1896.

[9](New York: Appleton, 1900); first published 1874.

[10]3d edition (New York: R.R. Bowker Co., 1970), p. 8.

[11]Quoted in Draper, op. cit. (note 9), p. 180.

[12](Chicago: University of Chicago Press, 1955).

The troubles of the scientist did not cease with Galileo's recantation.
Banned Books lists the works of giants like Descartes, Pascal and Darwin,
and later those of the prophets of the sexual revolution, Havelock Ellis,
Marie C. Stopes, Margaret Sanger and Alfred Kinsey. Darwin's work in par-
ticular brought forth an anguished reaction from the religious world, which
called on the power of government to save the souls of Christendom from the
Darwinian heresy. A description of Fundamentalist attacks in the United
States on Darwin's thinking is described in detail in Maynard Shipley's in-
dignant rejoinder, The War on Modern Science.[13] A highlight of that campaign was the trial in 1925 of John Thomas Scopes, a high school teacher in
Dayton, Tennessee, for violation of a statute which made it unlawful "to
teach any theory that denies the story of the Divine Creation of man as
taught in the Bible, and to teach instead that man has descended from a low-
er order of animals."[14]

The 20th century brought new political orthodoxies and persecution of
scientists by zealots of those ideologies, often backed by the full force
of the state's legal apparatus. On May 10, 1933, 25,000 volumes by Jewish
authors were burned by the Nazis at the University of Berlin, including
works by Karl Marx, Sigmund Freud, Alfred Adler, and Albert Einstein.[15]
The effect of the Nazi regime on one area of science, physics, is described
in Alan D. Beyerchen's recent study, Scientists Under Hitler: Politics and
the Physics Community in the Third Reich.[16] Although this book focuses on
but a single scientific field, it does provide an example of the modern to-
talitarian state's repressive impact on scientific freedom.

State persecution of scientists in the U.S.S.R. continues to occur from
time to time, usually stemming from non-scientific issues such as the politics or religion of the individuals involved. For example, the genetics
controversy associated with Lysenko involved the conflict between an offici-
ally-approved pseudo-scientific theory and its proponents, and the rest of
the traditional scientific community. Although initiated by Lysenko, him-
self a scientist, the establishment of a "Soviet" theory of genetics and the
ruthless repression of geneticists with different theories were carried out
by the government and the legal system--a campaign documented in The Rise
and Fall of T.D. Lysenko and other works.[17] Another form of political-legal

---

[13](New York: Alfred A. Knopf, Inc., 1927).

[14]The trial proceedings have been reported in detail, dramatized, and widely
discussed. See, for example, Raymond S. Ginger, Six Days or Forever? Tennessee vs. John Thomas Scopes (Boston: Beacon Press, 1958), and Jerry R.
Tompkins, ed., D-Days at Dayton: Reflections on the Scopes Trial (Baton
Rouge: Louisiana State University Press, 1965).

[15]Haight, op. cit. (note 10), p. 121.

[16](New Haven, CT: Yale University Press, 1977).

[17]See Julian Huxley, "Soviet Genetics: The Real Issue," in Versions of Cen-
sorship, An Anthology, edited by John McCormick and Mairi MacInnes (Garden
City, NY: Anchor Books, 1962). pp. 96-115. For a later study, see Z.A. Medvedev, The Rise and Fall of T.D. Lysenko (New York: Anchor Books/Doubleday,
1969/1971). Medvedev has written more broadly and collected documents on

repression of science is the use of psychiatric facilities for incarceration of political dissenters. A recent study of alleged psychiatric abuse in the Soviet Union is Psychiatric Terror: How Soviet Psychiatry is Used to Suppress Dissent by Sidney Bloch and Peter Reddaway.[18]

Some persons have seen a similarly repressive tendency in the 1954 U.S. Atomic Energy Commission administrative hearings on the security status of J. Robert Oppenheimer, and in the excesses of governmental concern with scientific loyalty and secrecy during the McCarthy era.[19] The author of The Crime of Galileo saw ominous parallels between the cases of Galileo and Oppenheimer, but he admitted that "today there is a tendency not to suppress physics but rather to exploit it...."[20]

Over the last 35 years or so, the importance of scientific research to national security has at times given the scientists a strong bargaining point and enabled them to achieve financial support and even political power. This new relationship between science and the political and legal structure in the United States has been described in a number of the publications listed in Section K of the Bibliography. The influence of scientists on the political process has fluctuated in recent years, however, as has access to federal funding for research.

LAW AND THE HEALING ARTS

Regulation of medical practice for the protection of the public was one of the earliest contacts between law and science. In addition to the development of a specialized literature of its own (i.e., medical jurisprudence) over the last hundred years, evidence of the relationship appears regularly in the separate writings of law and medicine.

Soviet control of science in The Medvedev Papers: Fruitful Meetings Between Scientists of the World [and] Secrecy of Correspondence is Guaranteed by Law (London: Macmillan, 1971).

[18](New York: Basic Books, 1977). See B.J. Ennis, Prisoners of Psychiatry: Mental Patients, Psychiatrists, and the Law (New York: Harcourt, Brace, Jovanovich, 1972) for a view of American practices in this regard. Also Amnesty International's Prisoners of Conscience in the USSR: Their Treatment and Conditions (London, 1975), especially Chapter 7, "Compulsory Detention in Psychiatric Hospitals."

[19]For detailed discussion of that problem, see Walter Gellhorn, Security, Loyalty and Science (Ithaca, NY: Cornell University Press, 1950); Eleanor Bontecore, Federal Loyalty-Security Program (Ithaca, NY: Cornell University Press, 1953); and Don K. Price, Government and Science: Their Dynamic Relation in American Democracy (New York: New York University Press, 1954).

[20]de Santillana, op. cit. (note 12), p. viii.

Henry E. Sigerist, the great medical historian, in his "History of Medical Licensure,"[21] mentions one of the earliest recorded regulations in the Persian Venidad of the Zend Avesta, the basic law of the Zoroastrian religion.[22] It rather cynically established the standard of admission to surgical practice among the worshippers of Mazda.

> 36(94) Maker of the material world, thou Holy One!
> If a worshipper of Mazda wants to practice the art
> of healing, on whom shall he first prove his skill?--
> on worshippers of Mazda or on worshippers of the Daevas?--
>
> 37(96) Ahura Mazda answered: "On worshippers of the Daevas
> shall he first prove himself, rather than on worshippers
> of Mazda. If he treat with the knife a worshipper of
> Daevas and he die; if he treat with the knife a second
> worshipper of the Daevas and he die; if he treat with
> the knife for the third time a worshipper of the Daevas
> and he die, he is unfit to practice the art of healing
> forever and ever."

Among the early Semites, medical practitioners were also subject to legal control. The Babylonian Code of Hammurabi, between its provisions governing Assault and Barbers, contains several relevant regulations of surgical practice. Sections 215 to 217 and 221 to 224 establish the fees for different types of operations,[23] relating them to the status of the patient, the nature of the operation, and the success of the surgeon's work. Sections 218 to 220, and 225, deal with the penalties for unsuccessful operations, ranging from a reduction in the surgeon's fee to the cutting off of his fore-hand.

Medical regulation was apparently not a matter of legal concern to the early Greeks and Romans, although they did recognize the special status of the physician. Hippocrates' Oath set standards of medical practice for at least some of the physicians of that time and became an enduring part of the professional tradition. However, the Hippocratic Oath did not have the force of law. Although the Romans gave practicing physicians special privileges--including exemption from taxation and military service--for many centuries there was no limitation on who might practice. Penalties for malpractice are indicated in the Lex Aemilia of 433 B.C. and the Lex Cornelia of 88 B.C. Benjamin Gordon, in Medicine Throughout Antiquity,[24] traces the gradual development of regulation until licensure was instituted under Lucius Septimius Severus in the second century.

---

[21]104 Journal of the American Medical Association 1057-1060 (1935), reprinted in On the Sociology of Medicine, edited by Milton I. Roemer (New York: MD Publications, 1960), pp. 308-318.

[22]In The Sacred Books of the East, Volume 4, edited by F.M. Muller (London: Oxford University Press, 1880). The last three chapters of the priestly code deal with medicine.

[23]G.R. Driver and John C. Miles, The Babylonian Laws, Volume 2 (London: Oxford University Press, 1955), pp. 79-81

[24](Philadelphia: F.A. Davis Co., 1949), Chapter 25.

Medicine was an integral part of the Jewish religion and is dealt with frequently in biblical law, particularly in matters of hygiene and ritual cleanliness. However, not until postbiblical writings is there evidence of regulation of medical practice. Medical licensure was apparently introduced under the Tannaim of the first two centuries of the Christian era. Regulation of physicians under Jewish law was quite liberal (although perhaps not as lenient as among the Greeks and Romans) and physicians were held responsible only if they intentionally hurt their patients.[25] The classic study of Jewish medicine, reflecting the development of medical practice, is Julius Preuss's Biblisch-talmudische Medizin;[26] a more recent survey is Immanuel Jakobovitz's Jewish Medical Ethics.[27]

Medical licensure as we know it today was initiated in Europe in the Middle Ages. Sigerist notes that the first medieval regulations promulgated in 1140 required certification of fitness by the medical faculty of Salerno. His writings describe the excellent and detailed ordinances of Frederick II[28] and survey the subsequent history of European regulation with its early emphasis on control by the universities. The first English statute requiring a license for medical practice was passed in 1511[29] and its preamble presents the rationale for such regulation:

> Forasmuch as the science and cunning of physick and surgery (to the perfect knowledge whereof be requisite both great learning and ripe experience) is daily within this realm exercised by a great multitude of ignorant persons, of whom the greater part have no manner of insight in the same, nor in any other kind of learning; [so far that] common artificers, as smiths, weavers and women boldly and accustomably take upon them great cures, and things of great difficulty in the which they partly use sorcery and witchcraft, partly apply such medicines unto the disease as be very noious...to the high displeasure of God, great infamy to the faculty, and the grievous hurt, damage, and destruction of many of the King's liege people, most especially of them that cannot discern the uncunning from the cunning: be it therefore... enacted that [none shall practice as a physician or surgeon in London, unless examined and approved by the bishop of London].

---

[25]A. Castiglioni, "The Contribution of the Jews to Medicine," in The Jews, Their History, Culture and Religion, Volume 2, edited by Louis Finkelstein (Philadelphia: Jewish Publication Society of America, 1960), p. 1355.

[26](Berlin: S. Karger, 1911).

[27](New York: Bloch Publishing Co., Inc., 1959).

[28]Sigerist, op. cit. (note 21), p. 1058.

[29]Great Britain. Statutes at Large. 3d regnal year of Henry VIII, Chapter 11.

The medical profession itself subsequently took steps to raise minimum qualifications and the College of Physicians was eventually given the responsibility of examining prospective physicians for licensing.

Parallel to the advancement of science and professional development in other areas, legal controls over medical practice grew more stringent throughout the world during the 19th and 20th centuries. The United States moved gradually from a virtual absence of controls in the colonial period to the establishment of the National Board of Medical Examiners in 1915 and the passage of regulatory legislation in every state. Today, this aspect of the law-science encounter is tightly regulated by licensure and by both civil and criminal law. Recent controversies over abortion, fetal research, and medical experimentation illustrate increasing involvement of criminal law in medical practice, while malpractice litigation grows in civil law.

SCIENCE AS A MATERIAL SOURCE OF LAW

From early times, the law has dealt with matters of personal status and kinship, crime, commerce and economics, inheritance, agriculture, public health, and property. In the formulation of regulations in those fields and others, legislators have drawn on the scientific knowledge of their time. In the application of those regulations to specific cases, government officials and tribunals required and obtained the expertise of scientists to guide and inform their deliberations. However, the scientific foundation of such laws was rarely explicit in their legal text and the study of legislative history was not highly developed before this century. Therefore, evidence of this aspect of the relationship between law and science is most difficult to document. Although the standard histories of law and those of science offer little help in this respect, some speculation is possible.

The relationship is perhaps clearest in medicine and hygiene. The ancient Semitic codes were much concerned with the control of disease, disposal of the dead, purity of food and water, status of the insane, and other problems of public health. The biblical concern with hygiene was particularly marked.

> The concept of purity is of eminent importance in biblical legislation.... Hygienic regulations were imposed on the people by law with the authority characteristic of divine maxims and in the form of religious ceremonies. Some of these regulations existed also in Egypt and in Babylonia, where they had a magic character...[30]

Regulation of such subjects involved considerable knowledge of the medical and natural sciences.

Laws governing agriculture and land tenure were fundamental to the economic life of ancient communities. Such regulations covered questions of cultivation, field rental, tenancies, flood losses, crop loans, irrigation,

---

[30]Castiglioni, op. cit. (note 25), p. 1353.

livestock, and distribution yields. They were treated in detail in the laws of the Babylonians,[31] the Assyrians,[32] the Hebrews,[33] and most other ancient peoples. G.R. Driver and John Miles, in their commentary on the Code of Hammurabi, note that "many processes continue to be carried out unchanged to the present day, and a knowledge of modern practice as well as the ancient agricultural contracts is essential to a right understanding of many passages of the Laws."[34]

Mathematics was important in the legal establishment and enforcement of uniform weights and measures and in questions of coinage and calendar stabilization. Algebra was helpful in problems of inheritance; geometry was employed in determining real property shares and boundaries. Salo Baron, in Social and Religious History of the Jews,[35] treats in detail the significance of science and mathematics in both Jewish and Muslim law.

Although these practical applications of mathematics to law are most significant, George Sarton notes a more subtle mathematical influence in Platonic jurisprudence.

> [Plato's] approach was not arithmetic (in our sense) but geometric. The secret of the universe (cosmos) is order and measure. Plato extended that conception to everything domestic and political and he did it without moderation. Everything in the perfect city must be regulated; no change is foreseen, therefore there is no opportunity, no choice, no fancy. The city will function like a machine. Some chapters of Laws regulate private life with so much detail and so little restraint that they are to the modern mind repulsive and obscene.[36]

The modern literature of forensic science and medical jurisprudence has developed widely and encompasses, in both civil and criminal law, questions of the extent and cause of physical injury, mental responsibility, birth control and abortion, the determination of paternity, research ethics and control, the definition of life and death, and numerous other scientific

[31]See Driver and Miles, op. cit. (note 23), Volume 2, pp. 27-33 and 87-93.

[32]G.R. Driver and John C. Miles, The Assyrian Laws (London: Oxford University Press, 1935), pp. 293-320.

[33]The Encyclopaedia Hebraica (Jerusalem: Encyclopaedia Publishing Co., 1965) notes in its article, "Agriculture" (Volume 17, p. 978), that "a substantial part of the precepts of the Torah deals, directly or indirectly, with agricultural subjects."

[34]Driver and Miles, op. cit. (note 23), Volume 1, p. 127.

[35](Philadelphia: Jewish Publication Society of America, 1958), Volume 8: Philosophy and Science, Chapter 35, "Scientific Exploration," pp. 153-54. See also W.M. Feldman, Rabbinical Mathematics and Astronomy (London: M.L. Cailingold, 1931).

[36]Sarton, op. cit. (note 6), p. 416.

problems. Only a small selection of the extensive writings in these fields is listed in the Bibliography which follows, but they reflect one of the most dramatic and controversial areas of contact between law and science.

The movement of science into new domains of research, experimentation, and technical achievement raises legal issues that expand the historic law-science interaction. As Judge David L. Bazelon has recently pointed out, "...the judiciary is increasingly being asked to grapple with scientific and technological issues of great complexity. Some two-thirds of the D.C. [District of Columbia] Circuit's caseload now involves review of action by federal administrative agencies; and more and more of such cases relate to matters on the frontiers of technology."[37] These issues are often stimulated by concerns about individual rights, public safety, community interests, and moral or ethical considerations.

The legal system's response to these developments can be seen in the tremendous expansion of some areas--e.g., environmental law--as well as in the creation of entirely new fields of law. Rapid advances in computer technology, for example, have not only brought about changes in legislative process and judicial administration, but also have required new fields of law to cope with problems arising from increased capabilities and uses of computers in society. Medical procedures, such as psychosurgery and organ transplantation, and the utilization of life-prolonging technologies have generated a host of legal problems and a rapidly growing literature. Efforts to exploit or protect the environment now frequently lead to confrontations in the courts, as do efforts to increase or diminish the regulation of drugs and other substances. Abortion, arms control, pollution, eavesdropping, and automobile hazards are only some of the diverse topics that fill daily newspapers and the scholarly journals of both the legal and scientific professions. As interaction between the legal system and the scientific world becomes more frequent and more intense, establishment of conditions to protect all relevant interests will require new understanding and new methods of resolving differences between the legal and scientific communities. This Bibliography is intended to facilitate that effort.

---

[37]David L. Bazelon, "Coping With Technology Through the Legal Process," 62 Cornell Law Review (June 1977), p. 817.

Law & Science

Bibliography

A. GENERAL DISCUSSION OF LAW AND SCIENCE

1. "AALS/AAAS Joint Panel Discussion on the Law-Science Interface," 16 Jurimetrics Journal 24-47 (1975).*

2. Aultman, M. "Technology and the End of Law," 17 American Journal of Jurisprudence 46-79 (1972).

3. Bazelon, D.L. "Coping with Technology through the Legal Process," 62 Cornell Law Review 817-832 (1977).

4. [Blaxland, G.] Elements of the Logical and Experimental Sciences Considered in Relation to the Practice of Law. London: Henry Butterworth, 1835. 500pp.

5. Brett, P. "The Implications of Science for the Law," 18 McGill Law Journal 170-205 (1972).

6. Caldwell, L.K. Science, Technology, and Public Policy: A Selected and Annotated Bibliography. Bloomington, IN: Indiana University, 1968-72. 3 volumes. (Vol. 1, Section 6--"Science, Technology, and the Law," pp.191-214; Vol. 2, Section 6--"Legal Aspects of Science and Technology," pp.207-226; Vol. 3, Section 6--"Legal Aspects of Science and Technology," pp.463-488.)

7. Caldwell, L.K., and T.A. Siddiqi. Science, Technology, and Public Policy: A Guide to Advanced Study. Bloomington, IN: Indiana University, School of Public and Environmental Affairs, 1972. 512pp. ("Science, Human Rights, and the Role of Law," pp.451-478.)

8. Daddario, E.Q. "Technology Assessment Legislation," 7 Harvard Journal of Legislation 507-532 (1970).

9. Douglas, R.I. Law for Technologists. London: Gee, 1964. 158pp.

10. Harvard University Program on Technology and Society, 1964-1972; A Final Review. Introduction by Emmanuel G. Mesthene. Cambridge, MA, 1972. 285pp.

---

*In entries for periodical articles, the number that appears before the title of the periodical indicates the VOLUME; the numbers following the title are the PAGE NUMBERS. Names given in brackets are the actual authors, although they may not have been specifically identified as author in the document.

11. Holmes, O.W. "Law in Science and Science in Law," in Collected
    Legal Papers, pp.210-243. New York: Harcourt, Brace and Howe,
    1920. Originally published in 12 Harvard Law Review 443-463
    (1899).

12. International Congress of Comparative Law, 9th, Teheran, 1974. Law
    in the United States of America in Social and Technological Re-
    volution, J.N. Hazard and W.J. Wagner, eds. Brussels: E. Bruy-
    lant, 1974. 697pp.

13. Jones, H.W., ed. Law and the Social Role of Science. New York:
    Rockefeller University Press, 1967. 242pp. Contents include:
    D.F. Cavers, "Law and Science: Some Points of Confrontation;"
    A.W. Murphy, "Law and Research Supported by Government;" B. Wolf-
    man, "Federal Tax Policy and the Support of Science;" J.H. Muns-
    ter and J.C. Smith, "Project Research and the Universities;"
    O.C. Lewis, "Restrictions on the Use of Animals and Persons in
    Scientific Research;" J.G. Palfrey, "Colleagueship in Law and
    Science;" O.M. Ruebhausen and O.G. Brim, "Privacy and Behavioral
    Research;" L.S. Cottrell, "The Interrelationships of Law and
    Social Science;" H.W. Jones, "Legal Inquiry and the Methods of
    Science."

14. Kalven, H., and H. Zeisel. "Law, Science and Humanism," in The
    Humanist Frame, edited by J.S. Huxley, pp.329-344. New York:
    Harper and Row, 1961.

15. Katz, M. "The Function of Tort Liability in Technology Assessment,"
    38 University of Cincinnati Law Review 587-662 (1969). Reprint-
    ed as Reprint No. 9, Harvard University Program on Technology
    and Society.

16. Law and the American Future. Englewood Cliffs, NJ: Prentice-Hall,
    1976. 212pp. (Background papers for the American Assembly on
    Law and a Changing Society. Stanford University Law School,
    1975.)

17. "Literature of the Law-Science Confrontation, 1965-1975," compiled
    by Morris L. Cohen and Jan Stepan, Newsletter of the Program on
    Public Conceptions of Science [now Science, Technology & Human
    Values]: Number 12, pp.28-54 (1975); Number 14, pp.32-84 (1976);
    and Number 15, pp.18-46 (1976).

18. Loevinger, L. "Law and Science as Rival Systems," 8 Jurimetrics
    Journal 63-82 (1966). Reprinted in 19 University of Florida Law
    Review 530-551 (1967).

19. Loth, D.G., and M.L. Ernst. How High is Up: Modern Law for Modern
    Man. Indianapolis, IN: Bobbs-Merrill, 1964. 275pp.

20. Loth, D.G., and M.L. Ernst. The Taming of Technology. New York:
    Simon & Schuster, 1972. 256pp.

21. Louisell, D.W. "Biology, Law and Reason: Man as Self-Creator," 16
    American Journal of Jurisprudence 1-24 (1971).

22. Markey, H.T.   "Science and Law: Toward a Happier Marriage," 59 Jour-
       nal of the Patent Office Society 343-361 (1977).

23. Miller, A.S.   "Science vs. Law: Some Legal Problems Raised by 'Big
       Science'," 17 Buffalo Law Review 591-630 (1968).

24. Patterson, E.W.   Law in a Scientific Age. New York: Columbia Univer-
       sity Press, 1963. 87pp. (Includes "Works cited," pp.77-84, a
       bibliography on the jurisprudential aspects of law and science.)

25. Sherman, J.G.   "A Note on Sources for Scientific Research for Law-
       yers," 70 Law Library Journal 364-367 (1977).

26. Symposium.   "Law and Science," 31 Texas Law Review 625-831 (1953).

27. Symposium.   "Law and Technology," 52 Chicago-Kent Law Review 545-
       620 (1976).

28. Symposium.   "Law, Science and Technology," 33 George Washington Law
       Review 1-456 (1964).

29. Symposium.   Report of Conference on Law and Science, London, 1964
       (F.C. Hodson and K. Lindsay, Chairmen). London: David Davies
       Memorial Institute, 1964. 154pp.

30. Symposium.   "Science and Technology," 17 Vanderbilt Law Review 1-
       272 (1963). (Part I: The Forces of Change; Part II: Social Ad-
       justment: Resources and Responsibility; Part III: The Law's Re-
       sponse to the Demand for Both Stability and Change.)

31. Symposium.   "Science and the Law," 63 Michigan Law Review 1325-1446
       (1965).

32. "Symposium on Technology Assessment," 14 Jurimetrics Journal 65-108
       (1973).

33. Thomas, W.A., ed.   Scientists in the Legal System: Tolerated Meddlers
       or Essential Contributors? Ann Arbor, MI: Ann Arbor Science
       Publishers, 1974. 141pp.

34. Tribe, L.H.   Channeling Technology through Law. Chicago: Bracton
       Press, 1973. 644pp.

35. Tribe, L.H.   "Technology Assessment and the Fourth Discontinuity:
       The Limits of Instrumental Rationality," 46 Southern California
       Law Review 617-660 (1973).

A.1 CURRENT SOURCES

Selected examples of subject headings under which law and science
materials may be found are included following the entries for indices.

36. Annual Legal Bibliography: A Selected List of Books and Articles Re-
        ceived by the Harvard Law School Library...including all items
        which have appeared in...Current Legal Bibliography.
        v.1-   1960/61-   .
        Cambridge, MA: Harvard Law School Library.
        Sample subject headings: Government Contracts, Natural Resources,
            Medical Jurisprudence, Legal Science and Research.
        [ALB is a principal source for this bibliography.]

37. Index to Foreign Legal Periodicals.
        v.1-   1960-   .
        London: Institute of Advanced Legal Studies, in cooperation with
            the American Association of Law Libraries.
        Sample subject headings: Science, Health, Pollution and Protec-
            tion of the Environment.

38. Index to Legal Periodicals.
        v.1-   1909-   .
        New York: H.W. Wilson, in cooperation with the American Associa-
            tion of Law Libraries.
        Sample subject headings: Science, Automation, Environmental Law,
            Health.

39. Index to Periodical Articles Related to Law: Selected from Journals
        not included in the Index to Legal Periodicals or the Index to
        Foreign Legal Periodicals.
        v.1-   1958-   .
        Dobbs Ferry, NY: Glanville.
        Reflects "an increasing concern with the legal implications of
            scientific technology." Sample subject headings: Law and
            Science, Environmental Law, Medical Jurisprudence.

40. Law Books in Print, 1957-1969, and its supplements Law Books Pub-
        lished, 1969-   .
        Dobbs Ferry, NY: Glanville.
        Sample subject headings: Law and Science, Law and Society.

41. Library of Congress Subject Headings.   8th edition, Washington, DC,
        1975.
        Many library card catalogues use Library of Congress subject
            headings, an applicable sample of which includes:
                Science and law
                Information storage and retrieval systems--Law
                Medical jurisprudence
                Natural resources--Law and legislation
                Research and development contracts
                Science and state
                Space law
                Technology assessment
                Technology and state

B. LAW AND SOCIAL SCIENCE, INCLUDING EMPIRICAL RESEARCH ON
    THE LAW

42. Akers, R.L., and R. Hawkins. Law and Control in Society. Engle-
        wood Cliffs, NJ: Prentice-Hall, 1975. 383pp.

43. Alker, H.R., et al. "Jury Selection as a Biased Social Process," 11
        Law & Society Review 9-41 (1976).

44. American Society for Political and Legal Philosophy. The Limits of
        Law, edited by J.R. Pennock and J.W. Chapman. New York: Lieber-
        Atherton, 1974. 276pp. (The Society's Yearbook, Nomos 15.)

45. American Society for Political and Legal Philosophy. Political and
        Legal Obligation, edited by J.R. Pennock and J.W. Chapman. New
        York: Atherton Press, 1970. 455pp. (The Society's Yearbook,
        Nomos 12.)

46. Anderson, D.C., and T.L. Whitman. "The Control of Behavior through
        Law," 47 Notre Dame Lawyer 815-852 (1972).

47. Aubert, V., ed. Sociology of Law: Selected Readings. Middlesex, Eng-
        land: Penguin, 1969. 366pp.

48. Barkun, M., ed. Law and the Social System. New York: Lieber-Ather-
        ton, 1973. 128pp.

49. Barkun, M. Law without Sanctions: Order in Primitive Societies and
        the World Community. New Haven, CT: Yale University Press, 1968.
        175pp.

50. Barry, B.M. The Liberal Theory of Justice: A Critical Examination
        of the Principal Doctrines in 'A Theory of Justice' by John
        Rawls. Oxford: Clarendon Press, 1973. 168pp.

51. Bechtler, T.W., ed. Law in a Social Context: Liber Amicorum Honour-
        ing Professor Lon L. Fuller. Deventer, Netherlands: Kluwer,
        1978. 227pp.

52. Bedau, H.A. Justice and Equality. Englewood Cliffs, NJ: Prentice-
        Hall, 1971. 185pp.

53. Bedau, H.A., and E. Currie. Social Science Research and the Death
        Penalty in America: An Interim Report to the Russell Sage Foun-
        dation. Medford, MA: Published by the authors, 1973. 46pp.

54. Beutel, F.K. Some Potentialities of Experimental Jurisprudence as a
        New Branch of Social Science. Lincoln, NE: University of Nebras-
        ka Press, 1957. 440pp.

55. Bienenfeld, F.R. "Prolegomena to a Psychoanalysis of Law and Jus-
        tice," 53 California Law Review 957-1028, 1254-1336 (1965).

56. Blum, W.J., and H. Kalven, Jr. "The Art of Opinion Research: A
        Lawyer's Appraisal of Emerging Science," 24 University of
        Chicago Law Review 1-69 (1956).

57. Bodenheimer, E.   "Philosophical Anthropology and the Law,"   59 California Law Review 653-682 (1971).

58. Bodenheimer, E.   Power, Law and Society: A Study of the Will to Power and the Will to Law.   New York: Crane, Russak, 1973. 202pp.

59. Brieland, D., and J. Lemmon.   Social Work and the Law.   St. Paul, MN: West, 1977.   830pp.

60. Cahn, E.N.   Confronting Injustice: The Edmond Cahn Reader, edited by L.L. Cahn.   Boston: Little, Brown, 1966.   428pp.

61. Cahn, E.N.   The Moral Decision: Right and Wrong in the Light of American Law.   Bloomington, IN: Indiana University Press, 1955. 342pp.

62. Cairns, H.   Law and the Social Sciences.   New York: Harcourt and Brace, 1935.   279pp.   (Reprinted by Rothman, 1970.)

63. Carlin, J.   Lawyers on Their Own: A Study of Individual Practitioners in Chicago.   New Brunswick, NJ: Rutgers University Press, 1962.   234pp.

64. Carlston, K.S.   Law and Structures of Social Action.   London: Stevens & Sons; New York: Columbia University Press, 1956. 288pp.

65. Cavers, D.F.   "Non-traditional Research by Law Teachers: Returns from the Questionnaire of the Council on Law-related Studies," 24 Journal of Legal Education 534-566 (1972).

66. Chambliss, W.J., and R.B. Seidman.   Sociology of the Law: A Research Bibliography.   Berkeley, CA: Glendessary Press, 1970. 113pp.

67. Church, V.A.   Behavior, Law and Remedies: Introducing the Juropsychologist.   Dubuque, IA: Kendall/Hunt, 1975.   234pp.

68. Commons, J.R.   Legal Foundations of Capitalism.   New York: Macmillan, 1924.   394pp.   Reprinted by University of Wisconsin Press, 1957.

69. Danzig, R.J.   "Hadley v. Baxendale: A Study in the Industrialization of the Law,"   4 Journal of Legal Studies 249-284 (1975).

70. Davis, A.L.   United States Supreme Court and the Uses of Social Science Data.   New York: MSS Information Corp., 1973.   150pp.

71. Davitt, T.E.   The Basic Values in Law: A Study of the Ethico-legal Implications of Psychology and Anthropology.   Philadelphia: American Philosophical Society, 1968.   144pp.

72. Devlin, P.A.   The Enforcement of Morals.   London: Oxford University Press, 1965.   139pp.

73. Dworkin, R.   "Lord Devlin and the Enforcement of Morals,"   75 <u>Yale Law Journal</u> 986-1006 (1966).

74. <u>Education, Social Science, and the Judicial Process</u>, edited by R.C. Rist and R.J. Anson. New York: Teachers College Press, Columbia University, 1977. 130pp.

75. Ehrlich, E.   <u>Fundamental Principles of the Sociology of Law</u>, translated by E. Moll. Cambridge, MA: Harvard University Press, 1936. 541pp. Reprinted by Russell & Russell, New York, 1962.

76. <u>Encyclopedia of the Social Sciences</u>, edited by E.R.A. Seligman and A. Johnson. New York: Macmillan, 1930-35. 13 vols; contains many articles on legal topics.

77. Evan, W.M., ed.   <u>Law and Sociology</u>. New York: Free Press of Glencoe, 1962. 235pp.

78. Frank, J.   <u>Law and the Modern Mind</u>. New York: Brentano's, 1930. 362pp.

79. Freedman, W.   <u>Society on Trial: Current Court Decisions and Social Change</u>. Springfield, IL: C.C. Thomas, 1965. 302pp.

80. "Freedom of Religion and Science Instruction in Public Schools,"   87 <u>Yale Law Journal</u> 515-570 (1978).

81. Friedman, L.M.   <u>Law and Society: An Introduction</u>. Englewood Cliffs, NJ: Prentice-Hall, 1977. 177pp.

82. Friedman, L.M.   "Legal Rules and the Process of Social Change,"   19 <u>Stanford Law Review</u> 786-840 (1967).

83. Friedman. L.M.   <u>The Legal System: A Social Science Perspective</u>. New York: Russell Sage Foundation, 1975. 338pp.

84. Friedman, L.M., and S. Macaulay.   <u>Law and the Behavioral Sciences</u>, 2d edition. Indianapolis, IN: Bobbs-Merrill, 1977. 1076pp.

85. Friedmann, W.G.   <u>Law in a Changing Society</u>, 2d edition. London: Stevens, 1972. 580pp.

86. Fuller, L.L.   <u>The Morality of Law</u>, revised edition. New Haven, CT: Yale University Press, 1969. 262pp.

87. Gluckman, M.   <u>The Allocation of Responsibility</u>. Manchester, England: Manchester University Press, 1972. 335pp.

88. Gould, W.L., and M. Barkun.   <u>Social Science Literature: A Bibliography for International Law</u>. Princeton, NJ: Published for the American Society of International Law, 1972. 641pp.

89. Green, L.C.   <u>Law and Society: Essays in the Sociology of Law</u>. Leyden: Sijthoff, 1975. 502pp.

8

90. Grossman, J.B. et al. "Law and Society: A Selected Bibliography," 2 Law and Society Review 291-340 (1968).

91. Gruter, M. "Law in Sociobiological Perspective," 5 Florida State University Law Review 181-218 (1977).

92. Gurvitch, G.D. Sociology of Law. New York: Philosophical Library, 1942. 309pp. The 1947 edition reprinted by Routledge and Kegan Paul, 1973; 248pp.

93. Hanson, P.O., III, and B. Boehnke. The Spatial Analysis of Crime: A Bibliography. Monticello, IL: Council of Planning Librarians, 1976. 25pp.

94. Harris, M. "Legal-Economic Interdisciplinary Research," 10 Journal of Legal Education 452-474 (1958).

95. Heyman, P.B. "The Problem of Coordination: Bargaining and Rules," 86 Harvard Law Review 797-877 (1973).

96. Hoebel, E.A. The Law of Primitive Man: A Study in Comparative Legal Dynamics. Cambridge, MA: Harvard University Press, 1954. 357pp. Includes a lengthy bibliography, pp.336-349, of works on the law of primitive societies.

97. Holmes, O.W. The Common Law. Boston: Little, Brown, 1881. 442pp. Also see M. DeW. Howe, ed., Harvard University Press, 1963; 338pp.

98. Horowitz, D.L. The Courts and Social Policy. Washington, DC: Brookings Institution, 1977. 309pp.

99. Horwitz, M.J. The Transformation of American Law, 1780-1860. Cambridge, MA: Harvard University Press, 1977. 356pp.

100. The Interaction of Economics and the Law, edited by B.H. Siegan. Lexington, MA: Lexington Books, 1977. 171pp.

101. International Encyclopedia of the Social Sciences, edited by D.L. Sills. New York: Macmillan and Free Press, 1968. 17 volumes; also contains articles on a variety of legal topics.

102. Keeton, R.E. Venturing to Do Justice: Reforming Private Law. Cambridge, MA: Harvard University Press, 1969. 183pp.

103. Lasswell, H.D., and M.S. McDougal. "The Relation of Law to Social Process: Trends in Theories about Law," 37 University of Pittsburgh Law Review 465-485 (1976).

104. Lasswell, H.D., and M.S. McDougal. "Trends in Theories about Law: Maintaining Observational Standpoint and Delimiting the Focus of Inquiry," 8 University of Toledo Law Review 1-50 (1976).

105. Leiser, B.M. Custom, Law, and Morality. Garden City, NY: Doubleday, 1969. 185pp.

106. Leiser, B.M.   Liberty, Justice and Morals: Contemporary Value Con-
     flicts. New York: Macmillan, 1973.   436pp.

107. Letwin, W.   Law and Economic Policy in America.   Edinburgh: Edin-
     burgh University Press, 1965.   304pp.

108. Llewellyn, K.N., and E.A. Hoebel.   The Cheyenne Way: Conflict and
     Case Law in Primitive Jurisprudence.   Norman, OK: University of
     Oklahoma Press, 1941.   360pp.

109. Luijpen, W.A.   Phenomenology of Natural Law.   Pittsburgh, PA:
     Duquesne University Press, 1967.   249pp.

110. McBride, W.L.   Fundamental Change in Law and Society: Hart and
     Sartre on Revolution.   The Hague: Mouton, 1970.   235pp.

111. Malinowski, B.   Crime and Custom in Savage Society.   London: Kegan
     Paul, Trench, Trubner, 1926.   132pp.

112. Michelman, F.I.   "In Pursuit of Constitutional Welfare Rights: One
     View of Rawls' Theory of Justice,"   121 University of Pennsylvan-
     ia Law Review 962-1019 (1973).

113. Morris, C.   The Justification of the Law.   Philadelphia: University
     of Pennsylvania Press, 1971.   214pp.

114. Nader, L., ed.   The Ethnography of Law.   Washington, DC: American
     Anthropological Association, 1965.   212pp.

115. Nader, L., ed.   Law in Culture and Society.   Chicago: Aldine, 1969.
     454pp.

116. Nader, L., and H.F. Todd, Jr., eds.   The Disputing Process in Ten
     Societies.   New York: Columbia University Press, 1978.   304pp.

117. Nagel, S.S.   The Legal Process from a Behavioral Perspective.   Home-
     wood, IL: Dorsey Press, 1969.   399pp.

118. Northrop, F.S.C.   The Complexity of Legal and Ethical Experience.
     Boston: Little, Brown, 1959.   331pp.

119. Olivecrona, K.H.K.   Law as Fact.   Copenhagen: Munksgaard, 1939.
     220pp.   (2d edition; London: Stevens, 1971;   320pp.)

120. Patterson, E.W.   "Jurisprudence and the Sciences," in Jurispru-
     dence, Men and Ideas of the Law, pp.50-65, edited by H.J. James.
     Brooklyn, NY: The Foundation Press, 1953.

121. Podgórecki, A.   Law and Society.   London: Routledge & Kegan Paul,
     1974.   302pp.

122. Posner, R.A.   Economic Analysis of Law, 2d edition.   Boston: Little,
     Brown, 1977.   572pp.

123. Pound, R. "The Need for a Sociological Jurisprudence," 19 Green
      Bag 607-615 (1907). (A pioneer article in the development of
      American sociological jurisprudence.)

124. Pound, R. Social Control through Law. New Haven, CT: Yale Univer-
      sity Press, 1942. 138pp.

125. Psychology in the Legal Process, edited by B.D. Sales. New York:
      Spectrum (distributed by Halsted Press), 1977. 291pp.

126. Rawls, J.B. A Theory of Justice. Cambridge, MA: Harvard Univer-
      sity Press, 1971. 607pp.

127. Riesman, D. "Law and Social Science," 50 Yale Law Journal 636-653
      (1941).

128. Scanlon, T.M., Jr. "Rawls' Theory of Justice," 121 University of
      Pennsylvania Law Review 1020-1069 (1973)

129. Schubert, G.A. Human Jurisprudence: Public Law as Political Sci-
      ence. Honolulu: University Press of Hawaii, 1975. 394pp.

130. Schwartz, R.D. "Social Factors in the Development of Legal Con-
      trol," 63 Yale Law Journal 471-491 (1954).

131. Schwartz, R.D., and J.H. Skolnick, eds. Society and the Legal
      Order. New York: Basic Books, 1970. 652pp.

132. Siegan, B.H., ed. Interaction of Economics and the Law. Lexington,
      MA: Lexington Books, 1977. 171pp.

133. Silber, J.R. "Being and Doing: A Study of Status Responsibility
      and Voluntary Responsibility," 35 University of Chicago Law
      Review 47-91 (1967).

134. Simon, R.J. The Sociology of Law. San Francisco, CA: Chandler,
      1968. 688pp.

135. Skolnick, J.H. "Social Control in the Adversary System," 11 Jour-
      nal of Conflict Resolution 52-70 (1967).

136. Smith, C.G. Conflict Resolution: Contributions of the Behavorial
      Sciences. Notre Dame, IN: University of Notre Dame Press, 1971.
      553pp.

137. Social Anthropology and Law, edited by I. Hamnett. London: Academic
      Press, 1977. 234pp.

138. Social Meaning of Legal Concepts, Numbers 1-5, 1948-53. New York:
      New York University School of Law, 1948-53.

139. Social Responsibility: Journalism, Law, Medicine. Lexington, VA:
      Washington and Lee University, 1975. 78pp.

140. Social Science Approaches to the Judicial Process: A Symposium, J.B.
      Grossman, et al. New York: Da Capo Press, 1971. 78pp. Cover-
      age of symposia on law and society; from 79 Harvard Law Review
      1551-1628 (1966).

141. "Social Science Research and the Law: A Symposium in Honor of Hans
      Zeisel," 41 University of Chicago Law Review 209-295 (1974).

142. Stanwood, C. Research on Violence: Some suggestions by D.J. West,
      and P. Wiles, together with a Bibliography. Cambridge: Univer-
      sity of Cambridge, Institute of Criminology, 1974. 124pp.

143. Stark, W. The Social Bond: An Investigation into the Bases of Law-
      Abidingness. New York: Fordham University Press, 1976-   .
      Volume 1, Antecedents of the Social Bond: The Phylogeny of soci-
      ality; 229pp.

144. Stone, J. Human Law and Human Justice. Stanford, CA: Stanford
      University Press, 1965. 415pp.

145. Stone, J. Law and the Social Sciences in the Second Half Century.
      Minneapolis, MN: University of Minnesota Press, 1966. 121pp.

146. Stone, J. The Province and Function of Law: Law as Logic, Justice,
      and Social Control. A Study in Jurisprudence. Cambridge, MA:
      Harvard University Press, 1950. 918pp.

147. Stone, J. Social Dimensions of Law and Justice. Stanford, CA:
      Stanford University Press, 1966. 933pp.

148. Symposium. "The Ethnography of Law," 67 American Anthropologist,
      Part 2, No. 6 (1965). Contents include: L. Nader, "The Anthro-
      pological Study of Law;" and B. Whiting, "Sex Identity Conflict
      and Physical Violence: A Comparative Study."

149. Symposium. "John Rawls' 'A Theory of Justice'," 40 University of
      Chicago Law Review 486-555 (1973).

150. "Symposium: Law and Social Change," 18 Catholic Lawyer 2-49 (1972).

151. Symposium. "Law and Society," a supplement to Social Problems,
      Summer 1965. Contents include: J.H. Skolnick, "The Sociology
      of Law in America;" H.W. Jones, "A View from the Bridge;"
      G.C. Hazard, "Reflections on Four Studies of the Legal Profes-
      sion;" and A. Rankin, "A Selected Bibliography in the Sociology
      of Law."

152. Symposium. "Social Research and the Law," 23 Journal of Legal
      Education 1-254 (1970).

153. Tapp, J.L., and F.J. Levine. "Legal Socialization: Strategies for
      an Ethical Legality," 27 Stanford Law Review 1-72 (1974).

154. Trubek, D.M. "Toward A Social Theory of Law," 82 Yale Law Journal
      1-50 (1972).

155. Unger, R.M.   Knowledge and Politics. New York: Macmillan, 1975.
     336pp.

156. Unger, R.M.   Law in Modern Society: Toward a Criticism of Social
     Theory. New York: Free Press, 1976. 309pp.

157. Watson, A.   Society and Legal Change. Edinburgh: Scottish Academic
     Press, 1977. 148pp.

158. Weber, M.   On Law in Economy and Society, edited by M. Rheinstein.
     Cambridge, MA: Harvard University Press, 1954. 363pp. Trans-
     lated from Wirtschaft und Gesellschaft, 2d edition, 1925.

159. Yale Review of Law and Social Action, Volumes 1-3, 1970-73. New
     Haven, CT: Yale Law School.

160. Zander, M.   Social Workers, Their Clients and the Law, 2d edition.
     London: Sweet & Maxwell, 1977. 140pp.

161. Zeisel, H.   "Reflections on Experimental Techniques in the Law,"
     15 Jurimetrics Journal 256-272 (1975). Reprinted from 2 Journal
     of Legal Studies (1973).

162. Zeisel, H.   "Social Research on the Law: The Ideal and the Practi-
     cal," in Law and Sociology, pp.124-143, edited by W.M. Evan.
     New York: Free Press of Glencoe, 1962.

163. Zeisel, H., H. Kalven, Jr., and B. Buchholz.   Delay in the Court.
     Boston: Little, Brown, 1959. 313pp.

164. Ziegel, J.S., ed.   Law and Social Change. Toronto: Osgoode Hall
     Law School, York University, 1973. 128pp. (Includes contribu-
     tions by H.W. Arthurs, et al.)

B.1   CURRENT SOURCES

165. American Behavioral Scientist.
          v.1-   1957-   6 times a year.
          Beverly Hills, CA: Sage Publications.

166. Columbia Journal of Law and Social Problems.
          v.1-   1965-   Quarterly.
          New York: Columbia University School of Law.

167. Journal of Law & Economics.
          v.1-   1958-   Semiannual.
          Chicago: University of Chicago Law School.

168. Law and Contemporary Problems.
         v.1-   1933-   Quarterly.
         Durham, NC: Duke University School of Law.
         [Each issue is devoted to a single topic and contains a list of
         topics covered previously.]

169. Law and Human Behavior.
         v.1-   1977-   Quarterly.
         New York: Plenum. Published in association with the American
             Psychology-Law Society, and with the assistance of students
             at the University of Virginia Law School.

170. Law & Society Review.
         v.1-   1966-   Quarterly.
         Denver, CO: Law and Society Association.

171. New York University Review of Law and Social Change.
         v.1-   1971-   Semiannual.
         New York: New York University School of Law.

C.   LAW AS SCIENCE: SCIENTIFIC METHODS, LOGIC, AND LEGAL
     REASONING

C.1 CURRENT SOURCE

172. Jurimetrics Journal.
         v.1-   1959-   Quarterly.
         Chicago: American Bar Association Section of Science and Technol-
         ogy. (Formerly M.U.L.L., Modern Uses of Logic in Law. Deals
         with "the uses of modern logic in law, the uses of modern methods
         of information retrieval in law, the uses of quantitative methods
         for the analysis of legal decision making, and the relationship
         between (a) developments in science and technology and (b) Law.")

C.2 JURISPRUDENCE AND LEGAL REASONING

173. Allen, L.E.   "Formalizing Hohfeldian Analysis to Clarify the Multi-
         ple Sources of Legal Right: A Powerful Lens for the Electronic
         Age," 48 Southern California Law Review 428-487 (1974).

174. Austin, J.   The Province of Jurisprudence Determined and the Uses
         of the Study of Jurisprudence. New York: Noonday Press, 1954.
         396pp. First published in 1832 and 1863. Intro. by H.L.A. Hart.

175. Becker, T.L.   Political Behavioralism and Modern Jurisprudence: A
         Working Theory and Study in Judicial Decision-Making. Chicago:
         McNally, 1964. 177pp.

176. Bentham, J.   The Limits of Jurisprudence Defined, Being Part Two of
     an Introduction to the Principles of Morals and Legislation.
     New York: Columbia University Press, 1945. 358pp. First print-
     ed in 1780.

177. Berman, H.J.   "The Origins of Western Legal Science," 90 Harvard
     Law Review 894-943 (1977).

178. Beutel, F.K.   Experimental Jurisprudence and the Scienstate.   Biele-
     feld: Gieseking, 1975. 404pp.

179. Boasson, C.   The Use of Logic in Legal Reasoning.   Amsterdam: Noord
     Hollandsche Uitgevers Maatschappij, 1966. 23pp.

180. Bodenheimer, E.   Jurisprudence: The Philosophy and Method of the
     Law, revised edition.   Cambridge, MA: Harvard University Press,
     1974. 463pp.

181. Cairns, H.   The Theory of Legal Science.   Chapel Hill, NC: Univer-
     sity of North Carolina Press, 1941. 155pp.

182. Cardozo, B.N.   The Paradoxes of Legal Science.   New York: Columbia
     University Press, 1928. 142pp.

183. Cohen, M.R.   "Philosophy and Legal Science" in Law and the Social
     Order: Essays in Legal Philosophy, pp.219-247.   New York: Har-
     court and Brace, 1933.   Originally published in 32 Columbia Law
     Review 1103-1127 (1932).

184. D'Amato, A.A.   "The Limits of Legal Realism," 87 Yale Law Journal
     468-513 (1978).

185. Dworkin, R.M.   "The Model of Rules," 35 University of Chicago Law
     Review 14-46 (1967).

186. Dworkin, R.M.   "Social Rules and Legal Theory," 81 Yale Law Review
     855-890 (1972).

187. Ehrenzweig, A.A.   Psychoanalytic Jurisprudence.   Leiden: Sijthoff;
     Dobbs Ferry, NY: Oceana, 1971. 395pp.

188. Fried, C.   An Anatomy of Values: Problems of Personal and Social
     Change.   Cambridge, MA: Harvard University Press, 1970. 265pp.

189. Fried, C.   Right and Wrong.   Cambridge, MA: Harvard University
     Press, 1978. 226pp.

190. Friedmann, W.G.   Legal Theory, 5th edition, revised.   London: Stev-
     ens, 1967. 607pp.

191. Fuller, L.L.   "An Afterword: Science and the Judicial Process," 79
     Harvard Law Review 1604-1628 (1966).

192. Fuller, L.L.   Anatomy of the Law.   New York: Praeger, 1968. 122pp.

193. Fuller, L.L. "The Case of the Speluncean Explorers," 62 Harvard Law Review 616-645 (1949).

194. Fuller, L.L. Legal Fictions. Stanford, CA: Stanford University Press, 1967. 192pp.

195. Golding, M.P., ed. The Nature of Law: Readings in Legal Philosophy. New York: Random House, 1966. 274pp.

196. Hart, H.L.A. The Concept of Law. Oxford: Clarendon Press, 1961. 263pp.

197. Hohfeld, W.N. Fundamental Legal Conceptions as Applied in Judicial Reasoning, and Other Legal Essays. New Haven, CT: Yale University Press, 1919. 114pp. Reprinted by Yale University Press, 1965. Originally published in 23 Yale Law Journal 16-59 (1913).

198. Horovitz, J. Law and Logic: A Critical Account of Legal Argument. New York: Springer-Verlag, 1972. 213pp.

199. Hughes, G.B.J., ed. Law, Reason, and Justice. New York: New York University Press, 1969. 269pp.

200. International Congress of Comparative Law, 8th, Pescara, 1970. Legal Thought in the United States of America under Contemporary Pressures. Brussels: Bruylant for the American Association for the Comparative Study of Law, 1970. 689pp.

201. Jaffe, L.L. English and American Judges as Lawmakers. Oxford: Clarendon Press, 1969. 116pp.

202. Jensen, O.C. The Nature of Legal Argument. Oxford: Blackwell, 1957. 166pp.

203. Jhering, R. von. Law as a Means to an End. New York: Macmillan, 1921. 483pp.

204. Kelsen, H. What is Justice? Justice, Law and Politics in the Mirror of Science. Berkeley, CA: University of California Press, 1957. 397pp.

205. Llewellyn, K.N. Jurisprudence: Realism in Theory and Practice. Chicago: University of Chicago Press, 1962. 531pp. (The major papers of the leader of the American school of realistic jurisprudence.)

206. Levi, E.H. An Introduction to Legal Reasoning. Chicago: University of Chicago Press, 1948. 74pp. Also see 15 University of Chicago Law Review 501-574 (1948).

207. McBride, W.L. "The Essential Role of Models and Analogies in the Philosophy of Law," 43 New York University Law Review 53-87 (1968).

208. McCarty, L.T. "Reflections on TAXMAN: An Experiment in Artificial
     Intelligence and Legal Reasoning," 90 Harvard Law Review 837-
     893 (1977). Also in 5 Datenverarbeitung im Recht (1977).

209. Morris, C. How Lawyers Think. Denver, CO: Alan Swallow, 1962.
     144pp.

210. Pound, R. Jurisprudence, 5 volumes. St. Paul, MN: West, 1959.
     (This monumental survey includes discussion of the question of
     law as a science.)

211. Radin. M. Law as Logic and Experience. New Haven, CT: Yale Univer-
     sity Press, 1940. 171pp. Reprinted by Hamden, CT: Shoestring
     Press, Archon Books, 1971.

212. Raz, J. The Concept of a Legal System. Oxford: Clarendon Press,
     1970. 212pp.

213. Stone, J. Legal System and Lawyers' Reasonings. Stanford, CA:
     Stanford University Press, 1964. 454pp. See particularly "Logic
     and Growth in Law," pp.209-234.

214. Thibaut, J., et al. "Adversary Presentation and Bias in Legal Deci-
     sion-Making," 86 Harvard Law Review 386-401 (1972).

215. Tribe, L.H. "Policy Science: Analysis or Ideology," 2 Philosophy
     and Public Affairs 66-110 (1972).

216. Yntema, H.E. "The Rational Basis of Legal Science," 31 Columbia
     Law Review 925-955 (1931).

C.3   SCIENTIFIC METHOD AND LOGIC

217. Allen, L.E. "Some Uses of Symbolic Logic in Law Practice," 8
     Practical Lawyer 51-72 (1962). Also in M.U.L.L. 119-136 (1962).

218. Allen, L.E. "Symbolic Logic: A Razor-Edged Tool for Drafting and
     Interpreting Legal Documents," 66 Yale Law Journal 833-879
     (1957).

219. Allen, L.E., and M.E. Caldwell. "Modern Logic and Judicial Deci-
     sion Making: A Sketch of One View," 28 Law & Contemporary Prob-
     lems 213-275 (1963).

220. Brkic, J. Norm and Order: An Investigation into Logic, Semantics,
     and the Theory of Law and Morals. New York: Humanities Press,
     1970. 159pp.

221. Buchanan, J., and G. Tulloch. The Calculus of Consent: Logical
     Foundations of Constitutional Democracy. Ann Arbor, MI: Univer-
     sity of Michigan Press, 1962. 361pp.

222. Cohen, F.S. "Field Theory and Judicial Logic," 59 Yale Law Journal 238-272 (1950).

223. Cohen, M.R. "Law and Scientific Method," in Law and the Social Order: Essays in Legal Philosophy, pp.184-197. New York: Harcourt and Brace, 1933.

224. Cowan, T.A. "Decision Theory in Law, Science and Technology," 17 Rutgers Law Review 499-530 (1963).

225. Edwards, T.H., and J.P. Barber. "A Computer Method for Legal Drafting Using Propositional Logic," 53 Texas Law Review 965-1004 (1975).

226. Hermann, D.H.J. "A Structuralist Approach to Legal Reasoning," 48 Southern California Law Review 1131-1194 (1975).

227. Lewis, O.C. "Phase Theory and the Judicial Process," 1 California Western Law Review 1-45 (1965).

228. Lewis, O.C. "Systems Theory and Judicial Behavioralism," 21 Case Western Reserve Law Review 361-465 (1970).

229. Loevinger, L. "An Introduction to Legal Logic," 27 Indiana Law Journal 471-522 (1952).

230. Loevinger, L. "Science and Legal Thinking," 25 Federal Bar Journal 153-166 (1965).

231. Noyes, C.R. "Law and the Scientific Method," 55 Political Science Quarterly 496-523 (1940).

232. Science of Legal Method: Select Essays by Various Authors. Boston: Boston Book Co., 1917. 593pp.

233. Shubik, M., and G.D. Brewer. Models, Simulations, and Games: A Survey. Santa Monica, CA: Rand Corporation, 1972. 160pp.

234. Tammelo, I. "Sketch for a Symbolic Juristic Logic," 8 Journal of Legal Education 277-306 (1955).

235. Tulloch, G. The Logic of the Law. New York: Basic Books, 1971. 278pp.

236. Waddell, W. Structure of Laws as Represented by Symbolic Methods. San Diego, CA: Published by the author, 1961. 99pp.

237. Wasserstrom, R.A. The Judicial Decision: Toward a Theory of Legal Justification. Stanford, CA: Stanford University Press, 1969. 197pp.

C.4   LINGUISTICS AND SEMANTICS

238. Bishin, W.R., and C.D. Stone. Law, Language, and Ethics: An Intro-
     duction to Law and Legal Method. Mineola, NY: Foundation Press,
     1972. 1315pp.

239. Blom-Cooper, L.J.   The Language of the Law. New York: Macmillan,
     1965. 397pp.

240. Bryant, M.M.   English in the Law Courts. New York: Columbia Univer-
     sity Press, 1930. 312pp. Reprinted by Frederick Ungar, 1962.

241. Eisele, T.D.   "Legal Imagination and Language: A Philosophical Crit-
     icism," 47 University of Colorado Law Review 363-420 (1976).

242. Mellinkoff, D.S.   The Language of the Law. Boston: Little, Brown,
     1963. 526pp.

243. Ostrower, A.   Language, Law, Diplomacy: A Study of Linguistic Diver-
     sity in Official International Relations and International Law,
     2 volumes. Philadelphia: University of Pennsylvania Press, 1965.

244. Probert, W.   "Law and Persuasion: The Language Behavior of Lawyers,"
     108 University of Pennsylvania Law Review 35-58 (1958).

245. Probert, W.   Law, Language and Communication. Springfield, IL: C.C.
     Thomas, 1972. 376pp.

246. Symposium.   "Language of Law," 9 Western Reserve Law Review 115-
     198 (1958). Contents include: E.B. Duffy, "Practicing Law and
     General Semantics;" W. Probert, "Law, Logic and Communication;"
     L. Loevinger, "Facts, Evidence and Legal Proof;" S.I. Hayakawa,
     "Semantics, Law and 'Priestly-Minded Man';" H.D. Lasswell, "Value
     Analysis of Legal Discourse."

247. Symposium.   "Law, Language and Communication," 23 Case Western Re-
     serve Law Review 307-390 (1972).

248. White, J.B.   Legal Imagination: Studies in the Nature of Legal
     Thought and Expression. Boston: Little, Brown, 1973. 986pp.

C.5   JURIMETRICS

249. Allen, L.E., and M.E. Caldwell, eds.   Communication Sciences and
     Law: Reflections from the Jurimetrics Conference. Indianapolis,
     IN: Bobbs-Merrill, 1965. 442pp.

250. "Education in Jurimetrics," 13 Jurimetrics Journal 67-107 (1972). A
     descriptive list of courses in jurimetrics.

251. "Jurimetrics in Education,"   16 Jurimetrics Journal 74-129 (1975).

252. Loevinger, L.   "Jurimetrics: Science and Prediction in the Field of Law," 46 Minnesota Law Review 255-275 (1961).

253. Loevinger, L.   "Jurimetrics: The Next Step Forward," 12 Jurimetrics Journal 3-41 (1971).

254. Symposium.   "Jurimetrics," 28 Law & Contemporary Problems 1-270 (1963). Published separately as Jurimetrics, edited by H. Baade. New York: Basic Books, 1963. 270pp.

C.6 QUANTITATIVE ANALYSIS AND PREDICTION

255. Dawson, J.M.   "Probabilities and Prejudice in Establishing Statistical Inferences," 13 Jurimetrics Journal 191-225 (1973).

256. Glueck, S., and E. Glueck.   Predicting Delinquency and Crime. Cambridge, MA: Harvard University Press, 1959. 283pp.

257. Haar, C.M., J.P. Sawyer, and S.J. Cummings.   "Computer Power and Legal Reasoning: A Case Study of Judicial Decision Prediction in Zoning Amendment Cases," American Bar Foundation Research Journal 651-768 (1977).

258. Kort, F.   "Simultaneous Equations and Boolean Algebra in the Analysis of Judicial Decisions," 28 Law & Contemporary Problems 143-163 (1963).

259. LaPatra, J.W.   Analyzing the Criminal Justice System. Lexington, MA: Lexington Books, 1978. 173pp.

260. Moskowitz, D.H.   "The Prediction Theory of Law," 39 Temple Law Quarterly 413-431 (1966).

261. Schubert, G.A.   The Judicial Mind Revisited: Psychometric Analysis of Supreme Court Ideology. New York: Oxford University Press, 1974. 183pp.

262. Schubert, G.A.   Quantitative Analysis of Judicial Behavior. Glencoe, IL: The Free Press, 1959. 392pp.

D.   SCIENCE AND THE ADJUDICATORY FUNCTION OF LAW

D.1   CURRENT SOURCES

263. American Criminal Law Review.
          v.1-   1962-   Quarterly.
      Chicago: American Bar Association Section of Criminal Justice.

264. American Journal of Criminal Law.
          v.1-   1972-   3 times a year.
      Austin, TX: University of Texas School of Law.

265. Crime & Delinquency.
          v.1-   1955-   Quarterly.
      Hackensack, NJ: National Council on Crime and Delinquency.

266. Criminology: an interdisciplinary journal.
          v.1-   1963-   Semiannual.
      Beverly Hills, CA: Sage, for the American Society of Criminology.

267. International Journal of Offender Therapy and Comparative Criminol-
          ogy.
          v.1-   1957-   3 times a year.
      London: Association for the Psychiatric Treatment of Offenders
          (APTO).

268. Journal of Criminal Law & Criminology.
          v.1-   1910-   Quarterly.
      Baltimore, MD: Williams & Wilkins for Northwestern University
          School of Law.

269. Polygraph.
          v.1-   1972-   Quarterly.
      Linthicum Heights, MD: American Polygraph Association.

270. Victimology: an international journal.
          v.1-   1976-   Quarterly.
      Washington, DC: Visage Press.

D.2   LEGAL EVIDENCE

271. Barwise, M.A.   "Scientific Proof and Legal Proof," 8 Maine Law Re-
          view 67-86 (1914-15).

272. Botein, B.,   and M.A. Gordon.   The Trial of the Future: Challenge to
          the Law.   New York: Simon and Schuster, 1963.   185pp.

273. Curran, W.J.   Medical Proof in Litigation.   Boston: Little, Brown,
          1961.   244pp.

274. Hart, H.M., Jr., and J.T. McNaughton. "Some Aspects of Evidence
     and Inference in the Law," in Evidence and Inference, pp.48-72.
     Glencoe, IL: The Free Press, 1959. Originally published in 87
     Daedalus (Journal of the American Academy of Arts and Sciences)
     40-64 (1958).

275. Loevinger, L. "Facts, Evidence and Legal Proof," 9 Western Re-
     serve Law Review 154-175 (1958).

276. Michael, J., and M.J. Adler. "The Trial of an Issue of Fact," 34
     Columbia Law Review 1224-1306, 1462-1493 (1934).

277. Moore, C.C. A Treatise on Facts: Or, The Weight and Value of Evi-
     dence, 2 volumes. Northport, NY: Edward Thompson, 1908.

278. Osborn, A.D. The Problem of Proof. Newark, NJ: Essex Press, 1926.
     539pp.

279. Ram, J. A Treatise on Facts as Subjects of Inquiry by a Jury, 3d
     edition. Mount Kisco, NY: Baker, Voorhis, 1873. 486pp.

280. Smith, H.W. "Scientific Proof," 16 Southern California Law Review
     120-160 (1943). Part of the symposium series on "Scientific
     Proof and Relations of Law and Medicine." Also published with
     modifications in 10 University of Chicago Law Review 243-284
     (1943).

281. Smith, H.W., ed. Scientific Proof and Relations of Law and Medi-
     cine (first and second series): A Symposium Series on Law-Sci-
     ence Problems with Particular Reference to Law-Medicine Problems.
     Urbana, IL, 1946. 26pp. Checklists of articles in these index-
     es, and their places of publication, also appear in 10 Univer-
     sity of Chicago Law Review 369-372 (1943) and 16 Southern Cali-
     fornia Law Review 213-219 (1943).

282. Tribe, L.H. "Trial by Mathematics: Precision and Ritual in the
     Legal Process," 84 Harvard Law Review 1329-1393 (1971). Also
     see M.O. Finkelstein and W.B. Fairley, "A Comment on 'Trial by
     Mathematics'," 84 Harvard Law Review 1801-1809 (1971); and L.H.
     Tribe, "A Further Critique of Mathematical Proof," 84 Harvard
     Law Review 1810-1820 (1971).

283. Wigmore, J.H. The Science of Judicial Proof, As Given by Logic,
     Psychology and General Experience, and Illustrated in Judicial
     Trials, 3d edition. Boston: Little, Brown, 1937. 1065pp.

D.2.a CAUSATION

284. Brecht, A.C., and F.W. Miller. The Test of Factual Causation in
     Negligence and Strict Liability Cases. St. Louis, MO: Washing-
     ton University Studies, 1961. 224pp.

22   CAUSATION/SOCIAL SCIENCE EVIDENCE

285. Coval, S.C., and J.C. Smith. "Causal Theory of Law," 36 Cambridge Law Journal 110-151 (1977).

286. Green, L. Rationale of Proximate Cause. Kansas City, MO: Vernon Law Book Co., 1927. 216pp.

287. [Green, N. St. John] "Proximate and Remote Cause," 4 American Law Review 201-206 (1870).

288. Hart, H.L.A., and A.M. Honore. Causation in the Law. London: Oxford University Press, 1959. 454pp.

289. James, F., Jr., and R.F. Perry. "Legal Cause," 60 Yale Law Journal 761-811 (1951).

290. Keeton, R.E. Legal Causes in the Law of Torts. Columbus, OH: Ohio State University Press, 1963. 137pp.

D.2.b   EVIDENCE AND SOCIAL SCIENCE RESEARCH

291. Arnold, G.F. Psychology Applied to Legal Evidence and Other Constructions of Law, 2d edition. Calcutta: Thacker, Spink, 1913. 607pp.

292. Barksdale, H.C. The Use of Survey Research Findings as Legal Evidence. Pleasantville, NY: Printers Ink Books, 1957. 166pp.

293. Frank, J. Court on Trial: Myth and Reality in American Justice. Princeton, NJ: Princeton University Press, 1949. 441pp. Reprinted by Atheneum Press, New York, 1963.

294. The Growing Role of Economic Data in Judicial and Administrative Proceedings. New York: Society of Business Advisory Professions, 1954. 56pp. Current Business Studies, Number 18.

295. Hutchins, R.M., and D. Slesinger. "Some Observations on the Law of Evidence," 28 Columbia Law Review 432-440 (1928); and five further articles, each with the above title and the following subtitles: ":Memory," 41 Harvard Law Review 860-873 (1928); ":The Competency Witness," 37 Yale Law Journal 1017-1028 (1928); ":Consciousness of Guilt," 77 University of Pennsylvania Law Review 725-740 (1929); ":State of Mind to Prove an Act," 38 Yale Law Journal 283-298 (1929); ":State of Mind in Issue," 29 Columbia Law Review 147-157 (1929).

296. Kubie, L.S. "Implications for Legal Procedure of the Fallibility of Human Memory," 108 University of Pennsylvania Law Review 59-75 (1959).

297. Levin, A.L., ed. Evidence and the Behavioral Sciences. Philadelphia: University of Pennsylvania Law School, Institute of Legal Research, 1956.

298. Munsterberg, H.   On the Witness Stand: Essays on Psychology and
        Crime. New York: Clark Boardman, 1923. 269pp. Reprinted, New
        York: AMS Press, 1976.

299. Robbins, I.P.   "The Admissibility of Social Science Evidence in Per-
        son-Oriented Legal Adjudication," 50 Indiana Law Journal 493-
        516 (1975).

D.3 EXPERT WITNESSES

300. American Association for the Advancement of Science. Reports on the
        Use of Expert Testimony in Court Proceedings in Foreign Coun-
        tries. Washington, DC: Press of B.S. Adams, 1918. 313pp. Col-
        lected by the United States Department of State for the use of a
        special committee of the association.

301. Donaldson, S.W.   Roentgenologist in Court, 2d edition. Springfield,
        IL: C.C. Thomas, 1954. 348pp.

302. Friedman, J.   "The Scientist as Expert Witness: Why Lawyers and
        Scientists Can't Talk to Each Other," 18 Jurimetrics Journal 99-
        106 (1977).

303. Hand, L.   "Historical and Practical Considerations Regarding Expert
        Testimony," 15 Harvard Law Review 40-58 (1901).

304. Kraft, M.D., ed.   Using Experts in Civil Cases. New York: Practis-
        ing Law Institute, 1977. 279pp.

305. Liebenson, H.A.   You, The Expert Witness. Chicago: Callaghan, 1962.
        169pp.

306. Rogers, H.W.   The Law of Expert Testimony, 3d edition, rewritten
        and enlarged by B. Werne. New York: Matthew Bender, 1941.
        1101pp. First published in 1883.

307. Symposium.   "Expert Testimony," 34 Temple Law Quarterly 357-486
        (1961). Contents include: S. Polsky, "Expert Testimony: Problems
        in Jurisprudence;" M.S. Guttmacher, "Problems Faced by the Impar-
        tial Expert Witness in Court: The American View;" H. Schroeder,
        "The Continental View;" and F.L. Van Dusen, "The Judicial Point
        of View."

308. "Symposium on the Adversary System and the Role of the Forensic Sci-
        entist," 18 Journal of Forensic Sciences 173-205 (1973).

D.3.a MEDICAL EXPERTS

309. Association of the Bar of the City of New York. Impartial Medical
     Testimony: A Report by a Special Committee on the Medical Expert
     Testimony Project. New York: Macmillan, 1956. 188pp.

310. Beeman, J. Pathologist as a Witness. Chicago: Callaghan, 1964.
     242pp.

311. Cooper, P. The Medical Detectives. New York: David McKay, 1973.
     238pp.

312. Houts, M. Lawyers' Guide to Medical Proof, 2 volumes (loose-leaf).
     Albany, NY: Matthew Bender, 1966.

313. Liebenson, H.A. You, The Medical Witness. Chicago: Year Book Med-
     ical Pub., 1961. 219pp.

314. Nordstrom, N. Rights and Rewards of the Medical Witness and Medi-
     cal and Dental Appraiser. Springfield, IL: C.C. Thomas, 1962.
     104pp.

315. Tilevitz, O.E. "Judicial Attitudes towards Legal and Scientific
     Proof of Cancer Causation," 3 Columbia Journal of Environmental
     Law 344-381 (1977).

316. Wick, W.A., and E.A. Kightlinger. "Impartial Medical Testimony
     under the Federal Civil Rules: A Tale of Three Doctors," Per-
     sonal Injury Annual 281-338 (1967).

D.3.b PSYCHIATRIC EXPERTS*

317. Allen, R.E.B. "Admission of Psychiatric Evidence," 8 Arizona Law
     Review 205-235 (1967).

318. Dix, G.E. "The Death Penalty, Dangerousness, Psychiatric Testimony,
     and Professional Ethics," 5 American Journal of Criminal Law
     151-214 (1977).

319. Ennis, B.J., and T. Litwack. "Psychiatry and the Presumption of
     Expertise: Flipping Coins in the Courtroom," 62 California Law
     Review 693-752 (1974).

320. Group for the Advancement of Psychiatry, Committee on Psychiatry and
     Law. Misuse of Psychiatry in the Criminal Courts: Competency
     to Stand Trial. New York, 1974. (Published as an internal re-
     port, no. 89, vol. 8, 853-919.)

---

* See also Sections G.4 through G.6.

321. Liebenson, H.A., and J.M. Wepman. The Psychologist as a Witness.
      Mundelein, IL: Callaghan, 1964. 288pp.

322. Louisell, D.W. "The Psychiatrist as an Expert Witness: Some Rumi-
      nations and Speculations," 63 Michigan Law Review 1335-1354
      (1965).

323. Practising Law Institute. The Effective Use of Psychiatric Evidence
      in Civil and Criminal Litigation (B.J. George, Jr., chairman).
      New York, 1974. 248pp.

324. Rothblatt, H.B. "The Preparation of the Psychiatric Defense and
      the Direct and Cross-Examination of the Psychiatric Witness,"
      Legal Medicine Annual 299-325 (1971).

325. Ziskin, J. Coping with Psychiatric and Psychological Testimony,
      2d edition. Beverly Hills, CA: Law and Psychology Press, 1975.
      385pp.

D.3.c PRIVILEGED COMMUNICATIONS

326. Cross, W. "Privileged Communications between Participants in Group
      Psychotherapy," Law and the Social Order 191-211 (1970).

327. DeWitt, C. Privileged Communications between Physician and Patient.
      Springfield, IL: C.C. Thomas, 1958. 528pp.

328. Fleming, J.G., and B. Maximov. "The Patient or His Victim: The
      Therapist's Dilemma," 62 California Law Review 1025-1068 (1974).

329. Group for the Advancement of Psychiatry, Committee on Psychiatry and
      Law. Confidentiality and Privileged Communication in the Prac-
      tice of Psychiatry. New York, 1960. 114pp. Published as its
      report--Number 45.

330. Hageman, J.F. Privileged Communications as a Branch of Legal Evi-
      dence. Somerville, NJ: Honeyman, 1889. 328pp.

331. Louisell, D.W., and K. Sinclair, Jr. "Reflections on the Law of
      Privileged Communications: The Psychotherapist-Patient Privilege
      in Perspective," 59 California Law Review 30-55 (1971).

D.4 SCIENTIFIC EVIDENCE

332. Bates, B.P. Typewriting Identification (I.S.Q.T.). Springfield,
      IL: C.C. Thomas, 1971. 101pp.

333. Brown, P.N. "Guilt by Physiology: The Constitutionality of Tests
      to Determine Predisposition to Violent Behavior," 48 Southern
      California Law Review 489-570 (1974).

334. Cederbaums, J.G., and S. Arnold, eds. Scientific and Expert Evi-
      dence in Criminal Advocacy. New York: Practising Law Institute,
      1975. 537pp.

335. Cullison, A.D. "Identification by Probabilities and Trial by Arith-
      metic," 6 Houston Law Review 471-518 (1969).

336. Finkelstein, M.O., and W.B. Fairley. "A Bayesian Approach to Iden-
      tification Evidence," 83 Harvard Law Review 489-517 (1970).

337. Freed, R.N. "Computer Printouts as Evidence," 16 Proof of Facts
      273-350 (1965).

338. Hughes, K.B., and B.J. Cantor. Photographs in Civil Litigation.
      Indianapolis, IN: Bobbs-Merrill, 1973. 796pp.

339. Korn, H. Law and the Determination of Facts Involving Science and
      Technology: A Preliminary Report of the Armstrong Project. New
      York: Columbia University Law School, 1965. 40pp. Reprinted as
      "Law, Fact and Science in the Courts," 66 Columbia Law Review
      1080-1116 (1966).

340. Los Angeles County Law Library. Scientific Tests in the Law: A Bib-
      liography. Los Angeles, CA, May 1963. 18pp.

341. "Scientific Evidence in Traffic Cases," 59 Journal of Criminal Law,
      Criminology and Police Science 57-73 (1968).

342. Smith, D.N. The Law of Confessions and Scientific Evidence. Chap-
      el Hill, NC: University of North Carolina, Institute of Govern-
      ment, 1963. 308pp.

343. Symposium. "Law and Medicine," 3 Journal of Public Law 209-736
      (1954). (Part 1--Law-Science Integrations and the Science of
      Human Behavior; Part 2--Law-Science Integrations and the Science
      of Proof.)

344. Tapper, C. "Evidence from Computers," 8 Georgia Law Review 562-
      613 (1974). Reprinted in 4 Rutgers Journal of Computers and the
      Law 324-406 (1975).

345. Tisdale, D.M. "Proposals for a Uniform Radar Speed Detection Act,"
      7 University of Michigan Journal of Law Reform 440-454 (1974).

346. Wood, D.J. "Commentary on the Law-Science Relationship in the Ad-
      missibility of Scientific Evidence," 18 Idea 5-21 (1976).

D.4.a   BLOOD AND CHEMICAL TEST EVIDENCE

347. American Medical Association, Committee on Medicolegal Problems.
      Alcohol & the Impaired Driver: A Manual on the Medicolegal As-
      pects of Chemical Tests for Intoxication, 2d edition. Chicago,
      1973. 234pp.

348. Andresen, P.H.   The Human Blood Groups Utilized in Disputed Pater-
      nity Cases and Criminal Proceedings. Springfield, IL: C.C.
      Thomas, 1952. 115pp.

349. Brownlee, A.   "Blood and the Blood Groups - A Developing Field for
      Expert Evidence," 5 Forensic Science Society Journal 124-175
      (1965).

350. Davis, C.D.   Breath, Blood and Vehicles. Asheville, NC: Biltmore
      Press, 1972. 253pp.

351. Donigan, R.L.   Chemical Tests and the Law: Legal Aspects of and Con-
      stitutional Issues Involved in Chemical Tests to Determine Alco-
      holic Influence. Chicago: Northwestern Traffic Institute, 1957.
      257pp.

352. Krause, H.D.   "Scientific Evidence and the Ascertainment of Pater-
      nity," 5 Family Law Quarterly 252-281 (1971).

353. Krause, H.D. et al.   "Joint AMA-ABA Guidelines: Present Status of
      Serologic Testing in Problems of Disputed Parentage," 10 Family
      Law Quarterly 247-285 (1976).

354. Lombard, J.F.   Adoption, Illegitimacy and Blood Tests. Boston: Bos-
      ton Law Book Co., 1952. 958pp. (Massachusetts Practice, volume
      3.)

355. Schatkin, S.B.   Disputed Paternity Proceedings. New York: Banks &
      Co., 1953. 823pp.

356. Symposium.   "Intoxication: Legal By-Products of Chemical Testing for
      Intoxication," 11 Cleveland-Marshall Law Review 1-118 (1962).
      Contents include: M.C. Slough and P.E. Wilson, "Legal By-Pro-
      ducts of Chemical Testing for Intoxication;" J.M. MacDonald,
      "Alcoholism as a Medicolegal Problem;" J.E. Martindale, "Intoxi-
      cation and Opinion Evidence;" J. Vamis, "Intoxication and Third
      Parties;" B.J. Conley, "Scientific Investigation of Intoxica-
      tion;" J.J. McGarry, "Habitual Drunkenness Affecting Family Re-
      lations."

357. Weiner, A.S.   Blood Groups and Transfusions. Springfield, IL: C.C.
      Thomas, 1943. 483pp.

D.4.b VOICEPRINTS

358. Barnett, R. "Voiceprints: The End of the Yellow Brick Road," 8
      University of San Francisco Law Review 702-727 (1974).

359. Bricker, P.L. "The Voiceprint Technique: A Problem in Scientific
      Evidence," 18 Wayne Law Review 1365-1402 (1972).

360. Jones, W.R. "Evidence vel non: The non Sense of Voiceprint Identi-
      fication," 62 Kentucky Law Journal 301-326 (1973/74).

361. Michigan, State Police. Voice Identification Research. Washington,
      DC: U.S. Government Printing Office, 1972. 147pp. (U.S. Na-
      tional Institute of Law Enforcement and Criminal Justice.)

362. "Voiceprint Identification," 61 Georgetown Law Journal 703-745
      (1973).

D.4.c LIE DETECTION

363. Abrams, S. A Polygraph Handbook for Attorneys. Lexington, MA: Lex-
      ington Books, 1977. 257pp.

364. Ansley, N. Legal Admissibility of the Polygraph. Springfield, IL:
      C.C. Thomas, 1975. 344pp.

365. Arons, H. Hypnosis in Criminal Investigation. Springfield, IL: C.
      C. Thomas, 1967. 211pp.

366. Block, E.B. Lie Detectors: Their History and Use. New York: McKay,
      1977. 211pp.

367. "The Emergence of the Polygraph at Trial," 73 Columbia Law Review
      1120-1144 (1973).

368. Hiller, L.D. "The Psychological Stress Evaluator: Yesterday's
      Dream -- Tomorrow's Nightmare," 24 Cleveland State Law Review
      300-340 (1975).

369. Inbau, F.E. "The Polygraph Technique," 4 Lawyer's Medical Journal
      355-473 (1969).

370. Inbau, F.E., and J.E. Reid. Lie Detection and Criminal Interroga-
      tion, 3d edition. Baltimore, MD: Williams & Wilkins, 1953.
      242pp.

371. Kubis, J.F. "Comparison of Voice Analysis and Polygraph as Lie De-
      tection Procedures," 3 Polygraph 1-47 (1974).

372. Lee, C.D. Instrumental Detection of Deception: The Lie Test.
      Springfield, IL: C.C. Thomas, 1952. 268pp.

373. Reid, J.E., and F.E. Inbau. Truth and Deception: The Polygraph ("lie-detector") Technique, 2d edition. Baltimore, MD: Williams and Williams, 1977. 430pp.

374. Trovillo, P. "A History of Lie Detection," 1 Polygraph 46-74, 151-160 (1972).

375. U.S. Congress, House of Representatives, Committee on Government Operations. The Use of Polygraphs and Similar Devices by Federal Agencies. Washington, DC: U.S. Government Printing Office, 1974. 790pp.

376. U.S. Congress, House of Representatives, Committee on Government Operations. Use of Polygraphs as "lie detectors" by the Federal Government, 6 parts. Washington, DC: U.S. Government Printing Office, 1964-66.

377. Wilhelm, P.L., and F.D. Burns. Lie Detection with Electrodermal Response. Michigan City, IN: B & W Associates, 1954. 100pp.

D.5 SCIENCE IN AID OF LAW ENFORCEMENT

378. Bailey, J.S., and R.G. Hann. Systems Analysis and the Corrections System in Ontario. Toronto: University of Toronto, Centre of Criminology, 1972. 40pp.

379. Biosocial Bases of Criminal Behavior, edited by S.A. Mednick and K.O. Christiansen. New York: Halsted Press, 1977. 298pp.

380. Criminological Colloquim, 2d, Strasbourg, 1975. Means of Improving Information on Crime. Strasbourg: Council of Europe, 1976. 150pp.

381. Forensic Sciences Foundation. Assessment of the Forensic Sciences Profession, 3 volumes. Washington, DC: U.S. Government Printing Office, 1977.

382. Gordon, R. Forensic Psychology: A Guide for Lawyers and the Mental Health Professions. Tucson, AZ: Lawyers and Judges, 1975. 133pp.

383. Hall, J. "Intoxication and Criminal Responsibility," 57 Harvard Law Review 1045-1084 (1944).

384. Inbau, F.E., A.A. Moenssens, and L.R. Vitullo. Scientific Police Investigation. Philadelphia: Chilton, 1972. 204pp.

385. Institute for Defense Analyses. Task Force Report: Science and Technology. Washington, DC: U.S. Government Printing Office, 1967. 228pp. (A report to the President's Commission on Law Enforcement and Administration of Justice.)

386. International Electronic Crime Countermeasures Conference, 1st, Edin-
     burgh, 1973. Proceedings. Springfield, VA: National Technical
     Information Service, 1973. 203pp.

387. International Symposium on Criminal Justice Information and Statis-
     tics Systems, 3d, Philadelphia, 1976. Proceedings. Sacramento,
     CA: SEARCH Group, 1976. 455pp.

388. Lucas, A. Forensic Chemistry and Scientific Criminal Investigation,
     4th edition. London: Edward Arnold, 1945. 340pp.

389. Mannheim, H. Comparative Criminology, 2 volumes. London: Rout-
     ledge & Kegan Paul, 1965.

390. Medico-Legal Conference, Boston, 1962. Medico-Legal Investigation
     in Murder and Suicide. Boston: Boston University Law-Medicine
     Research Institute, 1962. 219pp.

391. Morland, N. An Outline of Scientific Criminology, 2d edition. New
     York: St. Martin's Press, 1971. 242pp.

392. Munro, J. Classes, Conflict, and Control: Studies in Criminal Jus-
     tice Management. Cincinnati, OH: Anderson, 1976. 591pp.

393. National Symposium on Law Enforcement Science and Technology. Law
     Enforcement Science and Technology: Proceedings, 3 volumes.
     Washington, DC: Thompson Book Co., 1967-71.

394. National Symposium on Science and Criminal Justice, Washington, DC,
     1966. Proceedings. Washington, DC: U.S. Government Printing
     Office, 1967. 189pp. (Sponsored by the President's Commission
     on Law Enforcement and the Administration of Justice, the Pres-
     ident's Office of Science and Technology, and the Department of
     Justice, Office of Law Enforcement Assistance.)

395. Paulsen, M.G. "Intoxication as a Defense to Crime," University of
     Illinois Law Forum 1-24 (1961).

396. Peterson, J.L. Forensic Science: Scientific Investigation in Crim-
     inal Justice. New York: AMS Press, 1975. 450pp.

397. Polson, C.J., and D.J. Gee. The Essentials of Forensic Medicine,
     3d edition. Oxford: Pergamon, 1973. 729pp.

398. Practising Law Institute. Legal Problems of Correctional, Mental
     Health, and Juvenile Detention Facilities, edited by W.A. Carna-
     han. New York, 1975. 574pp.

399. Rape and Its Victims: A Report for Citizens, Health Facilities, and
     Criminal Justice Agencies, L. Brodyaga, et al. Washington, DC:
     U.S. Government Printing Office, 1976. 361pp. (U.S. National
     Institute of Law Enforcement and Criminal Justice.)

400. Thornton, J.I. "Criminalistics: Past, Present, and Future," 11 Lex
     et Scientia 1-44 (1975).

401. U.S. Congress, Senate, Committee on the Judiciary. Criminal Justice
      Data Banks, 1974: Hearings, 2 volumes. Washington, DC: U.S. Gov-
      ernment Printing Office, 1974.

402. U.S. Federal Bureau of Investigation. Handbook of Forensic Science.
      Washington, DC: U.S. Government Printing Office, 1975. 133pp.

403. U.S. Federal Bureau of Investigation. The Science of Fingerprints:
      Classification and Uses. Washington, DC: U.S. Government Print-
      ing Office, 1977. 209pp.

404. U.S. National Bureau of Standards. Standard Reference Collections
      of Forensic Science Materials: Status and Needs, by H.L. Stein-
      berg. Washington, DC: U.S. Government Printing Office, 1977.
      83pp. (For U.S. National Institute of Law Enforcement and Crim-
      inal Justice.)

405. U.S. President's Commission on Law Enforcement and Administration of
      Justice. Challenge of Crime in a Free Society. A Report. Wash-
      ington, DC: U.S. Government Printing Office, 1967. 340pp. Sup-
      porting materials are contained in nine task force reports.

406. Weston, P.B., and K.M. Wells. Criminal Investigation: Basic Per-
      spectives, 2d edition. Englewood Cliffs, NJ: Prentice-Hall,
      1974. 462pp.

407. Zavala, A., and J.J. Paley. Personal Appearance Identification.
      Springfield, IL: C.C. Thomas, 1972. 331pp.

E.   THE LAW OF COMPUTERS AND LEGAL USES OF COMPUTERS*

408. Bigelow, R.P., ed. Computers and the Law: An Introductory Hand-
          book, 2d edition. New York: Commerce Clearing House, 1969.
          226pp.

409. Bigelow, R.P., and S.H. Nycum. Your Computer and the Law. Engle-
          wood Cliffs, NJ: Prentice-Hall, 1975. 283pp.

410. Duggan, M.A. Law and the Computer: A KWIC Bibliography. New York:
          Macmillan, 1973. 323pp.

411. Freed, R.N. Computers and Law: A Reference Work, 5th edition. Bos-
          ton: Published by the author, 1976. 648pp.

412. Lautsch, J.C. "A Digest of State Legislation Relating to Computer
          Technology," 17 Jurimetrics Journal 39-94 (1976).

413. National Law and Electronics Conference, 1st, Lake Arrowhead, CA,
          1960. Law and Electronics: The Challenge of a New Era: A Pio-
          neer Analysis of the Implications of the New Computer Technology
          for the Improvement of the Administration of Justice, edited by
          E.A. Jones. Albany, NY: Matthew Bender, 1962. 373pp.

414. Roberts, J.J. "A Practitioner's Primer on Computer-Generated Evi-
          dence," 41 University of Chicago Law Review 254-280 (1974).

415. Soma, J.T. The Computer Industry: An Economic-Legal Analysis of Its
          Technology and Growth. Lexington, MA: Lexington Books, 1976.
          219pp.

416. "Symposium: Computers in Law and Society," Washington University
          Law Quarterly 372-540 (1977).

417. Tapper, C.F.H. Computers and the Law. London: Weidenfeld & Nicol-
          son, 1973. 314pp.

E.1 CURRENT SOURCES

418. Computer Law Service.
              R.P. Bigelow, editor.
              Chicago: Callaghan, 1972-   (loose-leaf service).

419. Le Court: Global Communications in Legal Information Systems.
              v.1-   1976-   Quarterly.
              Tempe, AZ: World Information Systems Exchange (WISE).

---

* See also Sections F and K.3

420. The Justice System Journal: A Management Review.
          v.1-   1974-   3 times a year.
      Denver, CO: Institute for Court Management.

421. Law and Computer Technology.
          v.1-   1968-   Quarterly.
      Washington, DC: World Peace Through Law Center.

422. Rutgers Journal of Computers and the Law.
          v.1-   1970-   Semiannual.
      Newark, NJ: Rutgers Law School
      An "Index and Selected Bibliography on Computers and the Law" is
      a regular feature of this journal.

E.2 COMPUTERS AND OTHER TECHNOLOGY IN LEGISLATIVE AND
     JUDICIAL ADMINISTRATION

423. Adams, E. Courts and Computers. Chicago: American Judicature So-
      ciety, 1972. 159pp.

424. American Assembly. The Courts, the Public and the Law Explosion,
      edited by H.W. Jones. Englewood Cliffs, NJ: Prentice-Hall, 1965.
      177pp.

425. Barber, J.P., and P.R. Bates. "Videotape in Criminal Proceedings,"
      25 Hastings Law Journal 1017-1042 (1974).

426. Bird Engineering-Research Associates. A Guide to Jury System Man-
      agement, one volume. Washington, DC: U.S. Government Printing
      Office, 1976. U.S. National Institute of Law Enforcement and
      Criminal Justice.

427. Chartrand, R.L., K. Janda, and M. Hugo, eds. Information Support,
      Program Budgeting, and the Congress. New York: Spartan Books,
      1968. 231pp.

428. Coleman, G.V. Video Technology in the Courts, revised edition.
      Washington, DC: U.S. Government Printing Office, 1977. 69pp.

429. Corasick, M.J., and B.G. Brockway. "Protection of Computer-Based
      Information," 40 Albany Law Review 113-153 (1975).

430. Council of State Governments. State Use of Electronic Data Proces-
      sing. Lexington, KY: Council of State Governments, 1974. 51pp.

431. Court Information Systems, B. Kreidel, et al. Washington, DC: U.S.
      Government Printing Office, 1977. 51pp. U.S. National Institute
      of Law Enforcement and Criminal Justice.

432. Elkins, J.S., Jr. A Survey of the Use of Electronic Data Processing
      by State Legislatures. Lexington, KY: Council of State Govern-
      ments, 1971. 119pp.

433. Gilchrist, B., and M.R. Wessel. Government Regulation of the Com-
      puter Industry. New York: AFIPS Press, 1972. 247pp.

434. Holmes, G.W., and C.H. Norville, eds. The Law of Computers. Ann
      Arbor, MI: Institute of Continuing Legal Education, 1971. 332pp.

435. Information Systems Technology in State Government: Developed by the
      National Association for State Information Systems in Conjunction
      with the States. Lexington, KY: Council of State Governments,
      1972. 53pp + appendixes.

436. Klein, F.J. The Administration of Justice in the Courts: A Selected
      Annotated Bibliography, 2 volumes. Dobbs Ferry, NY: Oceana,
      1976.

437. Navarro, J.A., and J.G. Taylor. "Data Analyses and Simulation of a
      Court System for the Processing of Criminal Cases," 9 Jurimet-
      rics Journal 101-126 (1968).

438. Practising Law Institute. Computer Abuse. New York: Practising
      Law Institute, 1975. 206pp.

439. Slivaka, R.T., and J.W. Darrow. "Methods and Problems in Computer
      Security," 5 Rutgers Journal of Computers and the Law 217-269
      (1976).

440. "Symposium: The Use of Videotape in the Courtroom" 1 Brigham Young
      University Law Review 327-541 (1975).

441. U.S. Congress, House of Representatives, Committee on Government Op-
      erations. Use of Computers in the Legislative Process. Wash-
      ington, DC: U.S. Government Printing Office, 1969. 39pp.

442. U.S. Library of Congress, Congressional Research Service, Automated
      Information Services Section. Modern Information Technology in
      the State Legislatures. Washington, DC: U.S. Government Print-
      ing Office, 1972. 137pp. Prepared for the U.S. Congress, Joint
      Committee on Congressional Operations.

443. U.S. Library of Congress, Science Policy Research Division. The
      Congress and Information Technology. Washington, DC: U.S. Gov-
      ernment Printing Office, 1974. 277pp. Prepared for the U.S.
      Congress, House of Representatives Select Committee on Commit-
      tees.

444. The Video Telephone in Criminal Justice: The Phoenix Project, Summary
      Volume, W.A. Eliot, et al. Washington, DC: U.S. Government
      Printing Office, 1977. 95pp. U.S. National Institute of Law
      Enforcement and Criminal Justice.

E.3   COMPUTERIZED LEGAL RESEARCH

445. Allen, L.E., R.B.S. Brooks, and P.A. James. Automatic Retrieval of Legal Literature: Why and How. New Haven, CT: Walter E. Meyer Research Institute of Law, 1962. 113pp.

446. American Bar Association. Application of Electronic Data Processing Systems to Legal Research. Washington, DC: Bureau of National Affairs, 1960. 48pp.

447. Bing, J., and T. Harvold. Legal Decisions and Information Systems. Oslo: Universitets-forlag, 1977. 272pp. Norwegian Research Center for Computers and Law Publication No. 5.

448. "Conference on Computerized Access to Secondary Legal Materials," 18 Idea (No. 3) 67-124 (1976).

449. Janda, K. Information Retrieval: Applications to Political Science. New York: Bobbs-Merrill, 1968. 230pp.

450. Kayton, I. "Retrieving Case Law by Computer: Fact, Fiction, and Future," 35 George Washington Law Review 1-49 (1966).

451. "Legal Information thru Electronics," 14 United States Air Force Judge Advocate General Law Review 3-74 (1972).

452. Mead Data Central, Inc. LEXIS: A Primer, 2d edition. Dayton, OH: Mead Data Central, 1975. 22pp.

453. Mead Data Central, Inc. LEXIS Deskbook, loose-leaf, one volume. Dayton, OH: Mead Data Central, 1978.

454. Meldman, J.A. "A Structural Model for Computer-Aided Legal Analysis," 6 Rutgers Journal of Computers and the Law 27-71 (1977).

455. National Association of Attorneys General, Committee on the Office of Attorney General. Computerized Research in the Law. Raleigh, NC: National Association of Attorneys General, 1976. 40pp.

456. National Conference on Automated Law Research, 1st, Georgia Institute of Technology, 1972. Automated Law Research. R.A. May, Chairman. Chicago: American Bar Association, 1973. 182pp.

457. National Conference on Automated Law Research, 2d, Monterey, CA, 1973. Sense & Systems in Automated Law Research, edited by R.A. May. Chicago: American Bar Association, Section of Science & Technology, 1975. 170pp.

458. Sager, A.M. An Evaluation of Computer-Assisted Legal Research Systems for Federal Court Applications. Washington, DC: Federal Judicial Center, 1977. 229pp.

459. Slayton, P. Electronic Legal Retrieval: A Report. Ottawa: Information Canada, 1974. 46pp.

460. Sprowl, J.A.   "Computer-Assisted Legal Research: An Analysis of
     Full-Text Document Retrieval Systems, Particularly the LEXIS
     System," 1 American Bar Foundation Research Journal 175-226
     (1976).

461. Sprowl, J.A.   A Manual for Computer-Assisted Legal Research. Chi-
     cago: American Bar Foundation, 1976. 115pp.

F. LEGAL PROBLEMS OF PRIVACY

462. Chief Justice Earl Warren Conference on Advocacy in the United
     States, Cambridge, MA, 1974. Privacy in a Free Society: Final
     Report. Cambridge, MA: Roscoe Pound-American Trial Lawyers
     Foundation, 1974. 104pp.

463. Clark, R.H.   "Constitutional Sources of the Penumbral Right to Pri-
     vacy," 19 Villanova Law Review 833-884 (1974).

464. Comparative Legislative Information Systems: The Use of Computer
     Technology in the Public Policy Process, edited by J.A. Worthley.
     Washington, DC: National Science Foundation, 1976. 179pp.

465. Cowan, P., N. Egleson, and N. Hentoff.   State Secrets: Police Sur-
     veillance in America. New York: Holt, Rinehart and Winston,
     1974. 333pp.

466. Dial, O.E., and E.M. Goldberg.   Privacy, Security, and Computers:
     Guidelines for Municipal and Other Public Information Systems.
     New York: Praeger, 1975. 169pp.

467. "Foreign Security Surveillance and the Fourth Amendment," 87 Har-
     vard Law Review 976-1000 (1974).

468. Gerety, T.   "Redefining Privacy," 12 Harvard Civil Rights-Civil
     Liberties Law Review 233-296 (1977).

469. Gross, H.   Privacy: Its Legal Protection, revised edition. Dobbs
     Ferry, NY: Oceana, 1976. 108pp.

470. Halperin, M.H., and D. Hoffman.   Freedom vs. National Security:
     Secrecy and Surveillance. New York: Chelsea House, 1977. 594pp.

471. Hermann, D.H.J., III.   "Privacy, The Prospective Employee and Em-
     ployment Testing: The Need to Restrict Polygraph and Personality
     Testing," 47 Washington Law Review 73-154 (1971).

472. Hofstadter, S.H., and G. Horowitz.   Right of Privacy. New York:
     Central Book Co., 1964. 377pp.

473. Latin, H.A.   Privacy: A Selected Bibliography and Topical Index of
     Social Science Materials. South Hackensack, NJ: Rothman, 1976.
     93pp.

474. Parker, D.B., S.H. Nycum, and S.S. Oüra. Computer Abuse. Spring-
     field, VA: National Technical Information Service, U.S. Dept. of
     Commerce, 1973. 131pp.

475. Pound, R. "Interests of Personality," 28 Harvard Law Review 343-
     365, 445-456 (1915).

476. "Privacy," 31 Law and Contemporary Problems 251-435 (1966).

477. Prosser, W.L. "Privacy," 48 California Law Review 383-423 (1960).

478. Public Affairs Press. Uncle Sam is Watching You: Highlights from
     the Hearings of the Senate Subcommittee on Constitutional Rights,
     S.J. Ervin, et al. Washington, DC: Public Affairs Press, 1971.
     244pp.

479. Smith, R.E. Compilation of State and Federal Laws on Privacy.
     Washington, DC: Privacy Journal, 1976. 167pp.

480. Surveillance, Dataveillance and Personal Freedoms: Use and Abuse of
     Information. Fair Lawn, NJ: R.E. Burdick, 1973. 247pp. (Orig-
     inally appeared as a symposium in 4 Columbia Human Rights Law
     Review 1-235 (1972); includes articles by A.R. Miller, S.J. Ervin,
     N. deB. Katzenbach, F. Askin, and M.A. Baker.

481. Symposium. "The Griswold Case and the Right of Privacy," 64 Michi-
     gan Law Review 197-288 (1965). (Includes contributions by R.G.
     Dixon, Jr., T.I. Emerson, P.G. Kauper, R.B. McKay, and A.E. Suth-
     erland.)

482. U.S. Congress, House of Representatives, Committee on Government Op-
     erations. The Computer and Invasion of Privacy: Hearings before
     the Special Subcommittee on Invasion of Privacy. Washington, DC:
     U.S. Government Printing Office, 1966. 318pp.

483. Warren, S.D., and L.D. Brandeis. "The Right to Privacy," 4 Har-
     vard Law Review 193-220 (1890).

484. Wessel, M.R. Freedom's Edge: The Computer Threat to Society. Read-
     ing, MA: Addison-Wesley, 1974. 137pp.

485. Westin, A.F., ed. Information Technology in a Democracy. Cam-
     bridge, MA: Harvard University Press, 1971. 499pp.

486. Westin, A.F. Privacy and Freedom. New York: Atheneum Press, 1967.
     487pp.

487. Young, J.B., ed. Privacy: A Multidisciplinary Study. New York:
     Wiley-Interscience, 1978. 358pp.

488. Zelermyer, W. Invasion of Privacy. Syracuse, NY: Syracuse Univer-
     sity Press, 1959. 161pp.

F.1   EAVESDROPPING AND WIRETAPPING

489. Carr, J.G.   The Law of Electronic Surveillance. New York: Clark
      Boardman, 1977. 594pp.

490. Courtney, J.   "Electronic Eavesdropping, Wiretapping and Your Right
      to Privacy," 25 Federal Communications Bar Journal 1-60 (1973).

491. Dash, S., R.F. Schwartz, and R.E. Knowlton.   The Eavesdroppers.
      New Brunswick, NJ: Rutgers University Press, 1959. 484pp.

492. Decker, J.F., and J. Handler.   "Electronic Surveillance: Standards,
      Restrictions and Remedies," 12 California Western Law Review 60-
      101 (1975).

493. "Electronic Surveillance by Law Enforcement Officers," 64 Northwest-
      ern University Law Review 63-86 (1969).

494. McGuire, J.M.   Evidence of Guilt: Restrictions upon Its Discovery or
      Compulsory Disclosure. Boston: Little, Brown, 1959. 295pp.

495. Murphey, W.F.   Wiretapping on Trial: A Case Study in the Judicial
      Process. New York: Random House, 1965. 176pp.

496. National Lawyers Guild.   Raising and Litigating Electronic Surveil-
      lance Claims in Criminal Cases, one volume. San Francisco: Lake
      Law Books, 1977.

497. Paulsen, M.G.   The Problems of Electronic Eavesdropping. Philadel-
      phia: American Law Institute-American Bar Association Committee
      on Continuing Professional Education, 1977. 136pp.

498. Pollock, D.A.   Methods of Electronic Audio Surveillance. Spring-
      field, IL: C.C. Thomas, 1973. 385pp.

499. Schwartz, H.   A Report on the Costs and Benefits of Electronic Sur-
      veillance. New York: American Civil Liberties Union, 1971.
      46pp.

500. Spritzer, R.S.   "Electronic Surveillance by Leave of the Magistrate:
      The Case in Opposition," 118 University of Pennsylvania Law Re-
      view 169-201 (1969).

501. Symposium.   "The Wiretapping-Eavesdropping Problem: Reflections on
      The Eavesdroppers," 44 Minnesota Law Review 813-940 (1960).
      (Includes consideration of the subject by E.B. Williams, T. Hen-
      nings, H.K. Lipset, Y. Kamisar, and E.S. Silver.

502. U.S. Congress, Senate, Committee on the Judiciary.   Surveillance
      Technology. Washington, DC: U.S. Government Printing Office,
      1976. 1280pp.

503. U.S. Congress, Senate, Committee on the Judiciary. Wiretapping and
     Eavesdropping: Summary Report, 1958-1961: Hearings Before the
     Subcommittee on Constitutional Rights. Washington, DC: U.S. Gov-
     ernment Printing Office, 1962. 71pp.

504. U.S. National Commission for the Review of Federal and State Law Re-
     lating to Wiretapping and Electronic Surveillance. Commission
     Hearings, 2 volumes. Washington, DC: U.S. Government Printing
     Office, 1976.

505. "Wiretapping and Electronic Surveillance: Title III of the Crime Con-
     trol Act of 1968," 23 Rutgers Law Review 319-388 (1969).

F.2 PERSONAL RECORDS

506. Boyer, B.B. "Computerized Medical Records and the Right to Privacy:
     The Emerging Federal Response," 25 Buffalo Law Review 37-118
     (1975).

507. Countryman, V. "The Diminishing Right of Privacy: The Personal Dos-
     sier and the Computer," 49 Texas Law Review 837-871 (1971). Re-
     printed in Law in Contemporary Society, pp.61-95 (Austin: Univ-
     ersity of Texas Press, 1973).

508. Draper, H.L. "Privacy and Police Intelligence Data Banks," 14 Har-
     vard Journal on Legislation 1-110 (1976).

509. Hayt, E., and J. Hayt. Legal Aspects of Medical Records. Berwyn,
     IL: Physicians Record Co., 1964. 371pp.

510. Hirsh, H.L. "Medicolegal Implications of Medical Records," Legal
     Medicine Annual 171-188 (1975).

511. Miller, A.R. The Assault on Privacy: Computers, Data Banks and Dos-
     siers. Ann Arbor, MI: University of Michigan Press, 1971. 333pp.

512. Ohio, State of, Legislative Service Commission. Computer Data Sys-
     tems and Their Effect on Individual Privacy. Columbus, OH: Ohio
     Legislative Service Comm., 1975. 81pp. Staff Research Report
     117.

513. Seminar on Data Protection and Privacy, Paris, 1974. Policy Issues
     in Data Protection and Privacy: Concepts and Perspectives. Par-
     is: Organisation for Economic Co-operation and Development, 1976.
     324pp.

514. U.S. Congress, Senate, Committee on Finance. Federal Tax Return
     Privacy: Hearings. Washington, DC: U.S. Government Printing Off-
     ice, 1975. 308pp.

515. U.S. Congress, Senate, Committee on the Judiciary. Invasions of
      Privacy (Government Agencies), Hearings before the Subcommittee
      on Administrative Practice and Procedure, 4 parts. Washington,
      DC: U.S. Government Printing Office, 1965-66.

516. U.S. Department of Health, Education and Welfare. Records, Compu-
      ters, and the Rights of Citizens. Washington, DC: U.S. Govern-
      ment Printing Office, 1973. 346pp.

517. U.S. Law Enforcement Assistance Administration, National Criminal
      Justice Information and Statistics Service. Confidentiality of
      Research and Statistical Data. Washington, DC: U.S. Government
      Printing Office, 1978. 33pp.

518. U.S. Law Enforcement Assistance Administration, National Criminal
      Justice Information and Statistics Service. Privacy and Secur-
      ity of Criminal History Information: Summary of State Plans.
      Washington, DC: Department of Justice, 1977. 33pp.

519. Westin, A.F. Computers, Health Records, and Citizen Rights. Wash-
      ington, DC: U.S. Government Printing Office, 1977. 381pp.

520. Westin, A.F., ed. Databanks in a Free Society: Computers, Record-
      keeping and Privacy. New York: Quadrangle Books, 1972. 522pp.
      Report of the Project on Computer Databanks of the Computer Sci-
      ence and Engineering Board, National Academy of Sciences.

521. Willy, F.J. "Right to Privacy in Personal Medical Information,"
      Medical Trial Technique Quarterly 164-183 (1977).

G. MEDICINE AND LAW

522. Alton, W.G., Jr. Malpractice: A Trial Lawyer's Advice for Physi-
      cians (How to Avoid, How to Win). Boston: Little, Brown, 1977.
      230pp.

523. American Bar Association, Commission on Medical Professional Lia-
      bility. Interim Report. Chicago: American Bar Association,
      1976. 68pp.

524. American Board of Legal Medicine, Inc. Collected Papers 1956-1959.
      New York: Central Book Co., 1960. 238pp.

525. American Hospital Association, Special Committee on the Regulatory
      Process. Hospital Regulation. Chicago: American Hospital As-
      sociation, 1977. 188pp.

526. Annas, G.J. The Rights of Hospital Patients. New York: Avon Books,
      1975. 246pp.

527. Association of American Law Schools. Law Books Recommended for
      Libraries, List No. 28, "Medical Jurisprudence" (1968), and "Sup-
      plement to List No. 28" (1974). South Hackensack, NJ: Rothman.
      This useful series of bibliographies also covers other fields,
      e.g., aeronautics, atomic energy, food, drugs, cosmetics, and
      water law.

528. Barrow, R.L. Epilepsy and the Law: A Proposal for Legal Reform in
      the Light of Medical Progress. New York: Harper & Row, 1956.
      177pp.

529. Beck, T.R. Elements of Medical Jurisprudence, 2 volumes. Albany,
      NY: Webster and Skinner, 1823.

530. Bornette, W.H.L., ed. Legal Aspects of Anesthesia. Philadelphia:
      F.A. Davis, 1972. 599pp.

531. Brecht, A., et al. Medical Malpractice Insurance and its Alterna-
      tives: The Legal, Medical, and Insurance Literature: A Biblio-
      graphy. Los Angeles: University of Southern California, Law Cen-
      ter Library, 1975. 25pp.

532. Brittain, R.P. Bibliography of Medico-Legal Works in English. Lon-
      don: Sweet & Maxwell, 1962. 252pp.

533. Brown, K.L. Medical Problems and the Law. Springfield, IL: C.C.
      Thomas, 1971. 280pp.

534. California at Davis, University of, School of Law. Problems in
      Law and Medicine. Davis, CA: University of California, 1974.
      567pp. Issued as Vol. 7, Univ. of Calif. at Davis Law Review.

535. Charfoos, L.S. The Medical Malpractice Case: A Complete Handbook.
      Englewood Cliffs, NJ: Prentice-Hall, 1974. 201pp.

536. Chayet, N.L. Legal Implications of Emergency Care. New York: Appleton-Century-Crofts, 1969. 342pp.

537. Chitty, J. A Practical Treatise on Medical Jurisprudence. Philadelphia: Carey, Lea & Blanchard, 1835. 509pp.

538. Courtroom Medicine. New York: Matthew Bender, 1962- . Publisher's series of loose-leaf volumes. Includes, e.g., L. Gelfand, The Low Back, 1962- ; L.F. Chapman, Pain and Suffering, 1967- ; M. Houts, Death, 1966- ; J.R. Kalisch, Abdominal Injuries, 1973- ; M.E. Lewis, and R.L. Sadoff, Psychic Injuries, 1975- .

539. Curran, W.J. How Lawyers Handle Medical Malpractice Cases: An Analysis of an Important Medicolegal Study. Springfield, VA: distributed by National Technical Information Service for U.S. Department of Health, Education, and Welfare, 1977. 46pp.

540. Curran, W.J., and D.D. Shapiro. Law, Medicine and Forensic Science, 2d edition. Boston: Little, Brown, 1970. 1046pp. Supplement. Boston: Little, Brown, 1974. 196pp.

541. Dean, A. Principles of Medical Jurisprudence: Designed for the Professions of Law and Medicine. Albany, NY: Gould, Banks & Gould, 1850. 664pp.

542. Elwell, J.J. A Medico-Legal Treatise on Malpractice and Medical Evidence, Comprising the Elements of Medical Jurisprudence. New York: J.S. Voorhies, 1860. 588pp.

543. Epilepsy Foundation of America. The Legal Rights of Persons with Epilepsy: A Survey of State Laws and Administrative Policies Relating to Persons with Epilepsy: With a Special Section of Model Legislation, 4th edition. Washington, DC: Epilepsy Foundation of America, 1976. 154pp.

544. Feldstein, P.J. Health Associations and the Demand for Legislation: The Political Economy of Health. Cambridge, MA: Ballinger, 1977. 255pp.

545. Fox, R.M. The Medicolegal Report: Theory and Practice. Boston: Little, Brown, 1969. 260pp.

546. Freed, R.N. "Legal Aspects of Computer Use in Medicine," 32 Law and Contemporary Problems 674-706 (1967).

547. Freedman, W. Allergy and Products Liability. New York: Central Book Co., 1961. 529pp.

548. Gilmer, W., Jr. "Lawyers in Medical Bookland: A Bibliographic Essay for Lawyers Concerning Medical Books," University of Illinois Law Forum 115-129 (1970).

549. Goldstein, I., and L.W. Shabat. Medical Trial Technique. Chicago: Callaghan, 1942. 875pp.

550. Gonzales, T.A. Legal Medicine, Pathology and Toxicology, 2d edi-
       tion. New York: Appleton-Century-Crofts, 1954. 1349pp.

551. Gosfield, A. PSROs: The Law and the Health Consumer. Cambridge,
       MA: Ballinger, 1975. 264pp.

552. Gots, R.E. The Truth about Medical Malpractice: The Patient's
       Rights, the Doctor's Rights. New York: Stein and Day, 1975.
       216pp.

553. Grad, F.P. Public Health Law Manual: A Handbook on the Legal As-
       pects of Public Health Administration and Enforcement. New York:
       American Public Health Association, 1965. 225pp.

554. Gray, R.N. Attorneys' Textbook of Medicine, 3d edition. Albany,
       NY: Matthew Bender, 1949- . Loose-leaf service. (From 1967
       the service is called Gordy-Gray and is supplemented by L.J.
       Gordy.)

555. Harney, D.M. Medical Malpractice. Indianapolis, IN: Allen Smith,
       1973. 595pp.

556. Holder, A.R. Legal Issues in Pediatrics and Adolescent Medicine.
       New York: Wiley, 1977. 350pp.

557. Holder, A.R. Medical Malpractice Law. New York: Wiley, 1975.
       561pp.

558. Houts, M., ed. Courtroom Medicine. Springfield, IL: C.C. Thomas,
       1958. 511pp.

559. Houts, M. Lawyers' Guide to Medical Proof, 2 volumes. Albany, NY:
       Matthew Bender, 1966- . Volume 2 is loose-leaf.

560. Humber, J.M., and R.F. Almeder, eds. Biomedical Ethics and the
       Law. New York: Plenum, 1976. 541pp.

561. Institute of Continuing Legal Education, University of Michigan-Wayne
       State University. New Developments in Law/Medicine, edited by
       G.H. Morris and M.L. Norton. Ann Arbor, MI, 1974. 399pp.

562. Interamerican Conference on Legal Medicine and Forensic Science, 1st,
       Rio Piedras, Puerto Rico, 1962. Law, Medicine, Science--and
       Justice, edited by L.A. Bear. Springfield, IL: C.C. Thomas,
       1964. 636pp.

563. "International Medical Law," 54 International Law Association. Con-
       ference Report 247-336 (1970).

564. International Symposium on Society, Medicine, and Law, Jerusalem,
       1972. Proceedings, edited by H. Karplus. Amsterdam: Elsevier,
       1973. 204pp.

565. Jaksetic, E. "Bioethics and the Law: A Bibliography, 1974-76," 2
       American Journal of Law & Medicine 263-281 (1976-77).

566. Keeton, R.E.   "Compensation for Medical Accidents," 121 <u>University of Pennsylvania Law Review</u> 590-617 (1973).

567. King, J.H., Jr.   "In Search of a Standard of Care for the Medical Profession: The Accepted Practice Formula," 28 <u>Vanderbilt Law Review</u> 1213-1276 (1975).

568. King, J.H., Jr.   <u>The Law of Medical Malpractice in a Nutshell</u>. St. Paul, MN: West, 1977. 340pp.

569. Kramer, C.   <u>Medical Aspects of Negligence Cases</u>. New York: Practising Law Institute, 1961. 96pp.

570. Kramer, C.   <u>Medical Malpractice</u>, 4th edition. New York: Practising Law Institute, 1976. 235pp.

571. Ladimer, I., and L.F. Brown.   <u>Medical Malpractice Arbitration: An Annotated Bibliography</u>. New York: American Arbitration Association, 1977. 40pp.

572. "The Law and Transsexualism: A Faltering Response to a Conceptual Dilemma," 7 <u>Connecticut Law Review</u> 288-345 (1975).

573. <u>Lawyers' Medical Cyclopedia of Personal Injuries and Allied Specialities</u>. Indianapolis, IN: Allen Smith, 1958- . Kept up to date by recompiled volumes. <u>Supplementary service</u>, 1963- .

574. <u>Legacies in Law and Medicine</u>, edited by C.R. Burns. New York: Science History Pub., 1977. 310pp.

575. "Legal Medicine in Europe: An Introduction," 10 <u>Forensic Science</u> 3-86 (1977).

576. <u>A Legislator's Guide to the Medical Malpractice Issue</u>. D.G. Warren, and R. Merritt. Washington, DC: Health Policy Center, Georgetown University, 1976. 81pp.

577. Louisell, D.W., and H. Williams.   <u>Medical Malpractice</u>. New York: Matthew Bender Co., 1960- . (loose-leaf).

578. Louisell, D.W., and H. Williams.   <u>The Parenchyma of Law: A Dissection of the Legal Principles Affecting the Doctor, His Practice and His Role as Citizen, Witness or Defendant</u>. Rochester, NY: Professional Medical Pub., 1960. 517pp.

579. McMahon, J.   "Directory of Organizations and Resource Centers of Medicolegal Interest," 3 <u>American Journal of Law & Medicine</u> 97-113 (1977).

580. <u>Malpractice and Product Liability Actions Involving Drugs</u>, edited by R.M. Patterson and H.N. Morse. Indianapolis, IN: A. Smith, 1976. 409pp.

581. Meaney, T.F., A.F. Lalli, and R.J. Alfidi.   <u>Complications and Legal Implications of Radiologic Special Procedures</u>. St. Louis: C.V. Mosby, 1973. 207pp.

582. Medical Malpractice: A Selected Annotated Bibliography. Silver Spring, MD: Macro Systems, 1975. 89pp.

583. Medicine, Law and Public Policy, Volume 1, edited by N.N. Kittrie, H.L. Hirsch, and G. Wegner. New York: AMS Press, 1975. 605pp.

584. Mersky, R.M., D.A. Kronick, and L.W. Sheridan. A Manual on Medical Literature for Law Librarians: A Handbook and Annotated Bibliography. Dobbs Ferry, NY: distributed by Oceana for Glanville, 1973. 196pp.

585. Morris, W.O. Dental Litigation, 2d edition. Charlottesville, VA: Michie, 1977. 419pp.

586. National Research Council, Committee on the Life Sciences and Social Policy. Assessing Biomedical Technologies: An Inquiry into the Nature of the Process, M. Katz, Committee Chairman. Washington, DC: National Academy of Sciences, 1975. 114pp.

587. National Society for Medical Research. National Conference on the Legal Environment of Medical Science: Report. Chicago: University of Chicago Press, 1959. 114pp.

588. Nemec, J. International Bibliography of Medicolegal Serials 1736-1967. National Library of Medicine. Washington, DC: U.S. Government Printing Office, 1969. 110pp.

589. Nemec, J. International Bibliography of the History of Legal Medicine. National Library of Medicine. Washington, DC: U.S. Government Printing Office, 1974. 224pp.

590. New York (State), Special Advisory Panel on Medical Malpractice. Report. New York: The Panel, 1976. 292pp.

591. Nick, W.V. Index of Legal Medicine 1940-1970: Annotated Bibliography. Columbus, OH: Legal Medicine Press, 1970. 994pp., and Supplements, 1970-72.

592. Pies, H.E., et al. "Topical Index to Selected Medicolegal Information," 2 American Journal of Law & Medicine 177-196 (1976).

593. Practising Law Institute. Medical Ethics and Legal Liability, C.H. Wecht, Chairman. New York: Practising Law Institute, 1976. 355pp.

594. Practising Law Institute. New Developments in Medical Malpractice, L.S. Goldsmith, Chairman. New York: Practising Law Institute, 1974. 352pp.

595. Ramsey, R.P. Ethics at the Edges of Life: Medical and Legal Intersections. New Haven, CT: Yale University Press, 1978. 353pp.

596. Regan, L.J. Doctor and Patient and the Law, 5th edition, by R.C. Morris and A.R. Moritz. St. Louis, MO: C.V. Mosby, 1971. 554pp.

597. Regan, L.J. Handbook of Legal Medicine, 4th edition, by A.R. Moritz and R.C. Morris. St. Louis, MO: C.V. Mosby, 1975. 286pp.

598. Roady, T.G., and W.R. Anderson. Professional Negligence. Nashville, TN: Vanderbilt University Press, 1960. 332pp.

599. Sagall, E.L. "Directory of Periodical Publications of Medicolegal Interest," 3 American Journal of Law & Medicine 115-141 (1977).

600. Schneller, E.S. "Interprofessional Legal Practitioners: The Case of the M.D.-LL.B.," 27 Journal of Legal Education 324-346 (1975).

601. Schroeder, O.C., Jr. "The Influence of Medical and Biological Progress on the Criminal Law," in International Congress of Comparative Law. 8th, Pescara, 1970. Legal Thought in the United States of America under Contemporary Pressures, pp. 633-655. Brussels: E. Bruylant, 1970.

602. Simpson, C.K. Modern Trends in Forensic Medicine. London: Butterworth, 1953. 327pp.

603. Southwick, A.F., and G.J. Siedel, Jr. The Law of Hospital and Health Administration. Ann Arbor, MI: Health Administration Press, 1978. 496pp.

604. Sussman, A.N., and S.J. Cohen. Reporting Child Abuse and Neglect: Guidelines for Legislation. Cambridge, MA: Ballinger, 1975. 255pp.

605. "Symposium: Federal Regulation of the Health Care Delivery System," 6 University of Toledo Law Review 577-836 (1975).

606. Titmuss, R.M. The Gift Relationship: From Human Blood to Social Policy. New York: Pantheon Books, 1971. 339pp.

607. Tort and Medical Yearbook, volume 1-2; 1961-62. Indianapolis, IN: Bobbs-Merrill.

608. "Transsexualism, Sex Reassignment Surgery, and the Law," 56 Cornell Law Review 963-1009 (1971).

609. U.S. Army, Walter Reed Army Institute of Nursing, Washington, DC. Legal Implications of Medical Emergency. Washington, DC: The Institute, 1975. 85pp.

610. Van Der Borght, R.B. "The Effect of Biology and Modern Medicine in Private Law," in International Congress of Comparative Law, 8th, Pescara, 1970. Legal Thought in the United States of America under Contemporary Pressures, pp. 203-226. Brussels: E. Bruylant, 1970.

611. Veatch, R.M., and R. Branson, eds. Ethics and Health Policy. Cambridge, MA: Ballinger, 1976. 332pp.

612. Waltz, J.R., and F.E. Inbau.   Medical Jurisprudence. New York:
      Macmillan, 1971. 398pp.

613. Wasmuth, C.E.   Anesthesia and the Law. Springfield: IL: C.C.
      Thomas, 1961.

614. Wecht, C.H.   "Legal Medicine: An Historical Review and Future Per-
      spective," 22 New York Law School Law Review 873-903 (1977).

G.1 CURRENT SOURCES

615. Abortion Bibliography for 1970-___.
         M.K. Floyd, compiler.
         1972-   annual.
         Troy, NY: Whitston Publishing Co.

616. American Journal of Law & Medicine.
         v.1-   1975-   Quarterly.
         Cambridge, MA: MIT Press for the American Society of Law and
            Medicine.
         Each issue includes "Medicolegal Reference Library," selected
            recent court decisions, highlights of federal legislative
            and executive action, selected annotated book releases,
            and a selected listing of journal articles.

617. Annual Review of Population Law: Constitutions, Legislation, Regu-
         lations, Legal Opinions and Judicial Decisions.
         International Advisory Committee on Population and Law.
         Variously published as part of the following series: 1974-75,
            Law and Population Monograph Series; 1976, Law and Popu-
            lation Book Series; 1977- , New York: United Nations Fund
            for Population Activities.

618. Bibliography of Society, Ethics and the Life Sciences.
         1973-   Annual.
         Hastings-on-Hudson, NY: Institute of Society, Ethics and the
            Life Sciences.

619. Bioethics Digest: Summaries of Literature on Biomedical Ethics.
         v.1-   1973-   Monthly.
         Rockville, MD: Information Planning Associates.

620. Bulletin of the American Academy of Psychiatry and the Law.
         v.1-   1973-   Quarterly.
         New York: American Academy of Psychiatry and the Law.

621. Cumulated Index Medicus.
         v.1-   1960-   Annual.
         Bethesda, MD: National Library of Medicine.
         Consult the annual volume containing the Bibliography of Medi-
            cal Reviews, "papers which are well documented surveys of

the recent biomedical literature," under the subject headings: Forensic Dentistry, Forensic Medicine, Forensic Psychiatry, Jurisprudence, Legislation.

622. Current Medicine for Attorneys.
          v.1-   1953-   Quarterly.
     South Miami, Florida: Current Medicine for Attorneys.
     "A quarterly report on the latest trends in medicine as these
          apply to the general practice of law, personal injury and
          casualty suits."

623. Family Law Quarterly: To Stabilize and Preserve Family Life.
          v.1-   1967-   .
     Chicago: American Bar Association Section of Family Law.

624. The Family Law Reporter.
     Washington, DC: Bureau of National Affairs, 1974-   . (loose-
          leaf service).

625. Family Planning/Population Reporter: A Review of State Laws and Pol-
          icies.
          v.1-   1972-   6 times a year.
     New York: Planned Parenthood Federation of America, Alan Gutt-
          macher Institute.

626. Forensic Science.
          v.1-   1972-   6 times a year; 2 volumes a year.
     Lausanne: Elsevier Sequoia.
     Absorbed Journal of Forensic Medicine.

627. Hastings Center Report.
          v.1-   1971-   6 times a year.
     Hastings-on-Hudson, NY: Institute of Society, Ethics and the
          Life Sciences.

628. International Bibliography of the Forensic Sciences.
          v.1-   1975-   Annual.
     Wichita, KS: INFORM.

629. International Digest of Health Legislation.
          v.1-   1948-   Quarterly.
     Geneva: World Health Organization.

630. International Journal of Law and Psychiatry.
          v.1-   1978-   Quarterly.
     Elmsford, NY: Pergamon.

631. Journal of Family Law.
          v.1-   1961-   Quarterly.
     Louisville, KY: University of Louisville School of Law.

632. Journal of Forensic Sciences.
          v.1-   1956-   Quarterly.
     Rockville, MD: American Academy of Forensic Sciences.

633. The Journal of Health Politics, Policy and Law.
         v.1-   1976-   Quarterly.
      Durham, NC: Duke University Press, for the Duke University De-
            partment of Health Administration and Committee on Health
            Politics.

634. Journal of Legal Medicine: Legal Aspects of Medical Practice.
         v.1-   1972-   Monthly.
      New York: GMT Medical Information Systems Division of MFI, for
            the American College of Legal Medicine.

635. Journal of Psychiatry and Law.
         v.1-   1973-   Quarterly.
      New York: Federal Legal Publications.

636. Law & Psychology Review.
         v.1-   1975-   Annual.
      University, AL: University of Alabama School of Law.

637. Lawyer's Medical Journal.
         1st series, volumes 1-7, 1965-71; 2d series, volumes 1- ,
            1972-   Quarterly.
      Rochester, NY: Lawyers Co-operative Publishing Co.

638. Legal Medicine Annual.
         v.1-   1969-   .
      New York: Appleton-Century-Crofts.

639. Medical Devices Reporter.
         Chicago: Commerce Clearing House, 1976-
         (loose-leaf service).

640. Medical Trial Technique Quarterly.
         v.1-   1954-   .
      Mundelein, IL: Callaghan.

641. Medicare and Medicaid Guide.
         Chicago: Commerce Clearing House, 1969-   .
         (loose-leaf service).
         "Produced in cooperation with the Blue Cross Association."

642. Medicine, Science and the Law.
         v.1-   1960-   Quarterly.
      London: John Wright, for the British Academy of Forensic Sciences.

643. The Medico-Legal Journal.
         v.1-   1933-   Quarterly.
      London: Dramrite, for the Medico-Legal Society.

644. Mental Disability Law Reporter.
         v.1-   1976-   6 times a year.
      Washington, DC: American Bar Association Commission on the Men-
            tally Disabled.

645. National Medicolegal Symposium Proceedings.
     1963-   Biennial.
     Chicago: Sponsored jointly by the American Bar Association and
         the American Medical Association.

646. Professional Liability Reporter.
     San Francisco: Professional Liability Reporter, 1976-   .
     (loose-leaf service).

647. Reporter on Human Reproduction and the Law.
     Boston: Legal-Medical Studies, Inc. 1971-   .
     (loose-leaf service).

G.2 ISSUES OF LIFE AND DEATH

648. Cantor, N.L.   "Quinlan, Privacy, and the Handling of Incompetent
     Dying Patients," 30 Rutgers Law Review 243-266 (1977).

649. Cantor, N.L., E.J. Cassell, and D.R. Coburn.   "Is There a Right to
     Die?" 12 Columbia Journal of Law and Social Problems 489-529
     (1976).

650. Group for the Advancement of Psychiatry, Committee on Aging.   The
     Right to Die: Decision and Decision Makers: Proceedings of a Sym-
     posium. New York: Mental Health Materials Center, for the Group
     for the Advancement of Psychiatry, 1973. (Published as the
     Group's Symposium, no. 12, volume 8, 665-753.)

651. Hendin, D.   Death as a Fact of Life. New York: Norton, 1973.
     255pp.

652. Hirsch, H.L.,   and R.E. Donovan.   "The Right to Die: Medico-Legal
     Implications of In re Quinlan," 30 Rutgers Law Review 267-303
     (1977).

653. Hyland, W.F.,   and D.S. Baime.   "In re Quinlan: A Synthesis of Law
     and Medical Technology," 18 Jurimetrics Journal 107-131 (1977).

654. Kaplan, R.P.   "Euthanasia Legislation: A Survey and a Model Act,"
     2 American Journal of Law & Medicine 41-99 (1976).

655. Kushnir, L.   "Bridging the Gap: The Discrepancy between the Medical
     and Legal Definitions of Death," 34 University of Toronto Facul-
     ty of Law Review 199-216 (1976).

656. Life or Death: Who Controls?, edited by N.C. Ostheimer and J.M. Osth-
     eimer. New York: Springer, 1976. 308pp.

657. Oever, R. van den.   "A Review of the Literature as to the Present
     Possibilities and Limitations in Estimating the Time of Death,"
     16 Medicine, Science and the Law 269-276 (1976).

658. Price, K. "Defining Death and Dying: A Bibliographic Overview," 71 Law Library Journal 49-67 (1978). (Includes examples of living wills.)

659. Quinlan, K.A. In the Matter of Karen Quinlan: The Complete Legal Briefs, 2 volumes. Arlington, VA: University Publications of America, 1975-76.

660. Russell, O.R. Freedom to Die: Moral and Legal Aspects of Euthanasia. New York: Human Sciences Press, 1975. 352pp.

661. Society for the Right to Die. Death with Dignity: Legislative Manual. New York: Society for the Right to Die, 1976. 96pp.

662. "Symposium Issue: Euthanasia," 27 Baylor Law Review 1-108 (1975). (Includes J.D. Bonnet, "Bill of Rights of the Dying Patient.")

663. "Symposium: Mental Incompetents and the Right to Die," 11 Suffolk University Law Review 919-973 (1977). (Includes C.P. Kindregan, "The Court as Forum for Life and Death Decisions.")

664. Temkin, O., W.K. Frankena, and S.H. Kadish. Respect for Life in Medicine, Philosophy, and the Law. Baltimore, MD: Johns Hopkins University Press, 1977. 107pp.

665. Triche, C.W., III, and D.S. Triche. The Euthanasia Controversy 1812-1974: A Bibliography with Select Annotations. Troy, NY: Whitston, 1975. 242pp.

666. U.S. Congress, Senate, Special Committee on Aging. Death with Dignity: An Inquiry into Related Public Issues: Hearings, 3 volumes. Washington, DC: U.S. Government Printing Office, 1972.

667. Veatch, R.M. Death, Dying, and the Biological Revolution: Our Last Quest for Responsibility. New Haven, CT: Yale University Press, 1976. 323pp.

668. Wilson, J.B. Death by Decision: The Medical, Moral and Legal Dilemmas of Euthanasia. Philadelphia, PA: Westminster Press, 1975. 208pp.

G.3 HUMAN REPRODUCTION

669. Daly, C.B. Morals, Law and Life: An Examination of the Book 'The Sanctity of Life and the Criminal Law.' Dublin: Clonmore & Reynolds, 1963. 153pp. (See G.L. Williams, Reference 678 below.)

670. Fletcher, J.F. Morals and Medicine: The Moral Problem of: The Patient's Right to Know the Truth, Contraception, Artificial Insemination, Sterilization, Euthanasia. Boston: Beacon Press, 1960. 243pp.

671. Group for the Advancement of Psychiatry, Committee on Preventive
     Psychiatry. Humane Reproduction. New York: Group for the Ad-
     vancement of Psychiatry, 1973. (Issued as the Group's Report,
     no. 86, volume 8, 383-516.)

672. Indiana University, Institute for Sex Research. Pregnancy, Birth,
     and Abortion. P.H. Gebhard, W.B. Pomeroy, C.E. Martin and C.V.
     Christenson. New York: Harper & Row, 1958. 282pp.

673. Kayden, S.M., and I.P. Karpf. "A Selective Bibliography on Law and
     Population," 6 Columbia Human Rights Law Review 505-534 (1974-
     75).

674. Law and Population Book Series. Medford, MA: Law and Population Pro-
     gramme, Fletcher School of Law and Diplomacy, Tufts University,
     1971- . Includes 20 books published through 1977: (1) L.T. Lee
     and A. Larson, eds. Population and Law. (Leyden: Sijthoff; Dur-
     ham, NC: Rule of Law Press, 1971.) 452pp.; (3) D.G. Partan, Pop-
     ulation in the United Nations System: Developing the Legal Capa-
     city and Programs of UN Agencies. (Leiden: Sijthoff, 1973.)
     219pp.; (4) P.T. Piotrow, World Population Crisis: The United
     States Response. (New York: Praeger, 1973.) 276pp.; (16) United
     Nations Fund for Population Activities, Survey of Contraceptive
     Laws: Country Profiles, Checklists and Summaries. (New York: Uni-
     ted Nations Fund for Population Activities, 1976.) 143pp.

675. Law and Population Monograph Series. Medford, MA: Law and Population
     Programme, Fletcher School of Law and Diplomacy, Tufts University,
     1971- . Among the 46 monographs published through May 1978 are:
     Symposium on Law and Population, Tunis, 1974, Text of Recommen-
     dations. (1974). 49pp.; E.H. Kellogg, D.K. Kline, and J. Stepan,
     The World's Laws and Practices on Population and Sexuality Edu-
     cation. (1975). 127pp.

676. St. John-Stevas, N.A.F. Life, Death and the Law. Bloomington, IN:
     Indiana University Press, 1961. 375pp.

677. Symposium on Law and Population. "Part I: Rights of Choice in Matters
     Relating to Human Reproduction," 6 Columbia Human Rights Law Re-
     view 273-534 (1974-75); "Part II: Tunis Symposium," 7 Columbia
     Human Rights Law Review 1-309 (1975).

678. Williams, G.L. The Sanctity of Life and the Criminal Law. New York:
     Knopf, 1957. 350pp. (Includes chapters on: abortion, artificial
     insemination, birth control, euthanasia, infanticide, suicide.)

G.3.a   ARTIFICIAL INSEMINATION

679. Carr, J.E., IV. "Artificial Insemination: Problems, Policies and
      Proposals," 26 Alabama Law Review 120-162 (1973).

680. Dienes, C.T. "Artificial Donor Insemination: Perspectives on Legal
      and Social Change," 54 Iowa Law Review 253-318 (1968).

681. Finegold, W.J. Artificial Insemination, 2d edition. Springfield,
      IL: C.C. Thomas, 1976. 141pp.

682. "Symposium on Artificial Insemination," 7 Syracuse Law Review 96-113
      (1955).

683. Symposium on Legal and Other Aspects of Artificial Insemination by
      Donor (A.I.D.) and Embryo Transfer, London, 1972. Law and Ethics
      of A.I.D. and Embryo Transfer. Amsterdam: Associated Scientific
      Pub., 1973. 110pp. (CIBA Foundation Symposium 17, new series.)

684. Wadlington, W. "Artificial Insemination: The Dangers of a Poorly
      Kept Secret," 64 Northwestern University Law Review 777-807
      (1970).

G.3.b   BIRTH AND POPULATION CONTROL, INCLUDING STERILIZATION

685. Bergman, E., et al., eds. Population Policymaking in the American
      States: Issues and Processes. Lexington, MA: Lexington Books,
      1974. 318pp.

686. "Birth Control and the Liability of Physicians and Pharmacists," in
      University of California, Davis. School of Law. Legal Problems
      in Family Law, pp.255-274. Davis, CA: University of California,
      1973.

687. Brodie, D.W. "The Family Planning Services and Population Research
      Act of 1972," 5 Family Law Quarterly 424-477 (1971).

688. Chasteen, E.R. The Case for Compulsory Birth Control. Englewood
      Cliffs, NJ: Prentice-Hall, 1971. 230pp.

689. Dienes, C. Law, Politics and Birth Control. Urbana, IL: University
      of Illinois Press, 1972. 374pp.

690. Driver, E.D. World Population Policies: An Annotated Bibliography.
      Lexington, MA: Lexington Books, 1972. 1280pp.

691. Gray, J.C. "Compulsory Sterilization in a Free Society," 41 Univer-
      sity of Cincinnati Law Review 529-587 (1972).

692. International Conference on Family Planning Programs, Geneva, 1965. *Family Planning and Population Programs: A Review of World Developments*, edited by B. Berelson. Chicago: University of Chicago Press, 1966. 848pp.

693. McCombs, W.L., and J. F. Szaller. "The Intrauterine Device: A Criticism of Governmental Complaisance and an Analysis of Manufacturer and Physician Liability," 24 *Cleveland State Law Review* 247-298 (1975).

694. Noonan, J.T. *Contraception: A History of Its Treatment by the Catholic Theologians and Canonists*. Cambridge, MA: Belknap Press of Harvard University Press, 1965. 561pp.

695. Planned Parenthood-World Population, Center for Family Planning Program Development. *Family Planning, Contraception, and Voluntary Sterilization: An Analysis of Laws and Policies of the United States, Each State and Jurisdiction*. Washington, DC: U.S. Government Printing Office, 1973. 337pp. (A report of the National Center for Planning Services.)

696. "Progress and Problems of Fertility Control Around the World," 5 *Demography* no. 2, 539-1001 (1968). (Special issue.)

697. Stepan, J, and E.H. Kellogg. *The World's Laws on Contraceptives*. Medford, MA: Law and Population Programme, Fletcher School of Law and Diplomacy, 1973. 105pp. (Law and Population Monograph Series, 17.)

698. Symposium. "Population Control," 25 *Law & Contemporary Problems* 377-629 (1960). (Contents include: F. Osborn, "Qualitative Aspects of Population Control: Eugenics and Euthenics;" A. Sulloway, "The Legal and Political Aspects of Population Control in the U.S.;" C. Tietze, "Current Status of Fertility Control.")

699. "Symposium: Population and the Law," 23 *Hastings Law Journal* 1345-1526 (1972).

700. "Symposium on Population Problems and the Law," 55 *North Carolina Law Review* 357-460 (1977).

701. United Nations Fund for Population Activities. *Law and Population*. New York: United Nations Fund for Population Activities, 1975. 42pp.

702. U.S. Commission on Civil Rights. *Constitutional Aspects of the Right to Limit Childbearing*. Washington, DC: U.S. Commission on Civil Rights, 1975. 223pp.

703. U.S. Commission on Population Growth and the American Future. *Population and the American Future: Report*. Washington, DC: U.S. Government Printing Office, 1972. 186pp.

704. U.S. Congress, House, Committee on Government Operations. *FDA Regulation of Oral Contraceptives*. Washington, DC: U.S. Government Printing Office, 1971. 118pp.

705. U.S. Congress, House, Committee on Government Operations. <u>Regulation</u>
     <u>of Medical Devices: Intrauterine Contraceptive Devices.</u> Washing-
     ton, DC: U.S. Government Printing Office, 1973. 576pp.

706. U.S. Congress, Senate, Committee on Small Business. Hearings on the
     Safety of Oral Contraceptives, in <u>Competitive Problems of the Drug</u>
     <u>Industry</u>, parts 15-17, pp.5921-7324. Washington, DC: U.S. Govern-
     ment Printing Office, 1970.

707. <u>The World Population Crisis: Policy Implications and the Role of Law.</u>
     Proceedings of a symposium at the University of Virginia School of
     Law, 1971, edited by J.M. Paxman. Charlottesville, VA: John Bas-
     sett Moore Society of International Law, 1971. 179pp.

G.3.c   ABORTION

708. Calderone, M.S., ed. <u>Abortion in the U.S.: A Conference Sponsored by</u>
     <u>the Planned Parenthood Federation of America.</u> New York: Hoeber-
     Harper, 1958. 224pp.

709. Callahan, D. <u>Abortion: Law, Choice and Morality</u>. New York: Macmil-
     lan, 1972. 524pp.

710. Canada, Committee on the Operation of the Abortion Law. <u>Report</u>.
     Ottawa: Minister of Supply and Services, 1977. 474pp.

711. Carmen, A., and H. Moody. <u>Abortion Counseling and Social Change</u>:
     <u>From Illegal Act to Medical Practice.</u> Valley Forge, PA: Judson
     Press, 1973. 122pp.

712. Destro, R.A. "Abortion and the Constitution: The Need for a Life-pro-
     tective Amendment," 63 <u>California Law Review</u> 1250-1351 (1975).

713. Edelin, K.C. <u>The Edelin Trial</u>. Boston: Legal-Medical Studies, Inc.,
     1975. 62pp.

714. Ely, J. "The Wages of Crying Wolf: A Comment on Roe v. Wade," 82
     <u>Yale Law Journal</u> 920-949 (1973).

715. Great Britain, Committee on the Working of the Abortion Act. <u>Report</u>.
     London: Her Majesty's Stationery Office, 1974. 287pp.

716. Guttmacher, A.F., ed. <u>The Case for Legalized Abortion Now</u>. Berkeley,
     CA: Diablo Press, 1967. 154pp.

717. Hall, R.E., ed. <u>Abortion in a Changing World</u>, 2 volumes. New York:
     Columbia University Press, 1970. Proceedings of an international
     conference convened in Hot Springs, VA, 1968, by the Association
     for the Study of Abortion.

718. Heymann, P.B., and D.E. Barzelay. "The Forest and the Trees: Roe v.
     Wade and Its Critics," 53 <u>Boston University Law Review</u> 765-784
     (1973).

719. Kellogg, E.H. "Reform of Laws Affecting Population Growth," 10
     Journal of International Law and Economics 1-36 (1975).

720. Lader, L. Abortion. Indianapolis, IN: Bobbs-Merrill, 1966; Boston:
     Beacon Press, 1967. 212pp.

721. Lader, L. Abortion II. Making the Revolution. Boston: Beacon Press,
     1973. 242pp.

722. Lee, L.T., and J.M. Paxman. "Pregnancy and Abortion in Adolescence:
     A Comparative Legal Survey and Proposals for Reform," 6 Columbia
     Human Rights Law Review 307-353 (1974-75).

723. Liberalization of Abortion Laws: Implications, edited by A.R. Omran.
     Chapel Hill, NC: Carolina Population Center, University of North
     Carolina, 1976. 303pp.

724. National Abortion Rights Action League. Abortion Law Reporter, 2
     volumes. Washington, DC: Antioch School of Law, Women's Rights
     Clinic, 1976- . (loose-leaf).

725. Noonan, J.T., Jr., ed. The Morality of Abortion: Legal and Histori-
     cal Perspectives. Cambridge, MA: Harvard University Press, 1970.
     276pp.

726. Perkins, R.L. Abortion: Pro and Con. Cambridge, MA: Schenkman,
     1974. 236pp.

727. Potts, M., P. Diggory, and J. Peel. Abortion. Cambridge: Cambridge
     University Press, 1977. 575pp. (Extensive review of abortion
     legislation.)

728. Reiterman, C., ed. Abortion and the Unwanted Child. New York:
     Springer, 1971. 181pp. (Papers delivered at the California Con-
     ference on Abortion, San Francisco, 1969.)

729. Rosen, H., ed. Therapeutic Abortion: Medical, Psychiatric, Legal,
     Anthropological and Religious Considerations. New York: Julian
     Press, 1954. 348pp.

730. Sarvis, B., and H. Rodman. The Abortion Controversy. New York:
     Columbia University Press, 1973. 222pp.

731. Schaefer, G. Legal Abortions in New York State: Medical, Legal, Nur-
     sing, Social Aspects, July 1 - December 31, 1970. New York: Har-
     per & Row, 1971. 324pp.

732. "Symposium: Abortion and the Law," 23 Case Western Reserve Law Review
     705-895 (1972).

733. U.S. Congress, Senate, Committee on the Judiciary. Abortion. Part 1.
     Hearings before the Subcommittee on Constitutional Amendments.
     Washington, DC: U.S. Government Printing Office, 1974. 729pp.

734. Walbert, D.F., and J.D. Butler. Abortion, Society, and the Law.
     Cleveland: Case Western Reserve University Press, 1973. 395pp.

735. Wojcichowsky, S.   Ethical-Social-Legal Annotated Bibliography of
      English Language Studies on Abortion, 1967-1972.   Toronto: Toron-
      to Institute of Public Communications, 1973.   86pp.

736. World Health Organization.   Abortion Laws: A Survey of Current World
      Legislation.   Geneva: World Health Organization, 1971.   78pp.

G.3.d   GENETICS AND EUGENICS

737. Annas, G.J., and B. Coyne.   "Fitness for Birth and Reproduction:
      Legal Implications of Genetic Screening," 9 Family Law Quarterly
      463-489 (1975).

738. Balmer, T.A.   "Recombinant DNA: Legal Responses to a New Biohazard,"
      7 Environmental Law 293-313 (Winter 1977).

739. Burke, K.J.   "The 'XYY Syndrome': Genetics, Behavior and the Law,"
      46 Denver Law Journal 261-284 (1969).

740. Fletcher, J.F.   The Ethics of Genetic Control: Ending Reproductive
      Roulette.   Garden City, NY: Anchor Press, 1974.   218pp.

741. Friedman, J.M.   "Legal Implications of Amniocentesis," 123 Univer-
      sity of Pennsylvania Law Review 92-156 (1974).

742. Golding, M.P.   "Ethical Issues in Biological Engineering," 15 Uni-
      versity of California Los Angeles Law Review 443-479 (1968).

743. Gorney, R.   "The New Biology and the Future of Man," 15 University
      of California Los Angeles Law Review 273-356 (1968).

744. Hilton, B., et al., eds.   Ethical Issues in Human Genetics.   New
      York: Plenum, 1973.   455pp.

745. National Symposium on Genetics and the Law, Boston, 1975.   Genetics
      and the Law, edited by A. Milunsky and G.J. Annas. New York: Ple-
      num, 1976.   532pp. (Symposium sponsored by National Genetics
      Foundation and American Society of Law and Medicine.)

746. "The Potential for Genetic Engineering: A Proposal for International
      Legal Control," 16 Virginia Journal of International Law 403-430
      (1976).

747. Psychiatry and Genetics: Psychosocial, Ethical, and Legal Considera-
      tions, edited by M.A. Sperber and L.G. Jarvik. New York: Basic
      Books, 1976.   204pp.

748. Reilly, P.   Genetics, Law, and Social Policy.   Cambridge, MA: Harvard
      University Press, 1977.   275pp.

749. Robertson, J.A.   "Involuntary Euthanasia of Defective Newborns: A
      Legal Analysis," 27 Stanford Law Review 213-269 (1975).

750. Rosenfeld, A.   The Second Genesis: The Coming Control of Life.
     Englewood Cliffs, NJ: Prentice-Hall, 1969. 327pp.

751. Rosenthal, D.   Genetic Theory and Abnormal Behaviour. New York:
     McGraw-Hill, 1970. 318pp.

752. Waltz, J.R., and C.R. Thigpen.   "Genetic Screening and Counseling:
     The Legal and Ethical Issues," 68 Northwestern University Law
     Review 696-768 (1973).

G.4   DEVELOPMENTS IN PSYCHIATRY, PSYCHOLOGY, AND TREATMENT OF MENTAL ILLNESS

753. Abrahamsen, D.   The Murdering Mind. New York: Harper & Row, 1973.
     245pp.

754. Abrahamsen, D.   Psychology of Crime. New York: Columbia University
     Press, 1960. 368pp.

755. Alexander, F., and H. Staub.   The Criminal, the Judge and the Pub-
     lic: A Psychological Analysis, revised edition. New York: Crow-
     ell-Collier, 1962. 255pp.

756. Allen, R.C., E.Z. Ferster, and J.A. Rubin.   Readings in Law and
     Psychiatry, revised edition. Baltimore, MD: Johns Hopkins Univ-
     ersity Press, 1975. 828pp.

757. American Bar Foundation.   The Mentally Disabled and the Law, edited
     by F.T. Lindman and D.N. McIntyre. Chicago: University of Chica-
     go Press, 1961. 444pp.

758. Association of the Bar of the City of New York, Special Committee to
     Study Commitment Procedures.   Mental Illness and Due Process:
     Report and Recommendations on Admissions to Mental Hospitals under
     New York Law. Ithaca, NY: Cornell University Press, 1962. 316pp.

759. Ayd, F.J., ed.   Medical, Moral and Legal Issues in Mental Health Care.
     Baltimore, MD: Williams & Wilkins, 1974. 220pp.

760. Beresford, H.R.   Legal Aspects of Neurologic Practice. Philadelphia:
     F.A. Davis, 1975. 150pp.

761. Berry, F.D., Jr.   "Self-incrimination and the Compulsory Mental Exam-
     ination: A Proposal," 15 Arizona Law Review 919-950 (1973).

762. Biggs, J.   Guilty Mind: Psychiatry and the Law of Homicide. New York:
     Harcourt, Brace, 1955. 236pp.

763. Brooks, A.D.   Law, Psychiatry and the Mental Health System. Boston:
     Little, Brown, 1974. 1150pp.

764. Browne, E.W.   The Right to Treatment under Civil Commitment. Reno,
     NV: National Council of Juvenile Court Judges, 1975. 160pp.

765. Cassity, J.H.   Quality of Murder: A Psychiatric and Legal Evaluation
      of Motives and Responsibilities Involved in the Plea of Insanity
      as Revealed in Outstanding Murder Cases of this Century. New
      York: Julian Press, 1958. 268pp.

766. Cohen, H.A.   "In Defense of the Insane: A Proposal to Abolish the
      Defense of Insanity," 2 Criminal Justice Quarterly 127-151
      (1974).

767. Davidson, H.A.   Forensic Psychiatry, 2d edition. New York: Ronald
      Press, 1965. 473pp.

768. "Due Process Limitations on Parental Rights to Commit Children to Men-
      tal Institutions," 48 University of Colorado Law Review 235-266
      (1977).

769. Farrell, R.T.   "The Right of an Indigent Civil Commitment Defendant
      to Psychiatric Assistance of His Own Choice at State Expense," 11
      Idaho Law Review 141-192 (1975).

770. Foley, H.A.   Community Mental Health Legislation. Lexington, MA:
      Lexington Books, 1975. 155pp.

771. Glueck, S.   Law and Psychiatry: Cold War or Entente Cordiale? Balti-
      more, MD: Johns Hopkins Press, 1962. 181pp.

772. Group for the Advancement of Psychiatry, Committee on Psychiatry and
      Law.   Psychiatry and Sex Psychopath Legislation: The 30's to the
      80's. New York, Group for the Advancement of Psychiatry, 1977.
      (Issued as the Group's Report, no. 98, volume 9, 831-956.)

773. Guttmacher, M.S.   The Role of Psychiatry in Law. Springfield: C.C.
      Thomas, 1968. 170pp.

774. Guttmacher, M.S., and H. Weihofen.   Psychiatry and the Law. New
      York: W.W. Norton, 1952. 476pp.

775. Guze, S.B.   Criminality and Psychiatric Disorders. New York: Oxford
      University Press, 1976. 181pp.

776. Herr, S.S.   "Rights into Action: Protecting Human Rights of the Men-
      tally Handicapped," 26 Catholic University Law Review 203-318
      (1977).

777. Highmore, A.   A Treatise on the Law of Idiocy and Lunacy. Exeter,
      NH: George Lamson, 1822. 194pp.

778. Hoffman, P.B., and L.L. Foust.   "Least Restrictive Treatment of the
      Mentally Ill: A Doctrine in Search of Its Senses," 14 San Diego
      Law Review 1100-1154 (1977).

779. Irvine, L.M., and T.B. Brelje.   Law, Psychiatry and the Mentally
      Disordered Offender, 2 volumes. Springfield, IL: C.C. Thomas,
      1972-73.

780. Keeton, G.W.   Guilty but Insane. London: MacDonald & Evans, 1961.
      206pp.

781. Lewis, D.O., D.A. Balla, and S.S. Shanok. Delinquency and Psycho-pathology. New York: Grune & Stratton, 1976. 209pp.

782. Lieberman, S.S. Forensic Psychology, 1950 to Present. New York, 1963. 205pp. (Reprinted from 5 Progress in Clinical Psychology, 1963.)

783. MacDonald, J.M. Psychiatry and the Criminal: A Guide to Psychiatric Examinations for the Criminal Courts, 3d edition. Springfield, IL: C.C. Thomas, 1975. 501pp.

784. "Mental Health: A Model Statute to Regulate the Administration of Therapy within Mental Health Facilities," 61 Minnesota Law Review 841-886 (1977).

785. The Mentally Retarded Citizen and the Law. M.J. Kindred, et al. New York: Free Press, 1976. 738pp.

786. Mesnikoff, A.M., and C.G. Lauterbach. "The Association of Violent Dangerous Behavior with Psychiatric Disorders: A Review of the Research Literature," 3 Journal of Psychiatry and Law 415-445 (1975).

787. National Association of Attorneys General, Committee on the Office of Attorney General. The Right to Treatment in Mental Health Law. Raleigh, NC: National Association of Attorneys General, 1976. 97pp.

788. Nice, R.W., ed. Crime and Insanity. New York: Philosophical Libra-ry, 1958. 280pp.

789. Page, J.D. Psychopathology: The Science of Understanding Deviance. Chicago: Aldine-Atherton, 1971. 482pp.

790. Paper Victories and Hard Realities: The Implementation of the Legal and Constitutional Rights of the Mentally Disabled; Selected Papers on the Supreme Court Decision, O'Connor v. Donaldson, edit-ed by V. Bradley and G. Clarke. Washington, DC: Health Policy Center, Georgetown University, 1976. 143pp.

791. Ray, I. Treatise on the Medical Jurisprudence of Insanity, edited by W. Overholser. Cambridge, MA: Belknap Press of Harvard University Press, 1962. 376pp. (Originally published in 1838.)

792. The Right to Treatment for Mental Patients, edited by S. Golann and W.J. Fremouw. New York: Irvington Pub., 1976. 246pp.

793. Roche, P.Q. The Criminal Mind: A Study of Communication between the Criminal Law and Psychiatry. New York: Farrar, Straus and Cudahy, 1958. 299pp. (Reprinted, Westport, CT: Greenwood, 1976.)

794. Sadoff, R.L. Forensic Psychiatry: A Practical Guide for Lawyers and Psychiatrists. Springfield, IL: C.C. Thomas, 1975. 251pp.

795. Schiffer, M.E. Mental Disorder and the Criminal Trial Process. Tor-onto: Butterworths, 1978. 342pp.

796. Schwartz, B.M.   "In the Name of Treatment: Autonomy, Civil Commit-
     ment, and the Right to Refuse Treatment," 50 Notre Dame Lawyer
     808-842 (1975).

797. Schwartz, S.J., and D.K. Stern.   A Trial Manual for Civil Commit-
     ment. Boston: Mental Health Legal Advisors Committee, 1976.
     (loose-leaf).

798. Share, D.   "The Standard of Proof in Involuntary Civil Commitment
     Proceedings," Detroit College of Law Review 209-259 (1977).

799. Slovenko, R.   Psychiatry and the Law. Boston: Little, Brown, 1973.
     726pp.

800. Social and Psychological Factors in Legal Processes Conference, Bat-
     telle Seattle Research Center, 1975.   Psychology and the Law:
     Research Frontiers, edited by G. Bermant, C. Nemeth, and N. Vid-
     mar. Lexington, MA: Lexington Books, 1976.   302pp.

801. Stone, A.   Mental Health and Law: A System in Transition. New York:
     J. Aronson, 1976.   292pp.

802. Swadron, B.B.   Detention of the Mentally Disordered, Including the
     Applicable Criminal Law. Toronto: Butterworths, 1964.   470pp.

803. "Symposium: Children's Rights, Psychiatry and the Law," 3 Journal of
     Psychiatry and Law 475-499 (1975).

804. "Symposium: Mental Illness, the Law and Civil Liberties," 13 Santa
     Clara Lawyer 367-612 (1973).

805. Szasz, T.S.   The Age of Madness. New York: J. Aronson, 1974.   372pp.

806. Szasz, T.S.   Law, Liberty, and Psychiatry: An Inquiry. New York:
     Macmillan, 1963.   281pp.

807. Szasz, T.S.   Psychiatric Justice. New York: Macmillan, 1965.   283pp.

808. Tancredi, L.R.,   J. Lieb, and A.E. Slaby.   Legal Issues in Psychiat-
     ric Care. Hagerstown, MD: Harper & Row, 1975.   164pp.

809. Toch, H., ed.   Legal and Criminal Psychology. New York: Holt, Rine-
     hart & Winston, 1961.   426pp.

810. Tompkins, D.L.C.   Insanity and the Criminal Law: A Bibliography. Ber-
     keley, CA: University of California, Bureau of Public Administra-
     tion, 1960.   64pp.

811. U.S. Congress, Senate, Committee on the Judiciary.   Protecting the
     Constitutional Rights of the Mentally Ill: Report. Washington,
     DC: U.S. Government Printing Office, 1964.   64pp.

812. U.S. President's Committee on Mental Retardation, Legal Rights Work
     Group.   Compendium of Law Suits Establishing the Legal Rights of
     Mentally Retarded Citizens. Washington, DC: U.S. Government Print-
     ing Office, 1975.   67pp.

813. Van Hoose, W.H., and J.A. Kottler. Ethical and Legal Issues in Counseling and Psychotherapy. San Francisco: Jossey-Bass, 1977. 224pp.

814. Venables, H.D.S. A Guide to the Law Affecting Mental Patients. London: Butterworths, 1975. 155pp.

815. Walker, N. Treatment and Justice in Penology and Psychiatry. Edinburgh: Edinburgh University Press, 1976. 23pp. (Sandoz Lecture, 1976.)

816. Weihofen, H. Mental Disorder as a Criminal Defense. Buffalo, NY: Dennis, 1954. 530pp.

817. Weihofen, H. The Urge to Punish: New Approaches to the Problem of Mental Irresponsibility for Crime. New York: Farrar, Straus and Cudahy, 1956. 213pp.

818. Western Reserve University, Cleveland. Law-Medicine Center. The Mind: A Law-Medicine Problem; Proceedings of an Institute, edited by O. Schroeder. Cincinnati: W.H. Anderson Co., 1962. 517pp.

819. Wexler, D.B. Criminal Commitments and Dangerous Mental Patients: Legal Issues of Confinement, Treatment, and Release. Washington, DC: U.S. Government Printing Office, 1976. 94pp.

820. Whitlock, F.A. Criminal Responsibility and Mental Illness. London: Butterworths, 1963. 156pp.

G.5   BEHAVIOR MODIFICATION AND PSYCHOSURGERY

821. Barnhart, B.A., et al. "Informed Consent to Organic Behavior Control," 17 Santa Clara Law Review 39-83 (1977).

822. "Behavior Modification in Prisons," 13 American Criminal Law Review 1-99 (1975).

823. "Bibliography on Behavior Modification," 13 American Criminal Law Review 101-113 (1975).

824. Budd, K.S., and D.M. Baer. "Behavior Modification and the Law: Implications of Recent Judicial Decisions," 4 Journal of Psychiatry and Law 171-244 (1976).

825. Greenblatt, S.J. "The Ethics and Legality of Psychosurgery," 22 New York Law School Law Review 961-980 (1977).

826. Knowles, S. "Beyond the Cuckoo's Nest: A Proposal for Federal Regulation of Psychosurgery," 12 Harvard Journal on Legislation 610-667 (1975).

827. Martin. R.   Legal Challenges to Behavior Modification: Trends in
Schools, Corrections and Mental Health. Champaign, IL: Research
Press, 1975. 179pp.

828. Psychosurgery: A Multidisciplinary Symposium. Lexington, MA: Lexington Books, 1974. 140pp. Sponsored by the Center for Law and
Health Sciences, Boston University School of Law.

829. Psychosurgery and Society: Symposium, edited by J.S. Smith and L.C.
Kiloh. Oxford: Pergamon, 1977. 184pp. Organized by the Neuro-
psychiatric Institute, Sydney, Australia, 1974.

830. Schedler, G.   Behavior Modification and "Punishment" of the Innocent:
Towards a Justification of the Institution of Legal Punishment.
Amsterdam: B.R. Grüner, 1977. 110pp.

831. Shuman, S.I.   Psychosurgery and the Medical Control of Violence: Autonomy and Deviance. Detroit, MI: Wayne State University Press,
1977. 360pp.

832. U.S. National Commission for the Protection of Human Subjects of Biomedical and Behavioral Research.   Psychosurgery: Report and Recommendations. Bethesda, MD: National Commission for the Protection of Human Subjects, 1977. 76pp.

G.6   MEDICAL AND PSYCHOLOGICAL EXPERIMENTATION

833. Annas, G.J.,   H.L. Glantz, and B.F. Katz.   Informed Consent to Human
Experimentation: The Subject's Dilemma. Cambridge, MA: Ballinger,
1977. 333pp.

834. DuVal, B.S., Jr.   "Educational Research and the Protection of Human
Subjects," American Bar Foundation Research Journal 477-519
(1977).

835. Ethical and Legal Issues of Social Experimentation, edited by A.M.
Rivlin and P.M. Timpane. Washington, DC: Brookings Institution,
1975. 188pp.

836. Forum on Experiments and Research with Humans: Values in Conflict,
Washington, DC, 1975.   Record of Proceedings. Washington, DC:
National Academy of Sciences, 1975. 234pp.

837. Frenkel, D.A.   "Human Experimentation: Codes of Ethics," 1 Legal
Medical Quarterly 7-14 (1977).

838. Freund, P.A., ed.   Experimentation with Human Subjects. New York:
Braziller, 1970. 470pp. Based on Daedalus (Spring 1969).

839. Fried, C.   Medical Experimentation: Personal Integrity and Social
Policy. Amsterdam: North Holland, 1974. 177pp.

840. Friedman, J.M.   "The Federal Fetal Experimentation Regulations: An
      Establishment Clause Analysis," 61 Minnesota Law Review 961-1005
      (1977).

841. Gilchrist, I.   Medical Experimentation on Prisoners Must Stop. Col-
      lege Park, MD: Urban Information Interpreters, 1974. 128pp.

842. Gray, B.H.   Human Subjects in Medical Experimentation: A Sociologi-
      cal Study of the Conduct and Regulation of Clinical Research.
      New York: Wiley, 1975. 298pp.

843. Hershey, N. and R.D. Miller.   Human Experimentation and the Law.
      Germantown, MD: Aspen Systems, 1976. 165pp.

844. Horan, D.J.   "Fetal Experimentation and Federal Regulation," 22 Vil-
      lanova Law Review 325-356 (1977).

845. Katz, J.   Experimentation with Human Beings. New York: Russell Sage
      Foundation, 1972. 1159pp.

846. Ladimer, I.   "Ethical and Legal Aspects of Medical Research on Human
      Beings," 3 Journal of Public Law 467-511 (1954).

847. Ladimer, I., and R.W. Newman, eds.   Clinical Investigation in Medi-
      cine: Legal, Ethical, and Moral Aspects: An Anthology and Biblio-
      graphy. Boston: Boston University Law-Medicine Research Insti-
      tute, 1963. 517pp.

848. Levy, C.L.   The Human Body and the Law: Legal and Ethical Consider-
      ations in Human Experimentation. Dobbs Ferry, NY: Oceana, 1975.
      108pp.

849. "Medical Experimentation: A Symposium on Behavior Control," 13 Duques-
      ne Law Review 673-936 (1975).

850. "On the Report and Recommendations of the National Commission for the
      Protection of Human Subjects of Biomedical and Behavioral Research:
      A Symposium," 22 Villanova Law Review 297-417 (1977).

851. Ramsey, R.P.   The Ethics of Fetal Research. New Haven, CT: Yale Uni-
      versity Press, 1975. 104pp.

852. Shultz, W.J.   The Humane Movement in the United States, 1910-1922.
      New York: Columbia University Press, 1924. 319pp. (Columbia
      Studies in History, Economics and Public Law, v. 113.)

853. "Symposium: Medical Experimentation on Human Subjects," 25 Case West-
      ern Reserve Law Review 431-648 (1975).

854. Symposium on Human Experimentation, Southern Methodist University,
      1975.   Human Experimentation, edited by R.L. Bogomolny. Dallas,
      TX: SMU Press, 1976. 148pp.

855. "Symposium: The Control of Behavior: Legal, Scientific and Moral Di-
      lemmas," 11 Criminal Law Bulletin 598-636 (1975).

856. Symposium. 13 Duquesne Law Review 673-936 (1975). Contents include: M.H. Shapiro, "Therapeutic Justifications for Intervention into Mentation and Behavior;" C.E. Curran, "Ethical Considerations in Human Experimentation;" P.R. Breggin, "Psychosurgery for Political Purposes."

857. Trials of War Criminals before the Nuremberg Military Tribunal... Washington, DC: U.S. Government Printing Office, 1949-53. "The Medical Case" (Vols. I and II).

858. U.S. National Commission for the Protection of Human Subjects of Biomedical and Behavioral Research. Contractor and Staff Papers, 16 volumes. Washington, DC: Department of Health, Education and Welfare, 1976.

859. U.S. National Commission for the Protection of Human Subjects of Biomedical and Behavioral Research. Report on Research on the Fetus, 1 volume. Washington, DC: The Commission, 1975.

860. U.S. National Commission for the Protection of Human Subjects of Biomedical and Behavioral Research. Research Involving Prisoners: Report and Recommendations: Draft. Washington, DC: The Commission, 1976. 80pp.

861. Van Eys, J., ed. Research on Children: Medical Imperatives, Ethical Quandaries, and Legal Constraints. Baltimore, MD: University Park Press, 1978. 152pp.

862. Wilson, J.P. "Fetal Experimentation: Legal Implications of an Ethical Conundrum," 53 Denver Law Journal 581-642 (1976).

G.7 TRANSPLANTS

863. Baron, C.H., M. Botsford, and G.F. Cole. "Live Organ and Tissue Transplants from Minor Donors in Massachusetts," 55 Boston University Law Review 159-193 (1975).

864. Dickens, B.M. "The Control of Living Body Materials," 27 University of Toronto Law Journal 142-198 (1977).

865. Dunlap-McCuller, J.F. Blood Transfusions and Your Legal Rights. East Brunswick, NJ, 1975. 99pp.

866. Katz, J., and A.M. Capron. Catastrophic Diseases--Who Decides What?: A Psychosocial and Legal Analysis of the Problems Posed by Hemodialysis and Organ Transplantation. New York: Russell Sage Foundation, 1975. 273pp.

867. Miller, G.W. Moral and Ethical Implications of Human Organ Transplants. Springfield, IL: C.C. Thomas, 1971. 135pp.

868. National Research Council, Ad Hoc Committee on Medical-Legal Problems. Medical-Legal Aspects of Tissue Transplantation: A Report. Washington, DC: National Research Council, 1968. 43pp.

H. LEGAL CONTROL OF HAZARDS TO PUBLIC HEALTH AND SAFETY

869. Calabresi, G. The Costs of Accidents: A Legal and Economic Analysis. New Haven, CT: Yale University Press, 1970. 340pp.

870. Crusz, R.W.G. Ralph Nader: A Bibliography. Waterloo, Ont.: Reference Department, Dana Porter Arts Library, University of Waterloo, 1973. 27pp.

871. Fellner, B.A., and D.W. Salveson. Occupational Safety and Health: Law and Practice. New York: Practising Law Institute, 1976. 417pp.

872. Grad, F.P. Public Health Law Manual, 2d edition. New York: American Public Health Association, 1970. 243pp.

873. Jackson, C.O. Food and Drug Legislation in the New Deal. Princeton, NJ: Princeton University Press, 1970. 249pp.

874. National Academy of Engineering, Committee on Public Engineering Policy. Perspectives on Benefit-Risk Decision Making: Report of a Colloquium. Washington, DC: The Academy, 1972. 157pp. (Includes M. Katz, "Legal Mechanisms.")

875. National Institute on Occupational Safety and Health Law, Washington, DC, 1976. Proceedings. Chicago: American Bar Association, 1976. 281pp.

876. Rosenthal, A.J., H. Korn, and S.B. Lubman. Catastrophic Accidents in Government Programs. Washington, DC: National Security Industrial Association, 1963. 175pp. (Prepared by the Legislative Drafting Research Fund of Columbia University.)

877. Tallman, R., and W.M. Treadwell, eds. Consumer Protection Compliance. New York: Practising Law Institute, 1971. 549pp.

878. Toulmin, H.A. A Treatise on the Law of Foods, Drugs and Cosmetics, 2d edition, 4 volumes. Cincinnati: W.H. Anderson Co., 1963. Supplement, 1969. 589pp.

879. U.S. Congress, House, Committee on Government Operations. Regulatory Policies of the Food and Drug Administration: Hearings. Washington, DC: U.S. Government Printing Office, 1970. 138pp.

880. Vernon, D.H. General State Food and Drug Laws. Chicago: Commerce Clearing House, 1955. 804pp.

H.1   CURRENT SOURCES

881. Automobile Law Reporter.
          Chicago: Commerce Clearing House, 1965-   .
          (loose-leaf service).

882. Chemical Regulation Reporter.
          Washington, DC: Bureau of National Affairs, 1977-   .
          (loose-leaf service).
          Includes "Hazardous materials transportation."

883. Consumer Product Safety Guide.
          Chicago: Commerce Clearing House, 1974-   .
          (loose-leaf service).

884. Contemporary Drug Problems.
          v.1-   1972-   Quarterly.
          New York: Federal Legal Publications.

885. Drug Enforcement.
          v.1-   1973-   Irregular.
          Washington, DC: U.S. Drug Enforcement Administration
          Formerly U.S. Bureau of Narcotics and Dangerous Drugs BNDD Bulle-
              tin.

886. Employment Safety and Health Guide.
          Chicago: Commerce Clearing House, 1976-   .
          (loose-leaf service).

887. Federal Consumer Product Safety Service: Current Developments.
          Washington, DC: Matthew Bender, 1974-   .
          (loose-leaf service).

888. Federation of Insurance Counsel Quarterly.
          v.1-   1950-   .
          Champaign, IL: Garrard Press.

889. Food Drug Cosmetic Law Journal.
          v.1-   1946-   Monthly.
          Chicago: Commerce Clearing House.

890. Food Drug Cosmetic Law Reporter.
          Chicago: Commerce Clearing House, 1975-   .
          (loose-leaf service).

891. Journal of Drug Issues.
          v.1-   1971-   Quarterly.
          Tallahassee, FL: Journal of Drug Issues.

892. Journal of Products Liability.
          v.1-   1977-   Quarterly.
          Elmsford, NY: Pergamon Press.

893. Occupational Safety & Health Reporter.
     Washington, DC: Bureau of National Affairs, 1971-   .
     (loose-leaf service).

894. Product Safety & Liability Reporter.
     Washington, DC: Bureau of National Affairs, 1972-   .
     (loose-leaf service).

895. Products Liability Reporter.
     Chicago: Commerce Clearing House, 1963-   .
     (loose-leaf service).

H.2   PRODUCT SAFETY AND LIABILITY

896. Caves, R.E., and M.J. Roberts, eds. Regulating the Product: Quality
     and Variety. Cambridge, MA: Ballinger, 1974. 268pp.

897. Hursh, R.D., and H.J. Bailey. American Law of Products Liability,
     2d edition. Rochester, NY: Lawyers Co-operative, 1974- . (loose-
     leaf).

898. Kimble, W. Federal Consumer Product Safety Act. St. Paul, MN: West,
     1975. 548pp.

899. Schreiber, S. Product Liability: Law, Practice, Science, 2d edition,
     by P.D. Rheingold and S.L. Birnbaum. New York: Practising Law In-
     stitute, 1975. 1111pp.

900. U.S. Congress, Senate, Committee on Labor and Public Welfare. Medi-
     cal Devices: Hearings. Washington, DC: U.S. Government Printing
     Office, 1973. 446pp.

901. U.S. Interagency Task Force on Product Liability. Final Report, 1
     volume. Springfield, VA: National Technical Information Service,
     1978.

902. U.S. Interagency Task Force on Product Liability. Product Liability:
     Final Report of the Industry Study, 2 volumes. Washington, DC:
     U.S. Government Printing Office, 1977.

903. U.S. Interagency Task Force on Product Liability. Product Liability:
     Final Report of the Insurance Study, 1 volume. Washington, DC:
     U.S. Government Printing Office, 1977.

904. U.S. Interagency Task Force on Product Liability. Product Liability:
     Final Report of the Legal Study, 7 volumes. Washington, DC: U.S.
     Government Printing Office, 1977.

H.3   FOOD PURITY AND QUALITY; AGRICULTURE

905. American Society of International Law.   The International Regulation of Pesticide Residues in Food: A Report to the National Science Foundation on the Application of International Regulatory Techniques to Scientific/Technical Problems. D.A. Kay. St. Paul, MN: West, 1976. 172pp. (Studies in Transnational Legal Policy, 13.)

906. Aspen Systems Corporation.   Compilation of Federal, State and Local Laws Controlling Nonpoint Pollutants: An Analysis of the Law Affecting Agriculture, Construction, Mining and Silviculture Activity, 1 volume. Washington, DC: U.S. Government Printing Office, 1975.

907. Bennett, E.H.   Farm Law: A Treatise on the Legal Rights and Liabilities of Farmers. Portland, ME: Hoyt, Fogg & Donham, 1880. 120pp.

908. Beuscher, J.H., and H.W. Hannah.   Law and the Farmer, 4th edition. New York: Springer, 1975. 452pp.

909. Bigwood, E.J., and A. Gérard.   Fundamental Principles and Objectives of a Comparative Food Law, 4 volumes. Basel: Karger, 1967-71.

910. Cano, G.J.   A Legal and Institutional Framework for Natural Resources Management. Rome: Food and Agriculture Organization of the United Nations, 1975. 44pp. (Legislative Studies, 9.)

911. Center for Study of Responsive Law.   Sowing the Wind. H. Wellford. New York: Grossman, 1972. 384pp. (A report from Ralph Nader's Center for Study of Responsive Law on food safety and the chemical harvest.)

912. Christopher, T.W.   Constitutional Questions in Food and Drug Laws. Chicago: Commerce Clearing House, 1960. 116pp.

913. Dickerson, R.   Products Liability and the Food Consumer. Boston: Little, Brown, 1957. 339pp.

914. Forte, W.E.   "The Food and Drug Administration and the Economic Adulteration of Foods," 41 Indiana Law Journal 346-402 (1966).

915. Gérard, A.   An Outline of Food Law: Structure, Principles, Main Provisions. Rome: Food and Agriculture Organization of the United Nations, 1975. 105pp. (Legislative Studies, 7.)

916. Hunter, B.T.   The Miracle of Safety: Food Additives and Federal Policy. New York: Scribner, 1975. 322pp.

917. National Academy of Sciences, Washington, DC.   How Safe Is Safe? The Design of Policy on Drugs and Food Additives. Washington, DC: The Academy, 1974. 241pp.

918. "Symposium: Agricultural Law and Policy," 7 University of Toledo Law Review 791-1105 (1976).

919. "Symposium: The Legal Environment of Agriculture," University of
      Illinois Law Forum 469-558 (1976).

920. Turner, J.S.   The Chemical Feast: The Ralph Nader Study Group Report
      on Food Protection and the Food and Drug Administration.   New
      York: Grossman, 1970. 273pp.

H.4   REGULATION OF MEDICAL DRUGS

921. Arthur, W.R.   Law of Drugs and Druggists, 4th edition.   St. Paul, MN:
      West, 1955. 399pp.

922. Brecher, E.M.   Licit and Illicit Drugs.   Boston: Little, Brown, 1972.
      623pp.

923. DeMarco, C.T.   Pharmacy and the Law.   Germantown, MD: Aspen Systems
      Corp., 1975. 381pp.

924. Dewar, T.   A Textbook of Forensic Pharmacy, 6th edition.   London:
      Edward Arnold, 1964. 322pp.

925. Dixon, M.G.   Drug Product Liability, 1 volume. New York: Matthew
      Bender, 1974- . (loose-leaf).

926. The Food and Drug Law Institute.   An Analytical Legislative History
      of the Medical Device Amendments of 1976, edited by D.F. O'Keefe
      and R.A. Spiegel. Washington, DC: The Institute, 1976. 328pp.

927. Goodman, R.M., and P.D. Rheingold.   Drug Liability: A Lawyers Hand-
      book. New York: Practising Law Institute, 1970. 726pp.

928. Kay, D.A.   The International Regulation of Pharmacautical Drugs: A
      Report to the National Science Foundation on the Application of
      International Regulatory Techniques to Scientific/Technical Prob-
      lems. St. Paul, MN: West, 1976. 98pp. (American Society of
      International Law. Studies in Transnational Legal Policy, 14.)

929. The London Times.   The Thalidomide Children and the Law. London:
      Andre Deutsch, 1973. 156pp.

930. Merrill, R.A.   "Compensation for Prescription Drug Injuries," 59
      Virginia Law Review 1-120 (1973).

931. Mintz, M.   By Prescription Only. Boston: Houghton Mifflin, 1967.
      443pp.

932. Pettit, W.   Manual of Pharmaceutical Law, 3d edition. New York: Mac-
      millan, 1962. 284pp.

933. Practising Law Institute.   Federal Regulation of the Drug Industry.
      V.A. Kleinfeld, Chairman. New York: Practising Law Institute,
      1974. 344pp.

934. Rosenthal, M.P.   "Dangerous Drug Legislation in the United States:
     Recommendations and Comments," 45 Texas Law Review 1037-1174
     (1967).

935. U.S. Congress, Senate, Committee on Government Operations.   Drug
     Literature. Washington, DC: U.S. Government Printing Office,
     1963. 171pp. (A factual survey on "The Nature and Magnitude of
     Drug Literature" by the National Library of Medicine; includes
     "World List of Pharmacy Periodicals.")

936. U.S. Congress, Senate, Committee on Labor and Public Welfare.   Pre-
     scription Drug Legislation: Hearings. Washington, DC: U.S. Gov-
     ernment Printing Office, 1970.   258pp.

937. U.S. Department of Health, Education and Welfare, Review Panel on New
     Drug Regulation.   Final Report. Washington, DC: Department of
     Health, Education and Welfare, 1977.   117pp.

938. U.S. Department of Health, Education and Welfare, Review Panel on New
     Drug Regulation.   Investigation of Allegations Relating to the
     Bureau of Drugs, Food and Drug Administration. Washington, DC:
     U.S. Government Printing Office, 1977.   766pp.

939. U.S. Drug Enforcement Administration, Office of Compliance and Regu-
     latory Affairs.   Comprehensive Final Report on State Regulatory
     Agencies and Professional Associations. Washington, DC: U.S. Gov-
     ernment Printing Office, 1977.   193pp.

H.5   NARCOTICS AND ADDICTION

940. Andrews, T.   Bibliography of Drug Abuse, Including Alcohol and Tobac-
     co. Littleton, CO: Libraries Unlimited, 1977.   250pp.

941. Ashley, R.   Heroin: The Myths and the Facts. New York: St. Martin's
     Press, 1972.   276pp.

942. Braceland, F., D. Freedman, K. Rickels, et al.   Drug Abuse: Medical
     and Criminal Aspects. New York: MSS Information Corp., 1972.
     221pp.

943. Canada. Commission of Inquiry into the Non-medical Use of Drugs.
     Final Report. Ottawa: Information Canada, 1973.   1148pp.

944. Duster, T.   The Legislation of Morality: Law, Drugs, and Moral Judg-
     ment. New York: Free Press, 1970.   274pp.

945. Eckert, W.G.   The Medical, Legal & Law Enforcement Aspects of Drugs
     and Drug Abuse: A Bibliography of Classic and Current References.
     Wichita, KS: Published by the author, 1972.   97pp.

946. Edwards, C.N   Drug Dependence: Social Regulation and Treatment Al-
     ternatives. New York: J. Aronson, 1974.   206pp. (Published in
     association with John A. Calhoun & the Justice Resource Institute.)

947. Eldridge, W.B.   Narcotics and the Law: A Critique of the American
     Experiment in Narcotic Drug Control.   Chicago: American Bar Foun-
     dation, 1962.   204pp.

948. Epstein, S.S., ed.   Drugs of Abuse: Their Genetic and Other Chronic
     Nonpsychiatric Hazards.   Cambridge, MA: MIT Press, 1971.   228pp.
     (Based on a symposium co-sponsored by the Center for Studies of
     Narcotic and Drug Abuse and the Environmental Mutagen Society.)

949. Fingarette, H.   "Addiction and Criminal Responsibility," 84 Yale
     Law Journal 413-444 (1975).

950. Ford Foundation.   Dealing with Drug Abuse.   New York: Praeger, 1972.
     396pp.

951. Grinspoon, L., and J.B. Bakalar.   Cocaine: A Drug and Its Social
     Evolution.   New York: Basic Books, 1976.   308pp.

952. Grinspoon, L., and P. Hedblom.   The Speed Culture: Amphetamine Use
     and Abuse in America.   Cambridge, MA: Harvard University Press,
     1975.   340pp.

953. Hotchen, J.S.   Drug Misuse and the Law: The Regulations.   London:
     Macmillan, 1975.   118pp.

954. International Conference on Drug Abuse, University of Michigan, Ann
     Arbor, 1970.   Drug Abuse: Proceedings, edited by C.J.D. Zarafon-
     etis.   Philadelphia: Lea & Febiger, 1972.   616pp.

955. Joint Committee of the American Bar Association and the American Medi-
     cal Association on Narcotic Drugs.   Drug Addiction: Crime or Dis-
     ease? Interim and Final Reports.   Bloomington, IN: Indiana Uni-
     versity Press, 1961.   173pp.

956. "Law Symposium on the Social Control of Drugs," 9 John Marshall Jour-
     nal of Practice and Procedure 1-293 (1975).

957. Lindesmith, A.R.   The Addict and the Law.   Bloomington, IN: Indiana
     University Press, 1965.   337pp.

958. Menditto, J.   Drugs of Addiction and Non-addiction: Their Use and
     Abuse: A Comprehensive Bibliography, 1960-1969.   Troy, NY: Whit-
     ston Pub. Co., 1970.   315pp. Supplement, Drug Abuse Bibliography
     for 1970.   198pp.

959. National Council on Crime and Delinquency.   Drug Abuse and the Crimi-
     nal Justice System: A Survey of New Approaches in Treatment and
     Rehabilitation.   Davis, CA: The Council, 1974.   221pp.

960. National Drug Abuse Conference, Chicago, 1974.   Developments in the
     Field of Drug Abuse, edited by E. Senay, V. Shorty, and A. Alksne.
     Cambridge, MA: Schenkman, 1975.   1129pp.

961. Perlman, H.S., and P.A. Jaszi.   Legal Issues in Addict Diversion: A
     Technical Analysis.   Washington, DC: Drug Abuse Council, 1975.
     129pp.

962. Schur, E.M.   Narcotic Addiction in Britain and America: The Impact of Public Policy. Bloomington, IN: Indiana University Press, 1962. 281pp.

963. Simmons, L.R.S., and M.B. Gold.   Discrimination and the Addict: Notes Toward a General Theory of Addict Rehabilitation. Beverly Hills, CA: Sage, 1973. 334pp. (International Yearbooks of Drug Addiction and Society, 1.)

964. Symposium.   "Narcotics,"   22 Law and Contemporary Problems 1-154 (1957).

965. Symposium.   "Narcotics Problem," 1 University of California Los Angeles Law Review 405-546 (1954).

966. Tompkins, D.L.C.   Drug Addiction: A Bibliography. Berkeley, CA: University of California, Bureau of Public Administration, 1960. 130pp.

967. "Treating Alcoholic and Drug Dependent Offenders," 18 International Journal of Offender Therapy and Comparative Criminology 3-108 (1974).

968. Uelmen, G.F., and V.G. Haddox.   Cases, Text and Materials on Drug Abuse and the Law. St. Paul, MN: West, 1974. 564pp.

969. U.S. Advisory Committee on Smoking and Health.   Smoking and Health: Report of the Advisory Committee to the Surgeon General of the Public Health Service. Washington, DC: U.S. Government Printing Office, 1964. 387pp. ("The Surgeon General's Report.")

970. U.S. Bureau of Narcotics.   Handbook of Federal Narcotic and Dangerous Drug Laws. Washington, DC: U.S. Government Printing Office, 1969. 89pp.

971. U.S. Congress, House, Committee on the Judiciary.   Narcotic Addiction Treatment and Rehabilitation Programs: Hearings. Washington, DC: U.S. Government Printing Office, 1974. 315pp.

972. U.S. Congress, House, Committee on Ways and Means.   Controlled Dangerous Substances, Narcotics and Drug Control Laws: Hearings. Washington, DC: U.S. Government Printing Office, 1970. 536pp.

973. U.S. Drug Abuse Task Force.   White Paper on Drug Abuse: A Report. Washington, DC: U.S. Government Printing Office, 1975. 116pp.

974. U.S. National Clearinghouse for Smoking and Health.   State Legislation on Smoking and Health, 1976. Atlanta, GA: The Clearinghouse, 1976. 73pp.

975. U.S. National Commission on Marihuana and Drug Abuse.   Drug Use in America: Problem in Perspective. Washington, DC: U.S. Government Printing Office, 1973. 481pp.

976. U.S. President's Advisory Commission on Narcotic and Drug Abuse. Final Report. Washington, DC: U.S. Government Printing Office, 1963. 123pp.

977. U.S. President's Commission on Law Enforcement and Administration of
      Justice. Task Force Report: Narcotics and Drug Abuse. Washing-
      ton, DC: U.S. Government Printing office, 1967. 158pp.

978. White House Conference on Narcotic and Drug Abuse. Proceedings.
      Washington, DC: U.S. Government Printing Office, 1963. 330pp.

979. Whitlock, F.A. Drugs, Morality, and the Law. St. Lucia, Australia:
      University of Queensland Press, 1975. 156pp.

H.5.a   ALCOHOL

980. Eckert, W.G., and T.T. Noguchi. A Bibliography of Classic and Cur-
      rent References on Alcohol and Alcoholism: The Medical, Legal, and
      Law Enforcement Aspects, 2 volumes. Wichita, KA: Published by the
      authors, 1973-74.

981. Grad, F.P., A.L. Goldberg, and B.A. Shapiro. Alcoholism and the
      Law. Dobbs Ferry, NY: Oceana, 1971. 311pp.

982. McAdam, D. The Legal and Medical Aspect of Drunkenness. New York:
      Society of Medical Jurisprudence, 1894. 57pp.

983. Pittman, D.J., and C.W. Gordon. Revolving Door: A Study of the
      Chronic Police Case Inebriate. Glencoe, IL: Free Press, 1958.
      154pp.

984. U.S. Congress, House, Committee on Interstate and Foreign Commerce.
      Comprehensive Alcohol Abuse and Alcoholism Legislation: Hearings.
      Washington, DC: U.S. Government Printing Office, 1970. 443pp.

985. U.S. National Institute of Law Enforcement and Criminal Justice.
      Alcohol and the Criminal Justice System: Challenge and Response.
      H. Erskine. Washington, DC: U.S. Department of Justice, 1972.
      29pp.

986. U.S. National Institute of Mental Health. Alcohol and Alcoholism.
      Washington, DC: U.S. Government Printing Office, 1967. 73pp.

987. U.S. President's Commission on Law Enforcement and Administration of
      Justice. Task Force Report: Drunkenness. Washington, DC: U.S.
      Government Printing Office, 1967. 131pp.

H.5.b MARIHUANA

988. Bonnie, R.J., and C.H. Whitebread, Jr. The Marihuana Conviction: A History of Marihuana Prohibition in the United States. Charlottesville, VA: University Press of Virginia, 1974. 368pp.

989. Canada. Commission of Inquiry into the Non-medical Use of Drugs. Cannabis: A Report. Ottawa: Information Canada, 1972. 462pp.

990. Grinspoon, L. Marihuana Reconsidered, 2d edition. Cambridge, MA: Harvard University Press, 1977. 474pp.

991. Hellman, A.D. Laws Against Marijuana: The Price We Pay. Urbana, IL: University of Illinois Press, 1975. 210pp.

992. Kaplan, J. Marijuana: The New Prohibition. New York: World Pub. Co., 1970. 387pp.

993. United Nations, Commission on Narcotic Drugs. The Question of Cannabis: Cannabis Bibliography. New York: United Nations, 1965. 250pp.

994. U.S. Congress, House, Committee on the Judiciary. Commission on Marihuana: Hearings. Washington, DC: U.S. Government Printing Office, 1970. 123pp.

995. U.S. Congress, House, Select Committee on Crime. Crime in America: Views on Marihuana: Hearings. Washington, DC: U.S. Government Printing Office, 1970. 115pp.

996. U.S. Congress, Senate, Committee on the Judiciary. Marihuana-Hashish Epidemic and Its Impact on United States Security: Hearings. Washington, DC: U.S. Government Printing Office, 1975. 430pp.

997. U.S. National Commission on Marihuana and Drug Abuse. Marihuana: A Signal of Misunderstanding. Washington, DC: U.S. Government Printing Office, 1972. 184pp. (Reprinted, New York: New American Library, 1972. 233pp.)

H.5.c INTERNATIONAL CONTROL OF NARCOTICS

998. Bassiouni, M.C. International Drug Control. Washington, DC: World Peace through Law Center, 1973. 90pp.

999. European Conference of Directors of Criminological Research Institutes. The Importance of Narcotics in Relation to Criminality: Proceedings of the 11th Conference. Strasbourg: Council of Europe, 1975. 213pp.

1000. Arthur D. Little, Inc., Cambridge, MA. International Narcotics Con-
       trol: A Source Book of Conventions, Protocols, and Multilateral
       Agreements, 1909-1971. Cambridge, MA, 1971. 82pp.

1001. Simmons, L.R.S., and A.A. Said. Drugs, Politics, and Diplomacy:
       The International Connection. Beverly Hills, CA: Sage, 1974.
       312pp. (International Yearbooks of Drug Addiction and Society, 2.)

1002. United Nations, Secretary-General. Multi-Lingual List of Narcotic
       Drugs under International Control. New York: United Nations,
       1968. 273pp.

1003. U.S. Congress, House, Committee on Foreign Affairs. International
       Aspects of the Narcotics Problem. Washington, DC: U.S. Government
       Printing Office, 1971. 224pp.

1004. U.S. Congress, Senate, Committee on Foreign Relations. Internation-
       al Traffic in Narcotics. Washington, DC: U.S. Government Printing
       Office, 1971. 126pp.

1005. U.S. Congress, Senate, Committee on the Judiciary. World Drug Traf-
       fic and Its Impact on U.S. Security, 7 parts. Washington, DC:
       U.S. Government Printing Office, 1972-73.

H.6   AUTOMOBILE AND TRAFFIC HAZARDS

1006. The Automobile and the Regulation of Its Impact on the Environment.
       F.P. Grad, et al. Norman, OK: University of Oklahoma Press, 1975.
       481pp.

1007. Averbach, A. Handling Automobile Cases, 2 volumes. Rochester, NY:
       Lawyers Cooperative, 1962.

1008. Baker, R.F. The Highway Risk Problem: Policy Issues in Highway Safe-
       ty. New York: Wiley, 1971. 175pp.

1009. Blashfield, DeW. C. Automobile Law and Practice, 3d edition, edited
       by F.D. Lewis. St. Paul, MN: West, 1965- . (First edition pub-
       lished in 1927 under title: Blashfield's Cyclopedia of Automobile
       Law.)

1010. Conard, A.F., et al. Automobile Accident Costs and Payments. Ann
       Arbor, MI: University of Michigan Press, 1964. 506pp.

1011. Erwin, R.E., L.A. Greenberg, and M.K. Minzer. Defense of Drunk
       Driving Cases: Criminal-Civil, 3d edition. New York: Matthew Ben-
       der, 1971- . (loose-leaf).

1012. Finch, J.R., and J.P. Smith. Psychiatric and Legal Aspects of Auto-
       mobile Fatalities. Springfield, IL: C.C. Thomas, 1970. 150pp.

1013. Fisher, E.C.   Vehicle Traffic Law, 1974 revised edition by R.H.
       Reeder. Evanston, IL: Traffic Institute, Northwestern University,
       1974. 339pp.

1014. Gillam, C.W.   Products Liability in the Automobile Industry: A Study
       in Strict Liability and Social Control. Minneapolis, MN: Univer-
       sity of Minnesota Press, 1960. 239pp.

1015. Keeton, R.E., and J. O'Connell.   After Cars Crash: The Need for
       Legal and Insurance Reform. Homewood, IL: Dow Jones-Irwin, 1967.
       145pp.

1016. Keeton, R.E., J. O'Connell, and J.H. McCord, eds.   Crisis in Car
       Insurance. Urbana, IL: University of Illinois Press, 1968.
       279pp.

1017. Little, J.W.   Administration of Justice in Drunk Driving Cases.
       Gainesville, FL: University Presses of Florida, 1975. 221pp.

1018. Nader, R.   Unsafe at Any Speed, expanded edition. New York: Gross-
       man, 1972. 417pp.

1019. National Committee on Uniform Traffic Laws and Ordinances.   Uniform
       Vehicle Code: Rules of the Road with Statutory Annotations, 1967.
       Charlottesville, VA: Michie, 1968. 654pp.

1020. U.S. Congress, Senate, Committee on Commerce.   Auto Safety Oversight:
       Hearings. Washington, DC: U.S. Government Printing Office, 1972.
       543pp.

H.7 NUCLEAR HAZARDS*

1021. Atomic Insurance Project.   Financial Protection Against Atomic Haz-
       ards. A.W. Murphy, et al. New York: Atomic Industrial Forum,
       1957. 65pp. (Legislative Drafting Research Fund of Columbia Uni-
       versity.)

1022. Berman, W.H., and L.M. Hydeman.   A Study: Federal and State Respon-
       sibilities for Radiation Protection: The Need for Federal Legis-
       lation. Ann Arbor, MI: University of Michigan Law School, 1959.
       120pp.

1023. Cavers, D.F.   "Improving Financial Protection of the Public Against
       the Hazards of Nuclear Power," 77 Harvard Law Review 644-688
       (1964).

1024. Conference on Atomic Radiation and the Law, University of Chicago Law
       School, 1961.   Papers. Chicago: University of Chicago Law School,
       1961. 58pp.

_____

* See also I.5 and J.5.b.

1025. Convention on Third Party Liability in the Field of Nuclear Energy.
       Convention sur la Responsabilité Civil dans le Domaine de l'Éner-
       gie Nucléaire. Paris: Organisation de Coopération et de Dévelop-
       pement Économiques, Agence pour l'Énergie Nucléaire, 1974. 75pp.
       (in French and English.)

1026. Harvard University Law School. International Problems of Financial
       Protection Against Nuclear Risk: A Study under the Auspices of
       Harvard Law School and Atomic Industrial Forum. Cambridge, MA:
       Harvard University Law School, 1959. 95pp.

1027. Hydeman, L.M., and W.H. Berman. International Control of Nuclear
       Maritime Activities. Ann Arbor, MI: University of Michigan Law
       School, 1960. 384pp.

1028. International Atomic Energy Agency. International Conventions on
       Civil Liability for Nuclear Damage, revised edition. Vienna,
       1976. 261pp. (The Agency's Legal Series no. 4.)

1029. Organization for Economic Co-operation and Development, European Nu-
       clear Energy Agency. Nuclear Legislation, Analytical Study: Nu-
       clear Third Party Liability. Paris: Organization for Economic Co-
       operation and Development, 1976. 190pp.

1030. U.S. Bureau of Radiological Health. Legislative History of Radia-
       tion Control for Health and Safety Act of 1968, 2 volumes. Wash-
       ington, DC: U.S. Government Printing Office, 1975.

1031. U.S. Congress, Joint Committee on Atomic Energy. Investigation of
       Charges Relating to Nuclear Reactor Safety, 2 volumes. Washing-
       ton, DC: U.S. Government Printing Office, 1976.

1032. Weinstein, J.L., ed. Law and Administration: Nuclear Liability.
       Oxford: Pergamon, 1962. 483pp.

I. NATURAL RESOURCES AND ENVIRONMENTAL CONTROLS, NATIONAL AND INTERNATIONAL

1033. Abbasi, S.A. Current Legal Literature on Three Aspects of Ecology: Air, Noise, and Water Pollution: A Selected and Partially Annotated Bibliography, 1969-1974. Monticello, IL: Council of Planning Librarians, 1975. 54pp.

1034. Ackerman, B.A. The Uncertain Search for Environmental Quality. New York: Free Press, 1974. 386pp.

1035. American Bar Association, Section of Natural Resources Law. Environmental Law: Practice and Procedure Handbook. Chicago: American Bar Association, 1976. 302pp.

1036. Appelbaum, G.D. "Controlling the Environmental Hazards of International Development," 5 Ecology Law Quarterly 321-376 (1976).

1037. Baldwin, M.F., and J.K. Page, Jr., eds. Law and the Environment. New York: Walker, 1970. 432pp.

1038. Baram, M.S., et al. Environmental Law and the Siting of Facilities: Issues in Land Use and Coastal Zone Management. Cambridge, MA: Ballinger, 1976. 255pp.

1039. Bennett, G.F., and J.C. Bennett. Environmental Literature: A Bibliography, 3d edition. Park Ridge, NJ: Noyes Data Corp., 1973. 134pp.

1040. Bilder, R.B. The Settlement of International Environmental Disputes. Madison, WI: University of Wisconsin Sea Grant College Program, 1976. 92pp.

1041. Brecher, J.J., and M.E. Nestle. Environmental Law Handbook. Berkeley, CA: California Continuing Education of the Bar, 1970. 343pp.

1042. Caldwell, L.K. In Defense of Earth: International Protection of the Biosphere. Bloomington, IN: Indiana University Press, 1972. 295pp.

1043. Conference on Environmental Law, Ann Arbor, MI, 1970. Environmental Law, edited by C.M. Hassett. Ann Arbor, MI: Institute of Continuing Legal Education, 1971. 195pp.

1044. Conference on Environmental Quality and Social Justice, Woodstock, IL, 1972. Environmental Quality and Social Justice in Urban America, edited by J.N. Smith. Washington, DC: Conservation Foundation, 1974. 145pp.

1045. Conference on International Environmental Law, London, 1975. Environmental Law: International and Comparative Aspects: A Symposium, edited by J. Nowak. London: British Institute of International and Comparative Law, 1976. 193pp.

1046. "Conservation of the Environment," 55 International Law Association. Conference Report 468-538 (1974).

1047. Degler, S.E.   Federal Pollution Control Programs: Water, Air, and
      Solid Wastes, revised edition. Washington, DC: Bureau of Nation-
      al Affairs, 1971. 176pp.

1048. Dickson, L.E.   Law and the Environment: An Annotated Bibliographic
      Guide to Materials in the Tarlton Law Library. Austin, TX: Uni-
      versity of Texas, Tarlton Law Library, 1973. 40pp.

1049. Ditton, R.B.   National Environmental Policy Act of 1969: Bibliogra-
      phy on Impact Assessment Methods and Legal Considerations. Monti-
      cello, IL: Council of Planning Librarians, 1973. 22pp.

1050. Enviro/Info.   Science Policy, Technology Assessment, and the Envi-
      ronment: An Annotated Bibliography of Selected U.S. Government
      Publications. Green Bay, WI: Enviro/Info., 1973. 18pp.

1051. Environmental Law Institute.   Federal Environmental Law, edited by
      E.L. Dolgin and T.G.P. Guilbert. St. Paul, MN: West, 1974.
      1600pp.

1052. "Environmental Law Symposium," 19 Wayne Law Review 73-219 (1972).

1053. Environmental Programmes of Intergovernmental Organizations: With Spe-
      cial Reference to the Sphere of Interest of the Chemical Industry,
      1 volume. P.L. deReeder. The Hague: Nijhoff, 1977- . (loose-
      leaf).

1054. Goldie, L.F.E.   "International Principles of Responsibility for Pol-
      lution," 9 Columbia Journal of Transnational Law 283-330 (1970).

1055. Grad, F.P.   Environmental Law: Sources and Problems, 2d edition, 2
      volumes. New York: Matthew Bender, 1978- . (loose-leaf).

1056. Grad, F.P., G.W. Rathjens, and A.J. Rosenthal.   Environmental Con-
      trol: Priorities, Policies and the Law. New York: Columbia Uni-
      versity Press, 1971. 311pp. (Study prepared by the Legislative
      Drafting Research Fund of Columbia University.)

1057. Grieves, F.L.   International Law, Organization, and the Environment:
      A Bibliography and Research Guide. Tucson, AZ: University of Ari-
      zona Press, 1974. 131pp.

1058. Grossman, G.S.   Legal Bibliography: A Critical Overview for Environ-
      mentalists. Monticello, IL: Council of Planning Librarians, 1973.
      21pp.

1059. Haskell, E.H., and V.S. Price.   State Environmental Management:
      Case Studies of Nine States. New York: Praeger, 1973. 283pp.

1060. Henkin, H., M. Merta, and J. Staples.   The Environment, the Estab-
      lishment, and the Law. Boston: Houghton Mifflin, 1971. 223pp.

1061. Institute on Mineral Law, Louisiana State University.   Proceedings.
      1st-17th; 1953-1970. Baton Rouge, LA: Louisiana State University
      School of Law.

1062. International Environmental Law. Multilateral Treaties, 1 volume, edited by W.E. Burhenne. Berlin: Schmidt, 1974. (loose-leaf).

1063. Jaffe, L.L., and L.H. Tribe. Environmental Protection. Chicago: Bracton Press, 1971. 702pp; and Supplement, 1972. 140pp.

1064. Johnson, B. International Environmental Law: A Study of the Inter-relationship between General International Law and Treaty Law in the Field of Environmental Management with an Examination of Legal Documents Relevant to the Preservation of Nature. Stockholm: LiberFörlag, 1976. 226pp.

1065. Kneese, A.V., S.E. Rolfe, and J.W. Harned, eds. Managing the Environment: International Economic Cooperation for Pollution Control. New York: Praeger, 1971. 356pp.

1066. Krash, M., D. Duke, and G. Juris. From Now On: An Environmental Bibliography. St. Louis, MO: St. Louis University, Pius XII Library, 1972. 82pp.

1067. Laitos, J.G. "A Leap of Faith: Some Observations on Law's Effect upon the Earth's Natural Resources," 25 American University La Review 131-172 (1975).

1068. Lutz, R.E., II. "The Laws of Environmental Management," 24 American Journal of Comparative Law 447-520 (1976).

1069. McCaffrey, S.C. Private Remedies for Transfrontier Environmental Disturbances. Morges, Switzerland: International Union for Conservation of Nature and Natural Resources, 1975. 156pp. (IUCN Environmental Policy and Law Paper, 8.)

1070. McKnight, A.D, P.K. Marstrand, and T.C. Sinclair. Environmental Pollution Control: Technical, Economic and Legal Aspects. London: Allen & Unwin, 1974. 324pp.

1071. Meek, W.F. Environmental Analysis: A Guide to Federal Environmental Concerns, 2d edition. Boulder, CO: Rocky Mountain Mineral Law Foundation, 1974. 107pp.

1072. Meyers, C.J., and A.D. Tarlock. Selected Legal and Economic Aspects of Environmental Protection. Mineola, NY: Foundation Press, 1971. 410pp.

1073. Morrisey, J.J. Pollution Control Problems and Related Federal Legislation. New York: MSS Information Corp., 1974. 290pp.

1074. Murphy, E.F. Nature, Bureaucracy and the Rules of Property: Regulating the Renewing Environment. New York: Elsevier North-Holland, 1977. 335pp.

1075. National Institute of Municipal Law Officers, Washington, DC. Law and the Municipal Ecology: Air, Water, Noise, Over-Population. S.F. Lewin, et al. Washington, DC, 1970. 243pp. (Issued as the Institute's Report, 156.)

1076. National Institute on Environmental Litigation, Dallas, 1973. Planning, Environmental Science, Aviation. Chicago: American Bar Association, 1974- .

1077. Nonnenmacher, G.G., et al. The International Law of the Human Environment: Papers of the Twenty-third A.A.A. Congress, in 41 Hague. Academy of International Law. Association of Auditors and Former Auditors. Annuaire 9-134 (1971).

1078. Northwestern University, Orrington Lunt Library. A Selected List of U.S. Government Publications on Environmental Pollution. Evanston, IL: Northwestern University Library, Government Publications Department, 1970. 34pp.

1079. Ontario, Ministry of the Environment. Bibliography, Reference Material and Information Sources on the Environment. Toronto: Information Services Branch, 1973. 16pp.

1080. Onyx Group, Inc. Environment U.S.A.: A Guide to Agencies, People, and Resources. New York: Bowker, 1974. 451pp.

1081. Practising Law Institute. Legal Control of the Environment. M.B. Durning, Chairman. New York: Practising Law Institute, 1972. 341pp.

1082. Reitze, A.W., Jr. Environmental Law, 2d edition, 2 volumes. Washington, DC: North American International, 1972.

1083. Sand, P.H. Legal Systems for Environment Protection: Japan, Sweden, United States. Rome: Food and Agriculture Organization of the United Nations, 1972. 60pp. (Legislative Studies, 4.)

1084. Schaumburg, F.D. Judgment Reserved: A Landmark Environmental Case. Reston, VA: Reston Pub., 1976. 265pp.

1085. Schwartz, M.D. Environmental Law: A Guide to Information Sources. Detroit: Gale, 1977. 191pp.

1086. Sive, M.R., ed. Environmental Legislation: A Sourcebook. New York: Praeger, 1976. 561pp.

1087. Stanford Environmental Law Society. Publications. Stanford, CA: Stanford University School of Law, 1969-   . Various studies, e.g., R.S. Mallory, The Legally Required Contents of a NEPA Environmental Impact Statement. 1976. 67pp.

1088. Study of Critical Environmental Problems, Williams College, Williamstown, MA, 1970. Man's Impact on the Global Environment: Assessment and Recommendations for Action. Cambridge, MA: MIT Press, 1970. 319pp.

1089. Summer Institute on the Impact of the Environmental Sciences and the New Biology on Law Libraries, Berkeley, CA, 1971. The Impact of the Environmental Sciences and the New Biology on Law Libraries. Dobbs Ferry, NY: Distributed by Oceana for Glanville, 1973. 174pp.

1090. "Symposium on Natural Resource Property Rights," 15 _Natural Resources Journal_ 639-789 (1975).

1091. Teclaff, L.S., and A.E. Utton. _International Environmental Law._
       New York: Praeger, 1974. 270pp.

1092. Tribe, L.H. "From Environmental Foundations to Constitutional Structures: Learning from Nature's Future," 84 _Yale Law Journal_ 545-566 (1975).

1093. Tribe, L.H. "Ways Not to Think about Plastic Trees: New Foundations for Environmental Law," 83 _Yale Law Journal_ 1315-1348 (1974).

1094. Tribe, L.H., C.S. Schelling, and J. Voss, eds. _When Values Conflict: Essays on Environmental Analysis, Discourse, and Decision._
       Cambridge, MA: Ballinger, 1976. 178pp.

1095. U.S. Congress, Senate, Committee on Interior and Insular Affairs.
       Law and the Environment: Selected Materials on Tax Exempt Status and Public Interest Litigation. Washington, DC: U.S. Government Printing Office, 1970. 43pp.

1096. U.S. Congress, Senate, Committee on Public Works. _The Impact of Growth on the Environment._ Washington, DC: U.S. Government Printing Office, 1973. 158pp.

1097. U.S. Environmental Protection Agency. _Index of EPA Legal Authority: Statutes & Legislative History, Executive Orders, Regulations._
       Washington, DC: U.S. Government Printing Office, 1974. 280pp.

1098. U.S. Laws, Statutes, etc., Public Health Law. _Current Laws, Statutes and Executive Orders..._ Washington, DC: U.S. Environmental Protection Agency, 1972- . (loose-leaf).

1099. U.S. Laws, Statutes, etc., Public Health Law. _Legal Compilation._
       Washington, DC: U.S. Environmental Protection Agency, 1973-74.
       (Separate volumes on air, water, solid waste, pesticides, radiation, noise.)

1100. U.S. Library of Congress, Environmental Policy Division. _Congress and the Nation's Environment._ Washington, DC: U.S. Government Printing Office, 1973. 1145pp.

1101. U.S. Library of Congress, Legislative Reference Service. _How Can Our Physical Environment Best Be Controlled and Developed?_ Washington, DC: U.S. Government Printing Office, 1970. 229pp.

1102. Voss, H.L., and D.M. Petersen. _Ecology, Crime and Delinquency._
       New York: Appleton-Century-Crofts, 1971. 328pp.

I.1 CURRENT SOURCES

1103. Atomic Energy Law Journal.
       v.1-   1959-   Quarterly.
       White Plains, NY: Invictus.

1104. Columbia Journal of Environmental Law.
       v.1-   1974-   Semiannual.
       New York: Columbia University School of Law.

1105. Earth Law Journal: Journal of International and Comparative Environ-
       mental Law.
       v.1-   1975-   Quarterly.
       Leyden: A.W. Sijthoff, in cooperation with Friends of the Earth
           (FOE), International Union for the Conservation of Nature and
           Natural Resources (IUCN), and Environmental Law Institute
           (ELI).

1106. Ecology Law Quarterly.
       v.1-   1970-   .
       Berkeley, CA: University of California School of Law.

1107. Energy Controls: The Energy User's Guide to Meeting the Energy Crisis.
       Englewood Cliffs, NJ: Prentice-Hall, 1974-   .
       (loose-leaf service).

1108. Energy Index.
       v.1-   1973-   Annual.
       New York: Environment Information Center, Inc.
       Each volume includes coverage of legal material. See also EIC's
           Envirofiche Microfiche Program, including State Laws & Re-
           gulations: A Guide to Environmental Legislation in the Fifty
           States and the District of Columbia.

1109. Energy Management and Federal Energy Guidelines.
       Chicago: Commerce Clearing House, 1973-   .
       (loose-leaf service).

1110. Energy Users Report.
       Washington, DC: Bureau of National Affairs, 1973-   .
       (loose-leaf service).

1111. Environment Law Review.
       v.1-   1970-   Annual.
       New York: Clark Boardman.

1112. Environment Reporter.
       Washington, DC: Bureau of National Affairs, 1970-   .
       (loose-leaf service).

1113. Environmental Affairs: A Quarterly of Law and Science.
       v.1-   1971-   Quarterly.
       Newton, MA: Boston College Law School, Environmental Law Center.

1114. Environmental Law.
          v.1-   1971-   3 times a year.
          Portland, OR: Northwestern School of Law, Lewis & Clark Law
              School.

1115. Environmental Law Reporter.
          v.1-   1971-   Monthly.
          Washington, DC: Environmental Law Institute.

1116. Environmental Policy and Law.
          v.1-   1975-   Quarterly.
          Lausanne: Elsevier Sequoia.
          Sponsored by the International Council of Environmental Law (ICEL).

1117. Federal Power Service.
          Washington, DC: Matthew Bender, 1974-   .
          (loose-leaf service).

1118. Harvard Environmental Law Review.
          v.1-   1976-   Annual.
          Cambridge, MA: Harvard Law School, Environmental Law Society.

1119. International Environment Reporter.
          Washington, DC: Bureau of National Affairs, 1978-   .
          (loose-leaf service).

1120. Journal of Planning and Environment Law.
          1948-   Monthly.
          London: Sweet & Maxwell.

1121. Land and Water Law Review.
          v.1-   1965-   Semiannual.
          Laramie, WY: University of Wyoming College of Law.

1122. Natural Resources Journal.
          v.1-   1961-   Quarterly.
          Albuquerque, NM: University of New Mexico School of Law.

1123. Natural Resources Lawyer.
          v.1-   1968-   Quarterly.
          Chicago: American Bar Association Section of Natural Resources.

1124. Noise Regulation Reporter.
          Washington, DC: Bureau of National Affairs, 1974-   .
          (loose-leaf service).

1125. Nuclear Law Bulletin.
          no.1-   1968-   Irregular.
          Paris: Organisation for Economic Co-operation and Development,
              Nuclear Energy Agency.

1126. Nuclear Regulation Reporter.
          Chicago: Commerce Clearing House, 1975-   .
          (loose-leaf service).
          Continues Atomic Energy Law Reporter, 1955-75.

1127. The Public Land and Resources Law Digest.
      v.1-   1963-   Semiannual.
      Boulder, CO: Rocky Mountain Mineral Law Foundation.

1128. Rocky Mountain Mineral Law Institute. Proceedings.
      1st-   1955-   Annual.
      New York: Matthew Bender.

1129. Utilities Law Reporter: Federal and State Regulation of Public Utili-
      ties.
      Chicago: Commerce Clearing House, 1947-   .
      (loose-leaf service).

I.2 AIR

1130. Air Pollution Publications: A Selected Bibliography, 1955/62-   .
      Washington, DC: U.S. Government Printing Office, 1964-   . (U.S.
      Library of Congress, Science and Technology Division, for the U.S.
      Public Health Service, Division of Air Pollution.)

1131. Christol, C.Q. The International Legal and Institutional Aspects of
      the Stratosphere Ozone Problem: Staff Report. Washington, DC: U.S.
      Government Printing Office, 1975. 132pp.

1132. Council of Europe. Committee of Experts on Air Pollution. Legal
      Aspects of Air Pollution Control. Strasbourg, 1972. 67pp.

1133. Downing, P.B. Air Pollution and the Social Sciences: Formulating
      and Implementing Control Programs. New York: Praeger, 1971.
      270pp.

1134. Duisin, X.W. Air Pollution Control: A Selected, Annotated Biblio-
      graphy. New York: Institute of Public Administration, 1971. 65pp.

1135. Garner, J.F., and R.K. Crow. Clean Air-Law and Practice, 3d edi-
      tion. London: Shaw, 1969. 506pp.

1136. Hertzendorf, M.S. Air Pollution Control: Guidebook to U.S. Regula-
      tions. Westport, CT: Technomic Pub. Co., 1973. 266pp.

1137. International Clean Air Congress. 1st, London, 1966. Proceedings.
      London: National Society for Clean Air, 1966. 292pp.

1138. International Clean Air Congress. 2d, Washington, DC, 1970. Proceed-
      ings. New York: Academic Press, 1971. 1354pp.

1139. Jacoby, H.D., J.D. Steinbrunner, et al. Clearing the Air: Federal
      Policy on Automotive Emissions Control. Cambridge, MA: Ballinger,
      1973. 213pp.

1140. Jones, C.O.   Clean Air: The Policies and Politics of Pollution Con-
      trol. Pittsburgh, PA: University of Pittsburgh Press, 1975.
      373pp.

1141. Krier, J.E.   Environmental Law and Policy: Readings, Materials and
      Notes on Air Pollution and Related Problems. Indianapolis, IN:
      Bobbs-Merrill, 1971. 480pp.

1142. Rhyne, C.S., and W.G. Van Meter.   City Smoke Control and Air Pol-
      lution Programs: Model Ordinance Annotated. Washington, DC: Na-
      tional Institute of Municipal Law Officers, 1947. 23pp.

1143. Tomany, J.P.   Air Pollution: The Emissions, the Regulations, and the
      Controls. New York: American Elsevier, 1975. 475pp.

1144. U.S. Congress, Senate, Committee on Public Works.   Air Pollution,
      1970: Hearings, 5 parts. Washington, DC: U.S. Government Printing
      Office, 1970.

1145. U.S. Library of Congress, Environmental Policy Division.   A Legisla-
      tive History of the Clean Air Amendments of 1970, 2 volumes. Wash-
      ington, DC: U.S. Government Printing Office, 1974.

1146. U.S. Public Health Service, Division of Air Pollution.   A Digest of
      State Air Pollution Laws. Washington, DC: Department of Health,
      Education and Welfare, 1966. 292pp.

1147. Van Nest, W.J.   Air Pollution and Urban Planning: A Selective Anno-
      tated Bibliography. Monticello, IL: Council of Planning Librar-
      ians, 1972. 64pp.

I.3 WATER

1148. Bracken, D.D.   Trends in Environmental Law Related to Water Resour-
      ces Planning. Auburn, AL: Water Resources Research Institute,
      Auburn University, 1973. 119pp.

1149. Cost-Benefit Analysis and Water Pollution Policy, edited by H.M. Pes-
      kin and E.P. Seskin. Washington, DC: Urban Institute, 1975.
      370pp.

1150. Duisin, X.W.   Water Pollution Control: A Selected Bibliography. New
      York: Institute of Public Administration, 1970. 15pp.

1151. Haber, D., and S.W. Bergen.   Law of Water Allocation in the Eastern
      United States. New York: Ronald Press, 1958. 643pp.

1152. Handl, G.   "International Liability for the Pollution of Internation-
      al Watercourses," 13 Canadian Yearbook of International Law 156-
      194 (1975).

1153. Jacobstein, J.M., and R.M. Mersky. Water Law Bibliography, 1847-
      1965: Source Book on U.S. Water and Irrigation Studies, Legal,
      Economic and Political, 2 volumes. Silver Spring, MD: Jefferson
      Law Book Co., 1966. 249pp. and Supplements 1-2, 1966/67-1968/73;
      1969-74.

1154. Murphy, E.F. Water Purity: A Study in Legal Control of Natural Re-
      sources. Madison, WI: University of Wisconsin Press, 1961.
      212pp.

1155. Nanda, V.P., ed. "Water Needs for the Future: Legal, Political,
      Economic and Technological Issues in National and International
      Perspectives," 6 Denver Journal of International Law and Policy
      225-587 (1976).

1156. Stanford Environmental Law Society. Interstate Environmental Prob-
      lems: A Guide to Water Pollution and Water Scarcity. R.W. Harris,
      et al. Stanford, CA, 1974. 161pp.

1157. U.S. Congress, Senate, Committee on Public Works. Water Pollution
      Control Legislation, 4 volumes. Washington, DC: U.S. Government
      Printing Office, 1971.

1158. U.S. Environmental Protection Agency. Cost of Clean Water: Annual
      Report of the Administrator. 1968-1973. Washington, DC: U.S.
      Government Printing Office.

1159. U.S. Library of Congress, Environmental Policy Division. A Legis-
      lative History of the Water Pollution Control Act Amendments of
      1972. Washington, DC: U.S. Government Printing Office, 1973.
      1766pp.

1160. Wright, G.P., and D.G. Olson. Designing Water Pollution Detection
      Systems: Environmental Law Enforcement on the U.S. Coastal Waters
      and the Great Lakes. Cambridge, MA: Ballinger, 1974. 227pp.

I.4 NOISE

1161. Blitch, S.G. "Airport Noise and Intergovernmental Conflict: A Case
      Study in Land Use Parochialism," 5 Ecology Law Quarterly 669-705
      (1976).

1162. Bragdon, C.R. Noise Pollution: The Unquiet Crisis. Philadelphia:
      University of Pennsylvania Press, 1971. 280pp.

1163. Findley, R.W., and S.J. Plager. "State Regulation of Nontranspor-
      tation Noise: Law and Technology," 48 Southern California Law
      Review 209-317 (1974).

1164. Harris, C.M. Handbook of Noise Control. New York: McGraw-Hill,
      1957.

1165. Kavaler, L. Noise: The New Menace. New York: John Day, 1975. 206pp.

1166. Kerse, C.S. The Law Relating to Noise. London: Oyez, 1975. 188pp.

1167. King, R.L. Airport Noise Pollution: A Bibliography of Its Effects on People and Property. Metuchen, NJ: Scarecrow Press, 1973. 380pp.

1168. National Institute of Municipal Law Officers, Washington, DC. Model Community Noise Control Ordinance. Washington, DC: U.S. Environmental Protection Agency, 1975. 48pp.

1169. National Institute of Municipal Law Officers, Washington, DC. Municipal Control of Noise: Sound Trucks, Sound Advertising, Aircraft, Unnecessary Noises, Model Annotated Ordinances. C.S. Rhyne. Washington, DC: The Institute, 1948. 43pp.

1170. "Port Noise Complaint," 6 Harvard Civil Rights-Civil Liberties Law Review 61-118 (1970).

1171. U.S. Congress, House, Committee on Interstate and Foreign Commerce. Noise Control. Washington, DC: U.S. Government Printing Office, 1971. 504pp.

1172. U.S. Congress, Senate, Committee on Public Works. Noise Pollution. Washington, DC: U.S. Government Printing Office, 1972. 604pp.

1173. U.S. Environmental Protection Agency. Report to the President and Congress on Noise, 1 volume. Washington, DC: U.S. Government Printing Office, 1972.

1174. U.S. Environmental Protection Agency, Office of Noise Abatement and Control. Toward a National Strategy for Noise Control. Washington, DC: U.S. Government Printing Office, 1977. 53pp.

I.5 ENERGY

1175. "Bibliography of Atomic Energy Law Articles: 1947-1959," 1 Atomic Energy Law Journal 220-235 (1959).

1176. Bloustein, E.K., ed. Nuclear Energy, Public Policy and the Law. Dobbs Ferry, NY: Oceana, 1964. 114pp.

1177. Breyer, S.G., and P.W. MacAvoy. Energy Regulation by the Federal Power Commission. Washington, DC: Brookings Institution, 1974. 163pp.

1178. Burke, J.G. "Bursting Boilers and the Federal Power," 7 Technology and Culture 1-23 (1966).

1179. Cavers, D.F.   "Administrative Decision-Making in Nuclear Facilities
      Licensing,"   110 University of Pennsylvania Law Review 330-370
      (1962).

1180. Cicchetti, C.J., and J.L. Jurewitz.   Studies in Electric Utility
      Regulation. Cambridge, MA: Ballinger, 1975. 266pp.

1181. Duchesneau, T.D.   Competition in the U.S. Energy Industry. Cam-
      bridge, MA: Ballinger, 1975. 401pp.

1182. Ebbin, S., and R.G. Kasper.   Citizen Groups and the Nuclear Power
      Controversy: Uses of Scientific and Technological Information.
      Cambridge, MA: MIT Press, 1974. 307pp.

1183. Eisenhard, R.M.   A Survey of State Legislation Relating to Solar
      Energy, 1 volume. Washington, DC: Department of Commerce, 1976.

1184. Energy and Environmental Analysis, Inc.   Laws and Regulations Affect-
      ing Coal: With Summaries of Federal, State, and Local Laws and Re-
      gulations Pertaining to Air and Water Pollution Control, Reclama-
      tion, Diligence and Health and Safety. Washington, DC: Department
      of the Interior, 1976. 560pp.

1185. "The Energy Crisis. Part 1: The Radiation Controversy," 27 Bulletin
      of the Atomic Scientists 2-53 (1971).

1186. Energy Policies of the World, edited by G.J. Mangon. New York: Else-
      vier, 1976- . (Vol. 1: Canada, China, Arab States of the Persian
      Gulf, Venezuela, Iran. 1976 387pp.)

1187. Environmental Law Institute, State and Local Energy Conservation Pro-
      ject. Cambridge, MA: Ballinger, 1977-   . Includes Vol. 1, I.J.
      Tether, Government Procurement and Operation, 1977. 208pp. Vol.
      7, C.C. Harwood, Using Land to Save Energy, 1977. 336pp.

1188. European Atomic Energy Community (Euratom).   Legal and Administra-
      tive Problems of Protection in the Peaceful Uses of Atomic Energy:
      Proceedings of the International Symposium, Brussels, 1960. Paris:
      Dalloz, 1961. 1264pp.

1189. George Washington University, Washington, DC. Program of Policy Stud-
      ies in Science and Technology. Legal-Institutional Implications
      of Wind Energy Conversion Systems, WECS: Final Report. Washington,
      DC: U.S. Government Printing Office, 1977. 320pp.

1190. Hazelton, P.   "Literature Labyrinth of Nuclear Power: A Bibliogra-
      phy," 6 Environmental Law 921-943 (1976).

1191. International Arrangements for Nuclear Fuel Reprocessing, edited by
      A. Chayes and W.B. Lewis. Cambridge, MA: Ballinger, 1977. 251pp.

1192. International Atomic Energy Agency.   Licensing and Regulatory Con-
      trol of Nuclear Installations: Papers. Vienna: The Agency, 1975.
      313pp.

1193. "The International Regulation of Nuclear Energy," 16 Columbia Jour-
       nal of Transnational Law 385-469 (1977).

1194. "The Legal Aspects of Atomic Power Plant Development: A Selective
       Bibliography," 13 Atomic Energy Law Journal 50-75 (1971).

1195. Lindsey, M.K., and P. Supton. Geothermal Energy: Legal Problems of
       Resource Development. Stanford, CA: Stanford Environmental Law
       Society, 1975. 144pp.

1196. Moody, R., Jr. Legal Analysis of Issues Relating to Natural Gas
       Transportation. Washington, DC, 1976. 100pp. (Prepared for the
       Alaskan Legislature, Joint Gas Pipeline Impact Committee.)

1197. Nader, R., and J. Abbotts. The Menace of Atomic Energy. New York:
       Norton, 1977. 414pp.

1198. National Conference on the Environment, Warrenton, VA, 1976. Energy
       Conservation and the Law. Philadelphia: American Bar Association
       Standing Committee on Environmental Law, 1976. 155pp.

1199. "Nuclear Power Symposium," 6 Environmental Law 621-943 (1976).

1200. Ocean Thermal Energy Conversion: Legal, Political, and Institutional
       Aspects, edited by H.G. Knight, J.D. Nyhart, and R.E. Stein. Lex-
       ington, MA: Lexington Books, 1977. 243pp.

1201. Organization for Economic Co-operation and Development, European Nu-
       clear Energy Agency. Nuclear Legislation. Paris: Organization
       for Economic Co-operation and Development, 1972. 492pp.

1202. "Overcoming Legal Barriers to the Utilization of Solar Energy," 19
       Idea (no.1) 1-51 (1977).

1203. Ruebhausen, O.M., and A.B. Von Mehren. "Atomic Energy Act and the
       Private Production of Atomic Power," 66 Harvard Law Review 1450-
       1496 (1953).

1204. Sato, S., and T.D. Crocker. "Property Rights to Geothermal Resour-
       ces," 6 Ecology Law Quarterly 481-569 (1977).

1205. Smith, D.N., and L.T. Wells, Jr. Negotiating Third-World Mineral
       Agreements. Cambridge, MA: Ballinger, 1975. 266pp.

1206. Solomon, L.D., and F.H. Riesmeyer. "The Development of Alternate
       Energy Sources: A Legal and Policy Analysis," 30 Oklahoma Law
       Review 319-353 (1977).

1207. Stason, E.B., S. Estep, and W.J. Pierce. Atoms and the Law. Ann
       Arbor, MI: University of Michigan Law School, 1959. 1512pp.

1208. "Symposium: The Nuclear Power Plant Licensing Process," 15 William
       and Mary Law Review 487-566 (1974).

1209. U.S. Congress, Joint Committee on Atomic Energy. Proposed Nuclear
       Powerplant Siting and Licensing Legislation: Hearings. Washing-
       ton, DC: U.S. Government Printing Office, 1976. 770pp.

1210. U.S. Library of Congress, Congressional Research Service. Polar
       Energy Resources Potential: Report. Washington, DC: U.S. Govern-
       ment Printing Office, 1976. 178pp.

1211. U.S. Office of Technology Assessment. Analysis of the Proposed Na-
       tional Energy Plan. Washington, DC: U.S. Government Printing Of-
       fice, 1977. 243pp.

1212. U.S. Office of Technology Assessment. Nuclear Proliferation and
       Safeguards, 2 volumes. 1977. Vol. 1, New York: Praeger; Vol. 2,
       Springfield, VA: National Technical Information Service.

1213. U.S. Task Force on Reform of Federal Energy Administration. Federal
       Energy Administration Regulation, edited by P.W. MacAvoy. Wash-
       ington, DC: American Enterprise Institute for Public Policy Re-
       search, 1977. 195pp.

1214. University of Michigan, Summer Institute on International and Compar-
       ative Law, 1952. Lectures on Atomic Energy: Industrial and Legal
       Problems. Ann Arbor, MI: University of Michigan Law School, 1952.
       280pp.

1215. Wood, L.D. "Enforced Standards of Competence, Full Disclosure, and
       Public Control for the U.S. Nuclear Power Industry," 18 Atomic
       Energy Law Journal 1-82 (1976).

1216. Workshop on Solar Energy and the Law, Arlington, VA, 1975. Proceed-
       ings... An Interim Report Submitted to the National Science Foun-
       dation. Chicago: American Bar Foundation, 1975. 28pp.

1217. Zillman, D.N., and R. Deeny. "Legal Aspects of Solar Energy Devel-
       opment," Arizona State Law Journal 25-58 (1976).

I.6 WEATHER MODIFICATION

1218. Corbridge, J.N., Jr., and R.J. Moses. "Weather Modification,"
       1970 Environmental Law Review 109-138 (1970). (Reprinted from 8
       Natural Resources Journal 1968.)

1219. Hassett, C.M. "Weather Modification and Control," 7 Texas Inter-
       national Law Journal 89-118 (1971).

1220. McKenzie, A.G. "Weather Modification: A Review of the Science and
       the Law," 6 Environmental Law 387-430 (1976).

1221. Taubenfeld, H.J. Weather Modification and the Law. Dobbs Ferry, NY:
       Oceana, 1968. 228pp.

1222.   Thomas, W.A., ed.   Legal and Scientific Uncertainties of Weather
        Modification. Durham, NC: Duke University Press, 1977. 155pp.
        (Proceedings of a symposium convened by the National Conference
        of Lawyers and Scientists.)

1223.   U.S. Congress, House, Committee on Foreign Affairs.   Weather Modi-
        fication As a Weapon of War: Hearing. Washington, DC: U.S. Gov-
        ernment Printing Office, 1974. 39pp.

1224.   U.S. Congress, House, Committee on International Relations.   Prohi-
        bition of Weather Modification As a Weapon of War: Hearing. Wash-
        ington, DC: U.S. Government Printing Office, 1975. 51pp.

1225.   U.S. Congress, Senate, Committee on Commerce.   Weather Modification:
        Hearings. Washington, DC: U.S. Government Printing Office, 1968.
        119pp.

1226.   U.S. Congress, Senate, Committee on Foreign Relations.   Prohibiting
        Hostile Use of Environmental Modification Techniques: Hearing.
        Washington, DC: U.S. Government Printing Office, 1976. 46pp.

1227.   U.S. Congress, Senate, Committee on Foreign Relations.   Prohibiting
        Military Weather Modification. Washington, DC: U.S. Government
        Printing Office, 1972. 162pp.

1228.   U.S. Congress, Senate, Committee on Foreign Relations.   Weather Mod-
        ification: Hearings. Washington, DC: U.S. Government Printing Of-
        fice, 1974. 123pp.

J.   SCIENCE AND INTERNATIONAL LAW*

1229. Boassen, C.   Sociological Aspects of Law and International Adjust-
       ment. Amsterdam: Noord-Hollandsche Uitgevers-Mij., 1950. 120pp.

1230. Brodie, B.   "The Impact of Technological Change on the International
       System: Reflections on Prediction," 25 Journal of International
       Affairs 209-223 (1971).

1231. Dessemontet, F.   "Transfer of Technology under UNCTAD and EED Draft
       Codifications: A European View on Choice of Law," 12 Journal of
       International Law and Economics 1-55 (1977).

1232. Fisher, R., ed.   International Conflict and Behavioral Science. New
       York: Basic Books, 1964. 290pp.

1233. Haas, E.G., M.P. Williams, and D. Babai.   Scientists and World Or-
       der: The Uses of Technical Knowledge in International Organiza-
       tions. Berkeley, CA: University of California Press, 1978. 378pp.

1234. Hochmuth, M.S.   Organizing the Transnational: The Experience with
       Transnational Enterprise in Advanced Technology. Leyden: Sijthoff,
       1974. 211pp.

1235. Kish, J.   The Law of International Spaces. Leyden: Sijthoff, 1973.
       236pp.

1236. Lasswell, H., and M.S. McDougal.   Studies in World Public Order.
       New Haven, CT: Yale University Press, 1960. 1058pp.

1237. Livingston, D.   "Science, Technology, and International Law: Present
       Trends and Future Developments," in The Future of the Internation-
       al Legal Order, volume 4, edited by R.A. Falk and E.E. Black,
       pp. 68-123. Princeton, NJ: Princeton University Press, 1972.

1238. McDougal, M.S., and F.P. Feliciano.   Law and Minimum World Order:
       The Legal Revolution and International Coercion. New Haven, CT:
       Yale University Press, 1961. 872pp.

1239. Panel. "The United Nations and Science," 64 American Journal of
       International Law 147-189 (1970).

1240. Regimes for the Ocean, Outer Space, and Weather. Seyom Brown, et al.
       Washington, DC: Brookings Institution, 1977. 257pp.

1241. Skolnikoff, E.B.   "The International Functional Implications of Fu-
       ture Technology," 25 Journal of International Affairs 266-286
       (1971).

1242. Symposium. "Law, Psychology, and World Government," 16 University
       of Chicago Law Review 389-414 (1949). (Includes contributions by
       R.M. Hutchins, R. West, and others.)

---

* See also Sections H and I.

1243. U.S. Congress, House, Committee on International Relations. Science, Technology, and American Diplomacy: An Extended Study of the Interactions of Science and Technology with United States Foreign Policy, 3 volumes. Washington, DC: U.S. Government Printing Office, 1977.

1244. U.S. Congress, House, Committee on Science and Astronautics. Panel on Science and Technology, 8th Meeting: Government, Science and International Policy. Proceedings. Washington, DC: U.S. Government Printing Office, 1967. 220pp.

1245. U.S. Congress, House, Committee on Science and Astronautics. Panel on Science and Technology, 12th Meeting: International Science Policy. Washington, DC: U.S. Government Printing Office, 1971. 373pp.

1246. Weisband, E., and T.M. Franck. A Rationale for International Technology Assessment: Towards an Ethical Science. New York: New York University Center for International Studies, 1971. 40pp.

1247. Wolff, C. On the Law of Nations Treated According to a Scientific Method. Washington, DC: Carnegie Endowment, 1934. (Reprinted, Dobbs Ferry, NY: Oceana, 1964. 565pp.)

J.1   CURRENT SOURCES

1248. Air Law.
      v.1-   1975-   Quarterly.
      Deventer, Netherlands: Kluwer.

1249. American Journal of International Law.
      v.1-   1907-   Quarterly.
      Washington, DC: American Society of International Law.

1250. Annals of Air and Space Law. Annales de Droit Aérien et Spatial.
      v.1-   1976-   .
      Toronto: Carswell, for the Institute of Air and Space Law, McGill University, Montreal.

1251. Aviation Cases.
      v.1-   1822/1945-   .
      Chicago: Commerce Clearing House.

1252. Aviation Law Reporter.
      Chicago: Commerce Clearing House, 1947-   .
      (loose-leaf service).

1253. Colloquium on the Law of Outer Space. Proceedings.
      Edited by M.D. Schwartz.
      1st-   1958-   .
      Various publishers; volume 19 (1976) published by Rothman.
      And Space Law Perspectives: Commentaries Based on Vols. 1-15

(1957-1972) of the Colloquia on the Law of Outer Space, edited by M.D. Schwartz. South Hackensack, NJ: Rothman, for the University of California, Davis, School of Law, 1976. 302pp.

1254. Journal of Air Law and Commerce.
v.1- 1930- Quarterly.
Dallas, TX: Southern Methodist University School of Law.

1255. Journal of Conflict Resolution: Research on War and Peace between and within Nations.
v.1- 1957- Quarterly.
Beverly Hills, CA: Sage Publications.

1256. Journal of Maritime Law and Commerce.
v.1- 1969- Quarterly.
Cincinnati, OH: Jefferson Law Book Division of Anderson Publishing.

1257. Journal of Space Law: A Journal Devoted to the Legal Problems Arising out of Man's Activities in Outer Space.
v.1- 1973- Semiannual.
University, MS: University of Mississippi Law Center.

1258. Law of the Sea Institute, Kingston, RI, Conference Proceedings.
1st- 1966- Annual.
Various publishers; volume 10 (1976) published by Ballinger.

1259. Nuclear Inter Jura Congress. Proceedings.
1st- 1973- .
Brussels: International Nuclear Law Association.

1260. Ocean Development and International Law: The Journal of Marine Affairs.
v.1- 1973- Quarterly.
New York: Crane, Russak.

1261. Stanford Journal of International Studies.
no.1- 1966- Annual.
Stanford, CA: Stanford University School of Law.
One theme per issue; for example: 4. Ocean Resources, 1969; 5. Telecommunications, 1970; 7. Arms Control, 1972; 8. International Environmental Control, 1973.

1262. U.S. Arms Control and Disarmament Agency. Documents on Disarmament.
1961- Annual.
Washington, DC: U.S. Government Printing Office.

1263. United States Aviation Reports.
1928- Annual.
Dobbs Ferry, NY: Oceana.

1264. World Armaments and Disarmament: SIPRI Yearbook.
1968/69- .
London: Taylor & Francis, for Stockholm International Peace Research Institute.
(Distributed in the U.S.A. by New York: Crane, Russak.)

1265. Worldwide Bibliography... of Space Law and Related Matters. Biblio-
       graphie Mondiale... de Droit Spatial et Matières Connexes.
       v.1-   1964-   Annual.
       Paris: International Institute of Space Law of the International
       Astronautical Federation.

J.2 AVIATION LAW

1266. Billyou, DeF.   Air Law, 2d edition. New York: AD Press, 1964.
       674pp.

1267. Bohlen, F.H.   "Aviation under the Common Law," 48 Harvard Law Re-
       view 216-237 (1935).

1268. Flynn, P.P.   "Aviation and the Law," 4 Southwestern University Law
       Review 176-249 (1972).

1269. Heere, W.P.   International Bibliography of Air Law, 1900-1971. Ley-
       den: Sijthoff, 1972. 569pp.; and Supplements, 1972/76-   .

1270. International Conference on Air Law, Montreal, 1975.   Proceedings,
       2 volumes. Montreal: International Civil Aviation Organization,
       1975.

1271. Kneifel, J.L.   Air Laws and Treaties of the COMECON States, 4 vol-
       umes. Berlin-West, 1974.

1272. Kreindler, L.S.   Aviation Accident Law, revised edition. New York:
       Matthew Bender, 1971-   . (loose-leaf).

1273. London University, Institute of Advanced Legal Studies.   Union List
       of Air and Space Law Literature in the Libraries of Oxford, Cam-
       bridge and London, 2d edition. London, 1975. 1 volume. (The Uni-
       versity's Union Catalogue, 4.)

1274. Power-Waters, B.   Safety Last: The Dangers of Commercial Aviation:
       An Indictment by an Airline Pilot. New York: Dial Press, 1972.
       264pp.

1275. Rhyne, C.S.   Aviation Accident Law. Washington, DC: Columbia Law
       Book Co., 1947. 315pp.

1276. Speiser, S.M.   Lawyers' Aviation Handbook: Guide to Cases, Statutes,
       Forms, Regulations, Law Reviews, Tables. Rochester, NY: Lawyers
       Cooperative Pub., 1964. 576pp.

1277. "Symposium: Products Liability in Aviation Litigation," 40 Journal
       of Air Law and Commerce 365-506 (1974).

1278. "Symposium: Selected Problems in Aviation Litigation," 41 Journal of
       Air Law and Commerce 173-330 (1975).

1279. U.S. Laws, Statutes, etc. Aviation Law. Aeronautical Statutes and
      Related Material: Revised to Dec. 31, 1974. Washington, DC: U.S.
      Government Printing Office, 1975. 675pp.

1280. Vlasic, I.A., and M.A. Bradley. The Public International Law of
      Air Transport: Materials and Documents, 2 volumes. Montreal: In-
      stitute of Air and Space Law, McGill University, 1974.

1281. Wassenbergh, H.A. Public International Air Transportation Law in a
      New Era. Deventer, Netherlands: Kluwer, 1976. 165pp.

1282. Wright, R.R. The Law of Airspace. Indianapolis, IN: Bobbs-Merrill,
      1968. 575pp.

J.3 OUTER SPACE

1283. American Assembly. Outer Space: Prospects for Man and Society, edi-
      ted by L.P. Bloomfield. Englewood Cliffs, NJ: Prentice-Hall, 1962.
      203pp.

1284. Brownlie, I. "The Maintenance of International Peace and Security
      in Outer Space," 40 British Year Book of International Law 1-31
      (1966).

1285. Cohen, M.A., ed. Law and Politics in Space: Specific and Urgent
      Problems in the Law of Outer Space. Montreal: McGill University
      Press, 1964. 220pp.

1286. Conference on Space Science and Space Law, University of Oklahoma,
      1963. Proceedings, edited by M.D. Schwartz. South Hackensack,
      NJ: Rothman, 1964. 176pp.

1287. Csabafi, I.A. The Concept of State Jurisdiction in International
      Space Law. The Hague: Nijhoff, 1971. 197pp.

1288. European Space Research Organization. Basic Texts, Rules and Regu-
      lations and Agreements, revised edition. Neuilly-sur-Seine: Euro-
      pean Space Research Organization, 1973. 661pp.

1289. Fasan, E. Relations with Alien Intelligences: The Scientific Basis
      of Metalaw. Berlin: Berlin Verlag, 1970, 110pp.

1290. Fawcett, J.E.S. International Law and the Uses of Outer Space. Man-
      chester: Manchester University Press, 1968. 92pp.

1291. Gorove, S. Studies in Space Law: Its Challenges and Prospects. Ley-
      den: Sijthoff, 1977. 228pp.

1292. Haley, A.G. Medical Jurisprudence in Outer Space. Rochester, NY:
      Medical Society of the State of New York, 1961. 60pp.

1293. Haley, A.G. Space Law and Government. New York: Appleton-Century,
      1963. 584pp.

1294. Hood, V., M.E. Kimball, and D.A. Kay. A Global Satellite Observa-
      tion System for Earth Resources: Problems and Prospects. A Report
      to the National Science Foundation on the Application of Interna-
      tional Regulatory Techniques to Scientific/Technical Problems.
      St. Paul, MN: West, 1977. 174pp. (American Society of Interna-
      tional Law. Studies in Transnational Legal Policy, 15.)

1295. Jenks, C.W. Space Law. New York: Praeger, 1965. 476pp.

1296. Jessup, P.C., and H.J. Taubenfeld. Controls for Outer Space and
      the Antarctic Analogy. New York: Columbia University Press, 1959.
      379pp.

1297. Lachs, M. The Law of Outer Space: An Experience in Contemporary Law-
      Making. Leyden: Sijthoff, 1972. 196pp.

1298. Lay, S.H., and H.J. Taubenfeld. The Law Relating to the Activities
      of Man in Space. Chicago: University of Chicago Press, 1970.
      333pp.

1299. Li, K.L. World Wide Space Law Bibliography. Toronto: Carswell,
      1978. 700pp. (Institute and Center of Air and Space Law, McGill
      University, Montreal, Publication 1.)

1300. Lipson, L.S., and N.deB. Katzenbach. Report to NASA on the Law of
      Outer Space. Chicago: American Bar Foundation, 1961. 179pp.

1301. McDougal, M.S., H.D. Lasswell, and I.A. Vlasic. Law and Public Or-
      der in Space. New Haven, CT: Yale University Press, 1963. 1147pp.

1302. Mateesco Matte, N. Aerospace Law: From Scientific Exploration to
      Commercial Utilization. Toronto: Carswell, 1977. 354pp.

1303. Mateesco Matte, N., and H. DeSaussure. Legal Implications of Re-
      mote Sensing from Outer Space. Leyden: Sijthoff, 1976. 197pp.

1304. New Frontiers in Space Law, edited by E. McWhinney and M.A. Bradley.
      Leyden: Sijthoff, 1969. 134pp.

1305. Ogunbanwo, O.O. International Law and Outer Space Activities. The
      Hague: Nijhoff, 1975. 272pp.

1306. Seara Vázquez, M. Cosmic International Law. Detroit: Wayne State
      University Press, 1965. 293pp.

1307. Sloup, G.P. "Peaceful Resolution of Outer Space Conflicts through
      the International Court of Justice," 20 DePaul Law Review 618-
      698 (1971).

1308. "Space Law," 54 International Law Association Conference Report 405-
      441 (1970).

1309. United Nations, Secretariat. International Space Bibliography. New
      York: United Nations, 1966. 166pp.

1310.   United Nations, Secretary-General.   Space Activities and Resources:
        Review of United Nations, International and National Programmes.
        New York: United Nations, 1965. 171pp.

1311.   U.S. Congress, Senate, Committee on Aeronautical and Space Sciences.
        Space Agreements with the Soviet Union. Washington, DC: U.S. Gov-
        ernment Printing Office, 1972. 97pp.

1312.   U.S. Congress, Senate, Committee on Aeronautical and Space Sciences.
        Treaty on Principles Governing the Activities of States in the
        Exploration and Use of Outer Space, Including the Moon and Other
        Celestial Bodies. Washington, DC: U.S. Government Printing Of-
        fice, 1967. 84pp.

1313.   U.S. Congress, Senate, Special Committee on Space and Astronautics.
        Space Law: A Symposium. Washington, DC: U.S. Government Printing
        Office, 1959. 573pp.

1314.   U.S. Library of Congress, Congressional Research Service.   Conven-
        tion on Registration of Objects Launched into Outer Space: Staff
        Report. Washington, DC: U.S. Government Printing Office, 1975.
        66pp.

1315.   U.S. Library of Congress, Legislative Reference Service.   Legal Prob-
        lems of Space Exploration: A Symposium. Washington, DC: U.S. Gov-
        ernment Printing Office, 1961. 1392pp.

1316.   Verplaetse, J.G.   International Law in Vertical Space: Air, Outer
        Space, Ether. South Hackensack, NJ: Rothman, 1960. 505pp.

1317.   White, I.L.   Decision-Making for Space: Law and Politics in Air, Sea,
        and Outer Space. West Lafayette, IN: Purdue Research Foundation,
        1970. 277pp.

1318.   White, I.L., C.E. Wilson, and J.A. Vosburgh.   Law and Politics in
        Outer Space: A Bibliography. Tucson, AZ: University of Arizona
        Press, 1972. 176pp.

1319.   Yearbook of Air and Space Law. Annuaire de Droit Aérien et Spatial, 3
        volumes. 1965-67. Montreal: McGill University Press, 1967-70.

1320.   Zhukov, G.P.   "Fundamental Principles of Space Law," in Contempor-
        ary International Law, edited by G.I. Tunkin. pp.263-290. Moscow:
        Progess Publishers, 1969.

J.4   SEA AND SEA RESOURCES

1321. Borgese, E.M., and D. Krieger. The Tides of Change: Peace, Pollu-
        tion, and Potential of the Oceans. New York: Mason/Charter, 1975.
        357pp.

1322. Brown, E.D.   The Legal Regime of Hydrospace. London: Stevens, 1971.
        236pp. (Published under the auspices of the London Institute of
        World Affairs.)

1323. Burke, W.T.   A Report on International Legal Problems of Scientific
        Research in the Oceans. Washington, DC, 1967. 143pp. (Prepared
        for the National Council on Marine Resources and Engineering De-
        velopment.)

1324. Burke, W.T., R. Legatski, and W.W. Woodhead.   National and Interna-
        tional Law Enforcement in the Ocean. Seattle, WA: University of
        Washington Press, 1975. 244pp.

1325. International Legal Conference on Marine Pollution Damage, Brussels,
        1969.   Final Act of the Conference with Attachments Including the
        Texts of the Adopted Conventions. London: Inter-Governmental Mari-
        time Consultative Organization, 1970. 88pp.

1326. International Peace Academy.   Conflict Management on the Oceans.
        New York: International Peace Academy, 1977. 56pp. (IPA Occasion-
        al Paper, 1; Includes L.B. Sohn, "Conflict Management under the
        Law of the Sea Convention.")

1327. Knight, H.G.   The Law of the Sea: Cases, Documents, and Readings, 1
        volume. Baton Rouge, LA: Claitor's Law Books, 1978- . (loose-
        leaf).

1328. The Law of the Sea: Issues in Ocean Resource Management. New York:
        Praeger, 1977. 268pp.

1329. Lay, S., R. Churchill, and M. Nordquist, eds.   New Directions in the
        Law of the Sea. Dobbs Ferry, NY: Oceana, 1973- . (6 volumes pub-
        lished through 1977.)

1330. Llana, C.B., J.K. Gamble, and C. Quinn.   Law of the Sea: A Biblio-
        graphy of the Periodical Literature of the 1970's. Kingston, RI:
        Law of the Sea Institute, 1975. 80pp.

1331. Lundquist, T.R.   "The Iceberg Cometh: International Law Relating to
        Antarctic Iceberg Exploitation," 17 Natural Resources Journal 1-41
        (1977).

1332. McDougal, M.S., and W.T. Burke.   Public Order of the Oceans: A Con-
        temporary International Law of the Sea. New Haven, CT: Yale Uni-
        versity Press, 1962. 1226pp.

1333. Marine Policy and the Coastal Community: The Impact of the Law of the
        Sea, edited by D.M. Johnston. New York: St. Martin's Press, 1976.
        338pp.

1334. Mitchell, B., and J. Mitchell. Law of the Sea and International
       Fisheries Management. Monticello, IL: Council of Planning Librar-
       ians, 1976. 48pp.

1335. Oda, S. International Control of Sea Resources. Leyden: Sijthoff,
       1963. 215pp.

1336. Oda, S. The International Law of the Ocean Development: Basic Docu-
       ments, 2 volumes. Leyden: Sijthoff, 1972-75.

1337. Oda, S. The Law of the Sea in Our Time, 2 volumes. Leyden: Sij-
       thoff, 1977.

1338. Papadakis, N. The International Legal Regime of Artificial Islands.
       Leyden: Sijthoff, 1977. 277pp.

1339. Pulle, A.I. Transnational Controls on Marine Pollution by Wastes
       Disposal. Cambridge, MA, 1975. 443pp. (S.J.D. Thesis, Harvard
       University Law School.)

1340. Shinn, R.A. The International Politics of Marine Pollution Control.
       New York: Praeger, 1974. 200pp.

1341. Sullivan, J.J. Pacific Basin Enterprise and the Changing Law of the
       Sea. Lexington, MA: Lexington Books, 1977. 218pp.

1342. Symposium. "Conference of Soviet and American Jurists on the Law of
       the Sea and the Protection of the Marine Environment," 6 Georgia
       Journal of International and Comparative Law 1-196 (1976).

1343. "Symposium on the Fishery Conservation and Management Act of 1976,"
       52 Washington Law Review 427-745 (1977).

1344. United Nations, Dag Hammarskjöld Library. The Sea: A Select Biblio-
       graphy on the Legal, Political, Economic and Technological Aspects,
       1975-1976. New York: United Nations, 1976. 24pp.

1345. United Nations, Office of Legal Affairs. National Legislation and
       Treaties Relating to the Law of the Sea. New York: United Nations,
       1974. 604pp.

1346. The United Nations and the Oceans: Current Issues in the Law of the
       Sea. L.B. Sohn, Chairman. New York: Commission to Study the Or-
       ganization of Peace, 1973. 46pp. (Issued as the Commission's Re-
       port, 23.)

1347. U.S. Congress, Senate, Committee on Public Works. Oil Pollution of
       the Marine Environment: A Legal Bibliography. C.Q. Christol.
       Washington, DC: U.S. Government Printing Office, 1971. 93pp.

1348. U.S. Office of Technology Assessment. Establishing a 200-Mile Fish-
       eries Zone. Washington, DC: U.S. Government Printing Office, 1977.
       132pp.

1349. U.S. Office of Technology Assessment. Working Papers: Establishing
       a 200-Mile Fisheries Zone. Springfield, VA: National Technical
       Information Service, 1977. 375pp.

1350. Von Pfeil, H.P.   Oceans, Coasts and Law: Holdings of Eighteen Li-
      braries with Union List, Plus Selected Additional Books, Papers,
      Foreign and U.S. Articles Categorized by Topic, 2 volumes. Dobbs
      Ferry, NY: Oceana, 1976.

1351. Waldichuk, M.   "Control of Marine Pollution: An Essay Review," 4
      Ocean Development and International Law Journal 269-296 (1977).

1352. Winner, R.   "Science, Sovereignty, and the Third Law of the Sea Con-
      ference," 4 Ocean Development and International Law Journal 297-
      342 (1977).

1353. Wurfel, S.W., ed.   Legal Measures Concerning Marine Pollution. Ra-
      leigh, NC: North Carolina State University Sea Grant Program,
      1975. 80pp.

1354. Wurfel, S.W.   The Surge of Sea Law. Chapel Hill: NC: University of
      North Carolina Sea Grant Program, 1973. 246pp.

J.5 ARMS CONTROL AND DISARMAMENT

1355. Arms Control and Disarmament, volumes 1-9; Winter 1964/65--Spring
      1973. Quarterly. Washington, DC: Arms Control and Disarmament
      Bibliography Section, Library of Congress, 1964-73.

1356. Arms, Defense Policy, and Arms Control, edited by F.A. Long and G.W.
      Rathjens. Racine, WI: Johnson Foundation, 1975. 218pp. (104
      Daedalus [1975].)

1357. Barnaby, F., and R. Huisken.   Arms Uncontrolled. Cambridge, MA:
      Harvard University Press, 1975. 232pp.

1358. Baxter, R.R.   "Legal Aspects of Arms Control Measures Concerning the
      Missile Carrying Submarines and Anti-Submarine Warfare," in The
      Future of the Seabased Deterrent, edited by K. Tsipis, A.H. Cahn,
      and B.T. Feld, pp.209-232. Cambridge, MA: MIT Press, 1973.

1359. Bloomfield, L.P., A.C. Leiss, et al.   Arms Control and Local Con-
      flict, 3 volumes. Cambridge, MA: MIT Center for International
      Studies, 1970.

1360. Brown, E.D.   Arms Control in Hydrospace. Washington, DC: Woodrow
      Wilson International Center for Scholars, 1971. 131pp.

1361. Chayes, A.   "An Inquiry into the Workings of Arms Control Agree-
      ments," 85 Harvard Law Review 905-969 (1972).

1362. Conference of Government Experts on Weapons that May Cause Unneces-
      sary Suffering or Have Indiscriminate Effects, 2d, Lugano, 1976.
      Conference of Government Experts on the Use of Certain Convention-
      al Weapons: Report. Geneva: International Committee of the Red
      Cross, 1976. 231pp.

1363. Conference on Science and World Affairs, 26th, Muhlhausen, 1976. Disarmament, Security and Development: Proceedings of the 26th Pugwash Conference on Science and World Affairs. London: The Conference, 1976. 223pp

1364. Conference on World Peace through Law. World Conference, 2d, Washington, DC, 1965. Building Law Rules and Legal Institutions for Peace. St. Paul, MN: West, 1967.

1365. Conventional Weapons, Their Deployment and Effects from a Humanitarian Aspect: Recommendations for the Modernization of International Law, by T. Wulff, et al. Stockholm: Royal Swedish Ministry for Foreign Affairs, 1973. 182pp.

1366. Deutsch, K.W. Arms Control in the European Political Environment: Report. New Haven, CT: Yale University Press, 1966. 171pp.

1367. Disarmament: Negotiations and Treaties, 1946-1971. New York: Scribner, 1972. 385pp. (Keesing's Research Report, 7.)

1368. Dupuy, T.N., and G.M. Hammerman. A Documentary History of Arms Control and Disarmament. New York: Bowker, 1973. 629pp.

1369. Epstein, W. Disarmament: Twenty-Five Years of Effort. Toronto: Canadian Institute of International Affairs, 1971. 97pp.

1370. Gotlieb, A.E. Disarmament and International Law. Toronto: Canadian Institute of International Affairs, 1965. 232pp.

1371. Henkin, L. Arms Control Inspection in American Law. New York: Columbia University Press, 1958. 304pp.

1372. Kaplan, M.A. SALT: Problems & Prospects. Morristown, NJ: General Learning Press, 1973. 251pp.

1373. Kintner, W.R., and R.L. Pfaltzgraff, Jr. SALT: Implications for Arms Control in the 1970's. Pittsburgh: University of Pittsburgh Press, 1973. 447pp.

1374. Lawrence, R.M. Arms Control and Disarmament. Minneapolis: Burgess, 1973. 72pp.

1375. Martin, A. Legal Aspects of Disarmament. London: Stevens & Sons, 1963. 133pp. (International and Comparative Law Quarterly, Supplementary publication, 7.)

1376. Millis, W. An End to Arms. New York: Atheneum Pub., 1965. 301pp.

1377. Myrdal, A.R. The Game of Disarmament: How the United States and Russia Run the Arms Race. New York: Pantheon, 1976. 397pp.

1378. Newhouse, J. Cold Dawn: The Story of SALT. New York: Holt, Rinehart & Winston, 1973. 302pp.

1379. Parker, J., and T.A. Meeker. SALT II: A Selected Research Biblio-
       graphy. Los Angeles: Center for the Study of Armament and Dis-
       armament, California State University, 1973. 36pp.

1380. Pugwash Symposium, 10th, Racine, Wisconsin, 1970. Impact of New
       Technologies on the Arms Race, edited by B.T. Feld, et al. Cam-
       bridge, MA: MIT Press, 1971. 379pp.

1381. Stanford Arms Control Group. International Arms Control: Issues and
       Agreements, edited by J.H. Barton and L.D. Weiler. Stanford, CA:
       Stanford University Press, 1976. 444pp.

1382. Stanley, J., and M. Pearton. The International Trade in Arms. New
       York: Praeger, for the Institute for Strategic Studies, 1972.
       244pp.

1383. Stockholm International Peace Research Institute (SIPRI). Armaments
       and Disarmament in the Nuclear Age: A Handbook, edited by M. Thee.
       Atlantic Highlands, NJ: Humanities Press, 1976. 308pp.

1384. Stockholm International Peace Research Institute (SIPRI). The Law
       of War and Dubious Weapons. B.V.A. Röling and O. Sukovic̆. Stock-
       holm: Almqvist & Wiksell, 1976. 78pp.

1385. Stockholm International Peace Research Institute (SIPRI). Strategic
       Arms Limitation, 2 volumes. Stockholm: Almqvist & Wiksell, 1972.

1386. Stockholm International Peace Research Institute (SIPRI). Strategic
       Disarmament, Verification and National Security. A. Karkoszka.
       New York: Crane, Russak, 1977. 174pp.

1387. Stone, J. Conflict through Consensus: United Nations Approaches to
       Aggression. Baltimore, MD: Johns Hopkins University Press, 1977.
       234pp.

1388. Tondel, H.M., Jr., ed. Disarmament: Background Papers and Proceed-
       ings of 4th Hammarskjöld Forum. Dobbs Ferry, NY: Oceana, 1964.
       98pp.

1389. United Nations, Dag Hammarskjöld Library. Disarmament: A Select Bib-
       liography, 1967-1972. New York: United Nations, 1973. 63pp.

1390. United Nations, Department of Political and Security Council Affairs,
       Disarmament Affairs Division. The United Nations and Disarmament
       1970-1975. New York: United Nations, 1976. 267pp.

1391. U.S. Arms Control and Disarmament Agency. Arms Control and Disarma-
       ment Agreements, 1959-1972. Washington, DC: U.S. Government Print-
       ing Office, 1972. 119pp.

1392. U.S. Arms Control and Disarmament Agency. Arms Control and Disarma-
       ment Agreements: Texts and History of Negotiation. Washington,
       DC: U.S. Government Printing Office, 1975. 159pp.

1393. U.S. Arms Control and Disarmament Agency. Arms Control and Disarm-
       ament Agreements: Texts and History of Negotiations. Washington,
       DC: U.S. Government Printing Office, 1977. 187pp.

1394. U.S. Congress, Senate, Committee on Foreign Relations. Strategic
       Arms Limitation Agreements. Washington, DC: U.S. Government
       Printing Office, 1972. 435pp.

J.5.a CHEMICAL AND BIOLOGICAL WARFARE

1395. Baxter, R.R. Statement to the Subcommittee on National Security
       Policy and Scientific Developments, Committee on Foreign Affairs,
       House of Representatives, on the Geneva Protocol of 1925 for the
       Prohibition of the Use in War of Asphyxiating, Poisonous or Other
       Gases, and of Bacteriological Methods of Warfare. Cambridge, MA,
       1974. 21pp.

1396. Carnegie Endowment for International Peace. The Control of Chemical
       and Biological Weapons. New York: The Endowment, 1971. 130pp.

1397. Decker, R.G., and M.C. Dunlap. "War, Genetics and the Law," 1
       Ecology Law Quarterly 795-837 (1971).

1398. Midwest Research Institute, Kansas City, Missouri. Studies on the
       Technical Arms Control Aspects of Chemical and Biological Warfare:
       Summary and Index, 4 volumes. Kansas City, MO: The Institute,
       1972.

1399. Moore, J.N. "Ratification of the Geneva Protocol on Gas and Bacte-
       riological Warfare," 58 Virginia Law Review 419-509 (1972).

1400. Stockholm International Peace Research Institute (SIPRI). The Prob-
       lem of Chemical and Biological Warfare, 6 volumes. Stockholm/New
       York: Almqvist & Wiksell, Humanities Press, 1971-1975.

1401. Thomas, A.P.V.W., and A.J. Thomas. Legal Limits on the Use of Che-
       mical and Biological Weapons. Dallas, TX: Southern Methodist Uni-
       versity Press, 1970. 332pp.

1402. U.S. Arms Control and Disarmament Agency. International Negotia-
       tions on the Biological-Weapons and Toxin Convention. R.W. Lam-
       bert and J.E. Mayer. Washington, DC: U.S. A.C.D.A., 1975. 324pp.

1403. U.S. Congress, House, Committee on Foreign Affairs. U.S. Chemical
       Warfare Policy: Hearings. Washington, DC: U.S. Government Print-
       ing Office, 1974. 379pp.

1404. U.S. Congress, Senate, Committee on Foreign Relations. Prohibition
       of Chemical and Biological Weapons: Hearing. Washington, DC: U.S.
       Government Printing Office, 1974. 71pp.

1405. Verwey, W.D. Riot Control Agents and Herbicides in War. Leyden:
       Sijthoff, 1977. 377pp.

J.5.b NUCLEAR WEAPONS

1406. Bright, F., Jr.   "Nuclear Weapons as a Lawful Means of Warfare,"
       30 Military Law Review 1-42 (October 1965).

1407. Brownlie, I.   "Some Legal Aspects of the Use of Nuclear Weapons,"
       14 International and Comparative Law Quarterly 437-451 (1965).

1408. Fischer, C.   The Non-Proliferation of Nuclear Weapons, translated
       by D. Willey. London: Europa, 1971. 270pp.

1409. International Atomic Energy Agency.   International Treaties Relat-
       ing to Nuclear Control and Disarmament. Vienna: IAEA, 1975.
       78pp.

1410. Nash, H.T.   Nuclear Weapons and International Behavior. Leyden:
       Sijthoff, 1975. 172pp.

1411. Paust, J.J.   "The Nuclear Decision in World War II," 8 Internation-
       al Lawyer 160-190 (1974).

1412. Rathjens, G.W., A. Chayes, and J.R. Ruina.   Nuclear Arms Control
       Agreements: Process and Impact. Washington, DC: Carnegie Endow-
       ment for International Peace, 1974. 72pp.

1413. Schwarzenberger, G.   Legality of Nuclear Weapons. London: Stevens,
       1958. 61pp.

1414. Singh, N.   Nuclear Weapons and International Law. London: Stevens,
       1959. 267pp.

1415. U.S. Congress, House, Committee on International Relations.   First
       Use of Nuclear Weapons: Preserving Responsible Control: Hearings.
       Washington, DC: U.S. Government Printing Office, 1976. 246pp.

1416. U.S. Congress, Senate, Committee on Foreign Relations.   ABM, MIRV,
       SALT, and the Nuclear Arms Race: Hearings. Washington, DC: U.S.
       Government Printing Office, 1970. 624pp.

1417. U.S. Congress, Senate, Committee on Foreign Relations.   Nonproli-
       feration Issues: Hearings. Washington, DC: U.S. Government Print-
       ing Office, 1977. 426pp.

1418. U.S. Congress, Senate, Committee on Foreign Relations.   Prospects
       for Comprehensive Nuclear Test Ban Treaty. Washington, DC: U.S.
       Government Printing Office, 1971. 153pp.

1419. U.S. Congress, Senate, Committee on Foreign Relations.   Toward a
       Comprehensive Nuclear Test Ban Treaty. Washington, DC: U.S. Gov-
       ernment Printing Office, 1972. 152pp.

1420. U.S. Library of Congress, Congressional Research Service.   Nuclear
       Weapons Proliferation and the International Atomic Energy Agency:
       Analytical Report. Washington, DC: U.S. Government Printing Of-
       fice, 1976. 193pp.

1421. U.S. Library of Congress, Environment and Natural Resources Policy
        Division. Bibliography, Nuclear Proliferation. Compiled by T.
        W. Graham and R.C. Evers. Washington, DC: U.S. Government Print-
        ing Office, 1978. 159pp.

1422. Wentz, W.B. Nuclear Proliferation. Washington, DC: Public Affairs
        Press, 1968. 216pp.

K. GOVERNMENT, LAW, AND SCIENTIFIC RESEARCH

1423. American Academy of Political and Social Science. Perspectives on
        Government and Science. Philadelphia, 1960. 204pp. (The Acad-
        emy's Annals, vol. 327.)

1424. Baldwin, G.B. "Law in Support of Science: Legal Control of Basic
        Research Resources," 54 Georgetown Law Journal 559-592 (1966).

1425. Baram, M.S. "The Social Control of Science and Technology," 47
        Denver Law Journal 567-586 (1970).

1426. Beresford, S.M. "Lawyers, Science and the Government," 33 George
        Washington Law Review 181-208 (1964).

1427. Boffey, P.M. The Brain Bank of America: An Inquiry into the Poli-
        tics of Science. New York: McGraw-Hill, 1975. 312pp.

1428. Conference on United States Government Research and Development Con-
        tracts, George Washington University, 1962. Research & Develop-
        ment Contracting. Washington, DC: National Law Center of George
        Washington University, and Federal Publications, Inc., 1963.
        208pp.

1429. Daddario, E.Q. "Science, Technology, and the American Congress,"
        15 Parliamentarian 253-262 (1970).

1430. Dupree, A.H. Science in the Federal Government: A History of Poli-
        cies and Activities to 1940. Cambridge, MA: Belknap Press of
        Harvard University Press, 1957. 460pp.

1431. Gellhorn, W. Security, Loyalty and Science. Ithaca, NY: Cornell
        University Press, 1950. 300pp.

1432. Gilpin, R., and C. Wright, eds. Scientists and National Policy-
        Making. New York: Columbia University Press, 1964. 307pp.

1433. Haberer, J. Politics and the Community of Science. New York: Van
        Nostrand Reinhold, 1969. 337pp.

1434. Kantrowitz, A. "Proposal for an Institution for Scientific Judg-
        ment," 156 Science 763-764 (1967). (Proposes "Science Court,"
        a tribunal for resolution of scientific controversies affecting
        public issues.)

1435. Lakoff, S.A.   "Congress and National Science Policy," 89 Political
       Science Quarterly 589-611 (1974).

1436. Levenson, R.   Contractual Services in Government: Selected Biblio-
       graphy on Practices in Federal, State, and Local Agencies, Educa-
       tion, and Foreign Countries. Monticello, IL: Council of Planning
       Librarians, 1976. 58pp.

1437. Lontai, E.   The Research Contracts: Civil-Law Means Promoting Sci-
       entific-Technical Progress. Leyden: Sijthoff; Budapest: Akadé-
       miai Kiadó, 1977. 235pp.

1438. McBride, J.C., and I.H. Wachtel.   Government Contracts: Cyclopedic
       Guide to Law, Administration, Procedure. New York: Matthew Ben-
       der, 1963- . (loose-leaf).

1439. Miller, A.S.   "Technology, Social Change, and the Constitution,"
       33 George Washington Law Review 17-46 (1964).

1440. National Academy of Sciences, Washington, DC.   Technology: Processes
       of Assessment and Choice. Washington, DC: U.S. Government Print-
       ing Office, 1969. 163pp. (Report prepared for U.S. Congress,
       House, Committee on Science and Astronautics.)

1441. Nelkin, D.   "Thoughts on the Proposed Science Court," 18 Newsletter
       on Science, Technology & Human Values 20-31 (1977).

1442. Phelan, M.E., and J.K. Jones.   "Taxability of Fellowship Grants or
       Scholarships," 52 Taxes 83-96 (1974).

1443. Price, D.K.   Government and Science: Their Dynamic Relation in Amer-
       ican Democracy. New York: New York University Press, 1954.
       203pp.

1444. Price, D.K.   The Scientific Estate. Cambridge, MA: Harvard Univer-
       sity Press, 1965. 323pp.

1445. Primack, J.R., and F. Von Hippel.   Advice and Dissent: Scientists
       in the Political Arena. New York: Basic Books, 1974. 299pp.

1446. Ruebhausen, O.M.   "Government and Science," 32 Virginia Law Review
       868-885 (1946).

1447. Schrag, P.C.   "Scientists and the Test Ban," 75 Yale Law Journal
       1340-1363 (1966).

1448. Shannon, J.A., ed.   Science and the Evolution of Public Policy. New
       York: Rockefeller University Press, 1973. 259pp.

1449. Snow, C.P.   Science and Government. Cambridge, MA: Harvard Univer-
       sity Press, 1961. 88pp.

1450. Social Research in Conflict with Law and Ethics, edited by P. Nejel-
       ski. Cambridge, MA: Ballinger, 1976. 224pp.

1451. Stover, C.F.   The Government of Science. Santa Barbara, CA: Center
       for the Study of Democratic Institutions, 1962. 47pp.

1452. Symposium. "Government Contracts," 29 Law and Contemporary Prob-
       lems 1-646 (Winter and Spring issues, 1964).

1453. "Technology Assessment: Legal and Policy Implications: Proceedings
       and Papers," 16 Jurimetrics Journal 157-200 (1976).

1454. U.S. Congress, House, Committee on Science and Astronautics.
       National Science Policy: Hearings. Washington, DC: U.S. Govern-
       ment Printing Office, 1970. 963pp.

1455. U.S. Congress, House, Select Committee on Government Research.
       Studies. Washington, DC: U.S. Government Printing Office, 1964-
       65. This series includes the following monographs:
       No. 1. Administration of Research and Development Grants. 1964.
               106pp.
       No. 2. Manpower for Research and Development. 1964. 71pp.
       No. 3. Federal Facilities for Research and Development. 1964.
               246pp.
       No. 4. Documentation and Dissemination of Research and Develop-
               ment Results. 1964. 148pp.
       No. 5. Federal Student Assistance in Higher Education. 1964.
               100pp.
       No. 6. Impact of Federal Research and Development Programs.
               1964. 265pp.
       No. 7. Contract Policies and Procedures for Research and Develop-
               ment. 1964. 154pp.
       No. 8. Interagency Coordination in Research and Development.
               1964. 70pp.
       No. 9. Statistical Review of Research and Development. 1964.
               231pp.
       No. 10. National Goals and Policies. 1964. 64pp.
       No. 10/Part 2.   Staff Resume of Activities of Select Committee on
               Government Research. 1965. 78pp.

1456. U.S. Congress, Senate, Committee on Government Operations.   An In-
       ventory of Congressional Concern with Research and Development,
       88th-   Congress. Washington, DC: U.S. Government Printing Of-
       fice, 1966- . (A Bibliography Prepared for the Subcommittee on
       Government Research.)

1457. U.S. Library of Congress, Science Policy Research Division.   Statu-
       tory Provisions Related to Federal Research and Development, 2
       volumes. Washington, DC: U.S. Government Printing Office, 1976.

1458. U.S. Office of Technology Assessment.   Hearings: Technology Assess-
       ment Activities in the Industrial, Academic, and Governmental Com-
       munities. Washington, DC: U.S. Government Printing Office, 1976.
       391pp.

1459. U.S. President's Science Advisory Committee.   Science, Government,
       and Information. Washington, DC: U.S. Government Printing Office,
       1963. 52pp.

1460. U.S. President's Science Advisory Committee. Scientific Progress,
       the Universities and the Federal Government: Statement. Washing-
       ton, DC: U.S. Government Printing Office, 1960. 33pp.

1461. U.S. President's Scientific Research Board. Science and Public Pol-
       icy: A Report to the President, 5 volumes. J.R. Steelman. Wash-
       ington, DC: U.S. Government Printing Office, 1946.

K.1 CURRENT SOURCES

1462. APLA Quarterly Journal: A Forum for the Patent, Trademark and Copy-
       right Practitioner.
       v.1-   1972/73-   .
       Arlington, VA: American Patent Law Association.

1463. Bulletin of the Copyright Society of the U.S.A.
       v.1-   1953-   6 times a year.
       New York: New York University Law Center; distributed by Rothman.

1464. CIS Index: Congressional Information Service Index to Publications
       of the United States Congress.   -AND-
       CIS/Microfiche Service.
       Washington, DC: Congressional Information Service, Inc. 1970- .
       See, for example, relevant entries under "House Committee, H-700,
       Science and technology" and under "Science and technology"
       in the subject index.

1465. College and University Reporter.
       Chicago: Commerce Clearing House, 1964-   .
       (loose-leaf service).

1466. Copyright Bulletin: Quarterly Review.
       v.1-   1967-   .
       Paris: UNESCO

1467. Copyright Law Reporter.
       Chicago: Commerce Clearing House, 1978-   .
       (loose-leaf service).

1468. Federal Communications Bar Journal.
       v.1-   1937-   3 times a year.
       Washington, DC: Federal Communications Bar Association.

1469. Federal Contracts Report.
       Washington, DC: Bureau of National Affairs, 1964-   .
       (loose-leaf service).

1470. Government Contracts Reporter.
       Chicago: Commerce Clearing House, 1946-   .
       (loose-leaf service).

1471. Idea: The Journal of Law and Technology.
      v.1-   1957-   Quarterly.
      Buffalo, NY: Hein, for PTC (Patent, Trademark and Copyright) Re-
          search Foundation of the Franklin Pierce Law Center, Concord,
          NH.

1472. Industrial Property: Monthly Review of the World Intellectual Proper-
      ty Organization.
      v.1-   1962-   .
      Geneva: WIPO.

1473. Institute on Patent Law. Proceedings: Patent Law Annual.
      1st-   1963-   .
      New York: Matthew Bender, for the Continuing Legal Education Cen-
          ter of the Southwestern Legal Foundation, Dallas, TX.

1474. International Review of Industrial Property and Copyright Law (IIC).
      v.1-   1970-   6 times a year.
      Weinheim, Germany: Verlag Chemie, for the Max Planck Institute
          for Foreign and International Patent, Copyright, and Compe-
          tition Law, Munich.

1475. Journal of the Patent Office Society.
      v.1-   1918-   Monthly.
      Arlington, VA: Patent Office Society.

1476. Media Law Reporter.
      Washington, DC: Bureau of National Affairs, 1977-   .
      (loose-leaf service).

1477. Monthly Catalog of United States Government Publications.
      no.1-   1895-   .
      Washington, DC: U.S. Superintendent of Documents.

1478. Monthly Checklist of State Publications.
      v.1-   1910-   .
      Washington, DC: Library of Congress Processing Department.

                          [The preceding two monthly indexes are use-
                          ful also for works in most areas of this bib-
                          liography.]

1479. Oil & Gas Tax Quarterly.
      v.1-   1951-   .
      New York: Matthew Bender.

1480. Patent Law Review.
      v.1-   1969-   Annual.
      New York: Clark Boardman.

1481. Patent, Trademark & Copyright Journal.
      Washington, DC: Bureau of National Affairs, 1970-   .
      (loose-leaf service).

1482. Private Foundations Reporter.
      Chicago: Commerce Clearing House, 1971-   .
      (loose-leaf service).

1483. Public Contract Law Journal.
      v.1-   1967-   Semiannual.
      Chicago: American Bar Association Section of Public Contract Law.

1484. Radio Regulation: Second Series.
      Washington, DC: Pike and Fischer, 1963-   .
      (loose-leaf service).
      Covers communications industry generally.

1485. Science.
      1883-   Weekly.
      Washington, DC: American Association for the Advancement of Science.
      Science frequently reports on current developments relating to
          the impact of law and government policy on science and scientific research.

1486. Science, Technology & Human Values.
      no.1-   1972-   Quarterly.
      Cambridge, MA: Science, Technology & Human Values, Harvard University.
      An annotated "General Bibliography" appears in each issue.
      Numbers 1-16 (1972-1976) are titled Newsletter of the Program on
          Public Conceptions of Science; Numbers 17-24 (1976-1978) are
          titled Newsletter on Science, Technology & Human Values.

1487. The Trademark Reporter.
      v.1-   1911-   Monthly.
      New York: United States Trademark Association.

1488. United States Patents Quarterly.
      Washington, DC: Bureau of National Affairs, 1929-   .
      (loose-leaf service).

K.2 TAXATION AND RESEARCH

1489. Backus, D.C. "The Private Foundation Faces the Tax Reform Act of
      1969 - What to Do?" 16 Practical Lawyer (no.6) 13-17 (1970).

1490. Bischel, J.E. "Exportation of American Technology and the Federal
      Income Tax," 17 Tax Counselor's Quarterly 1-72 (1973).

1491. Bischel, J.E. Taxation of Patents, Trademarks, Copyrights, and
      Know-How, 1 volume. Boston: Warren, Gorham & Lamont, 1974- .
      (loose-leaf).

1492. Commerce Clearing House. The Private Foundation and the Tax Reform
      Act. Chicago, 1970. 157pp.

1493. Conference on Tax Planning for Foundations, Tax Exempt Status and
      Charitable Contributions, 4th, Los Angeles and New York, 1972.
      Foundations, Tax Exempt Status and Charitable Contributions.
      New York: Practising Law Institute, 1972. 312pp.

1494. Eliasberg, K.C. "Sec. 501(c)(3) - The Private Foundation: New Pro-
      cedural Requirements and Noncompliance Penalties," 49 Taxes 87-
      191 (1971).

1495. Hoorn, J.V., Jr. Tax Treatment of Research and Development: A Com-
      parative Survey of National Fiscal Measures and of Their Impact
      on Research. Paris: Organization for Economic Cooperation and
      Development, 1962. 280pp.

1496. Hopkins, B.R. "Scholarships and Fellowship Grants: Current Tax
      Developments and Problems," 3 Journal of College and University
      Law 54-71 (1975).

1497. Hopkins, B.R., and J.H. Myers. The Law of Tax-Exempt Organiza-
      tions. Washington, DC: Lerner Law Book Co., 1975. 356pp.

1498. Labovitz, J.R. "The Impact of the Private Foundation Provisions of
      the Tax Reform Act of 1969," 3 Journal of Legal Studies 63-105
      (1974).

1499. Lore, J.S. A Study of the Effects of the 1969 Tax Reform Act on
      Private Grant-Making Foundation Support of Charitable Activities.
      Ann Arbor, MI: University Microfilms, 1975. 140pp. (Thesis,
      Western Michigan University.)

1500. "Tax Consequences of Transfers of Bodily Parts," 73 Columbia Law Re-
      view 842-866 (1973).

1501. U.S. Office of Technology Assessment. A Preliminary Analysis of
      the IRS Tax Administration System. Springfield, VA: National
      Technical Information Service, 1977. 206pp.

1502. U.S. Treasury Department. Treasury Department Report on Private
      Foundations. Washington, DC: U.S. Government Printing Office,
      1965. 110pp.

1503. Wolfman, B. "Professors and the 'Ordinary and Necessary' Business
      Expense," 112 University of Pennsylvania Law Review 1089-1115
      (1964).

K.3 PROTECTION OF IDEAS

1504. American Bar Association, Section of Patent, Trademark and Copy-
      right Law. Two Hundred Years of English and American Patent,
      Trademark and Copyright Law. Chicago: American Bar Center, 1977.
      136pp.

1505. Blaustein, A.P., and R.A. Gorman. Cases and Materials on Intel-
      lectual Property 1960-1971. Mineola, NY: Foundation Press, 1972.
      319pp.

1506. "Computer Programs and Proposed Revisions of the Patent and Copy-
      right Laws," 81 Harvard Law Review 1541-1557 (1968).

1507. Conference of Plenipotentiaries of the Hague Union Concerning the
      International Deposit of Industrial Designs, Geneva, 1975.
      Records. Geneva, 1976. 196pp.

1508. Corasick, M.J., and B.G. Brockway. "Protection of Computer-Based
      Information," 40 Albany Law Review 113-153 (1975).

1509. Design Protection, edited by H. Cohen Jehoram. Leyden: Sijthoff,
      1976. 203pp.

1510. Dessemontet, F. The Legal Protection of Know-How in the United
      States of America, 2d edition. Translated by H.W. Clark. Geneva:
      Droz, 1976. 487pp.

1511. Goldstein, P. Copyright, Patent, Trademark and Related State Doc-
      trines: Cases and Materials. Chicago: Callaghan, 1973. 938pp.

1512. Hanifin, J.F., and J.K. Haskell. "Incentives for Inventors," 11
      Institute on Patent Law. Proceedings. Patent Law Annual 141-156
      (1973).

1513. Harris, L.J., ed. Nurturing New Ideas: Legal Rights and Economic
      Roles. Washington, DC: Bureau of National Affairs, 1969. 647pp.

1514. Hawkland, W.D. "Some Recent American Developments in the Protec-
      tion of Know-How," in International Congress of Comparative Law,
      8th, Pescaro, 1970. Legal Thought in the United States of Amer-
      ica under Contemporary Pressures, pp.389-416. Brussels, 1970.

1515. Kase, F.J. Designs: A Guide to Official Literature on Design Pro-
      tection. Leyden: Sijthoff, 1975. 411pp.

1516. Kimball, A.B., Jr. "An Analysis of Recent Supreme Court Assertions
      Regarding a Constitutional Standard on Invention," 1 APLA Quar-
      terly Journal 203-236 (1973).

1517. Kirtz, F.G. The Law of Electrical Invention. New York: Clark
      Boardman, 1954. 742pp.

1518. Ladas, S.P. Patents, Trademarks, and Related Rights: National and
      International Protection, 3 volumes. Cambridge, MA: Harvard Uni-
      versity Press, 1975. (Originally published in 1930.)

1519. Miller, R.I. Legal Aspects of Technology Utilization. Lexington,
      MA: Lexington Books, 1974. 164pp.

1520. Patent Resources Group. Software Protection by Trade Secret, Con-
      tract, Patent: Law, Practice and Forms. D. Bender, et al. Wash-
      ington, DC: Patent Resources Group, 1969. 358pp.

1521. "Protection of Computer Programs," 1973/1 International Associa-
      tion for the Protection of Industrial Property. Annuaire 401-442
      (1973).

1522. Puckett, A.W.   "The Limits of Copyright and Patent Protection for
      Computer Programs," 16 Copyright Law Symposium 81-142 (1968).

1523. Rossman, J.   "Selected General Bibliography: Patents, Trademarks,
      Copyrights," in The Law of Chemical, Metallurgical and Pharma-
      ceutical Patents, pp. 795-816, edited by H.I. Forman. New York:
      Central Book Co., 1967.

1524. Symposium.   "Intellectual Property," 9 Cleveland-Marshall Law Re-
      view 1-136 (1960).

1525. Ulmer, E.   Intellectual Property Rights and the Conflict of Laws: A
      Study Carried Out for the Commission of the European Communities.
      Deventer, Netherlands: Kluwer, 1978. 113pp.

1526. World Intellectual Property Organization. Current Trends in the
      Field of Intellectual Property. Geneva: World Intellectual Pro-
      perty Organization, 1971. 399pp.

1527. World Intellectual Property Organization. Legal Aspects of License
      Agreements in the Field of Patents, Trademarks and Know-How, 1 vol-
      ume. Geneva: World Intellectual Property Organization, 1972.

K.3.a PATENTS

1528. Amdur, L.H..   Patent Office Rules and Practice, edited by I. Seid-
      man and L. Horowitz. Albany, NY: Matthew Bender, 1959- .
      (loose-leaf).

1529. Baker, B.   Outline of Patent Office Interference Practice, 18th edi-
      tion, 1 volume. Chicago: United States Law Printing Co., 1975.

1530. Barton, J.H.   "Technology Transfer and LDC's: A Proposal for a Pre-
      ferential Patent System," 6 Stanford Journal of International
      Studies 27-50 (1971).

1531. Baxter, J.W.   World Patent Law and Practice, 2d edition. London:
      Sweet & Maxwell, 1973. 455pp.

1532. Bowman, W.S., Jr.   Patent and Antitrust Law: A Legal and Economic
      Appraisal. Chicago: University of Chicago Press, 1973. 272pp.

1533. "Computer Programming and Patent Law," 5 APLA Quarterly Journal 8-70 (1977).

1534. Deller, A.W. Dellar's Walker on Patents, 2d edition, 9 volumes. Mount Kisco, NY: Baker, Voorhis, 1964-76.

1535. Dunner, D.R., and P.M. Janicke. Court Review of Patent Office Decisions: Court of Claims and Patent Appeals, 2d edition, 2 volumes. New York: Matthew Bender, 1973- . (loose-leaf).

1536. Forman, H.I. Patents, Their Ownership and Administration by the United States Government. New York: Central Book Co., 1957. 354pp.

1537. Kase, F.J. Foreign Patents: A Guide to Official Patent Literature. Dobbs Ferry, NY: Oceana, 1972. 358pp.

1538. Kayton, I., et al. "Fraud in Patent Procurement: Genuine and Sham Charges," 43 George Washington Law Review 1-151 (1974).

1539. Leibesny, F. Mainly on Patents: The Use of Industrial Property and Its Literature. Hamden, CT: Archon Books, 1972. 210pp.

1540. Naimark, G.M. Patent Manual for Scientists and Engineers. Springfield, IL: C.C. Thomas, 1961. 108pp.

1541. Orkin, N. "The Legal Rights of the Employed Inventor: New Approaches to Old Problems," 56 Journal of the Patent Office Society 648-662, 719-745 (1974).

1542. Pagenberg, B.A. "Patentability of Computer Programs on the National and International Level," 5 International Review of Industrial Property and Copyright Law 1-43 (1974).

1543. Palmer, A.M. University Research and Patent Policies, Practices and Procedures. Washington, DC: National Academy of Sciences, 1962. 291pp.

1544. Practising Law Institute. International Patent Law and Practice. New York: Practising Law Institute, 1972. 400pp.

1545. Robbins, F.E. The Defense of Prior Invention: Patent Infringement Litigation. New York: Practising Law Institute, 1977. 277pp.

1546. Schramm, F.B. Handbook on Patent Disputes. Atlanta, GA: Harrison, 1974. 475pp.

1547. Sinnott, J.P. World Patent Law and Practice: Patent Statutes, Regulations and Treaties. New York: Matthew Bender, 1974- . (loose-leaf).

1548. Soltysinski, S.J. "Computer Programs and Patent Law: A Comparative Study," 3 Rutgers Journal of Computers and the Law 1-82 (1973).

1549. "Standards of Obviousness and the Patentability of Chemical Compounds," 6 Patent Law Review 151-172 (1974). (Reprinted from 87 Harvard Law Review 1974.)

1550. Symposium on the Role of Patent Information in Research and Development, Moscow, 1974. Collection of Lectures. Geneva: World Intellectual Property Organization, 1975. 372pp.

1551. Thomas, E. Chemical Patents and Chemical Inventions, 1 volume, edited by M.A. Auslander. New York: Clark Boardman, 1964- . (loose-leaf).

1552. Ullrich, H. Standards of Patentability for European Inventions: Should an Inventive Step Advance the Art? New York: Chemie Verlag, 1977. 116pp. (Studies in Industrial Property and Copyright Law, vol. 1.)

1553. U.S. Congress, Senate, Committee on the Judiciary. Studies. Washington, DC: U.S. Government Printing Office, 1956-63. This series of thirty studies for the Subcommittee on Patents, Trademarks and Copyrights covered all aspects of U.S. patent policy and procedure. The following are most relevant to this bibliography:
    No. 5. International Patent System and Foreign Policy. 1957. 52pp.
    No. 6. Patents and Nonprofit Research. 1957. 66pp.
    No. 8. Role of Court Expert in Patent Litigation. 1958. 96pp.
    No. 10. Exchange of Patent Rights and Technical Information under Mutual Aid Programs. 1958. 51pp.
    No. 11. Impact of Patent System on Research. 1958. 62pp.
    No. 16. Research and Development Factor in Mergers and Acquisitions. 1958. 35pp.
    No. 21. Technical Research Activities of Cooperative Associations. 1959. 59pp.
    No. 22. Government Assistance to Invention and Research: A Legislative History. 1960. 199pp.
    No. 24. Patent and Technical Information Agreements. 1960. 79pp.
    No. 25. Court Decisions as Guides to Patent Office. 1960. 18pp.
    No. 28. Independent Inventors and Patent System. 1961. 40pp.
    No. 30. Law of Employed Inventors in Europe. 1963. 156pp.

K.3.b COPYRIGHT

1554. [Banzhaf, J.F.] "Copyright Protection for Computer Programs," 64 Columbia Law Review 1274-1300 (1964).

1555. Baumgarten, J.A. US-USSR Copyright Relations under the Universal Copyright Convention. New York: Practising Law Institute, 1973. 172pp.

1556. Breyer, S. "The Uneasy Case for Copyright: A Study of Copyright in Books, Photocopies, and Computer Programs," 84 Harvard Law Review 281-351 (1970).

1557. Bush, G.P., ed. Technology and Copyright: Annotated Bibliography and Source Materials. Mt. Airy, MD: Lomond Systems, 1972. 454pp.

1558. Carnahan, W.H. Protection of Computer Programs: A Dilemma, 1 volume. Colorado Springs, CO: U.S. Air Force Academy, 1972.

1559. Copinger, W.A., and S. James. On Copyright, Including International Copyright, 11th edition. London: Sweet & Maxwell, 1971. 920pp.

1560. David, H. "Basic Principles of International Copyright," 21 Bulletin of the Copyright Society 1-24 (1973).

1561. Dreher, N.C. "Community Antenna Television and Copyright Legislation," 17 Copyright Law Symposium 102-132 (1969).

1562. Gorman, R.A. "Copyright Protection for the Collection and Representation of Facts," 76 Harvard Law Review 1569-1605 (1963); also in 12 Copyright Law Symposium 30-75 (1963).

1563. Hattery, L.H. and G.P. Bush, eds. Reprography and Copyright Law. Washington, DC: American Institute of Biological Sciences, 1964. 203pp.

1564. Henry, N. Copyright, Information Technology, Public Policy. New York: M. Dekker, 1975- .

1565. Howell, H.A. Copyright Law, 4th edition, edited by A. Latman. Washington, DC: Bureau of National Affairs, 1962. 385pp.

1566. Huang, Te-Hsien, comp. Bibliography on Copyright, 2d edition. Halifax, N.S.: Published by the compiler, 1972. 118pp.

1567. Huang, Te-Hsien, comp. Union List of Copyright Publications in West European Libraries. Halifax, N.S.: Publ. by compiler, 1974. 621pp.

1568. Johnston, D.F. Copyright Handbook. New York: Bowker, 1978. 309pp. (Includes text of the Copyright Acts of 1909 and 1976.)

1569. Kase, F.J. Copyright Thought in Continental Europe: Its Development, Legal Theories and Philosophy: A Selected and Annotated Bibliography. South Hackensack, NJ: F.B. Rothman, 1967. 85pp.

1570. Klaver, F. "The Legal Problems of Video-Cassettes and Audio-Visual Discs," 23 Bulletin of the Copyright Society 152-185 (1976).

1571. Legal Protection of Computer Software: An Industrial Survey. Boston: Harbridge House, Inc., 1977. 28pp. (Prepared for U.S. National Commission on New Technological Uses of Copyrighted Works [CONTU].)

1572. Levy, H.A. "Copyright Law and Computerized Legal Research," 20 Bulletin of the Copyright Society 159-180 (1973).

1573. Meadow, R. "Television Formats," 20 Copyright Law Symposium 73-111 (1972).

1574. Nimetz, M. "Design Protection," 15 Copyright Law Symposium 79-133 (1967).

1575. Nimmer, M.B.   Nimmer on Copyright: A Treatise on the Law of Liter-
      ary, Musical and Artistic Property and the Protection of Ideas.
      New York: Matthew Bender, 1963- . (loose-leaf).

1576. Nimmer, M.B.   A Preliminary View of the Copyright Act of 1976: Anal-
      ysis and Text. Albany, NY: Matthew Bender, 1977. 142pp.

1577. Oberman, M.S.   "Copyright Protection for Computer-Produced Director-
      ies," 22 Copyright Law Symposium 1-52 (1977).

1578. Prasinos, N.   "Worldwide Protection of Computer Programs by Copy-
      right," 4 Rutgers Journal of Computers and the Law 42-85 (1974).

1579. Roberts, M.   Copyright: A Selected Bibliography of Periodical Liter-
      ature Relating to Literary Property in the United States. Metu-
      chen, NJ: Scarecrow Press, 1971. 416pp.

1580. Russell-Clarke, A.D.   Copyright in Industrial Designs, 5th edition,
      edited by M. Fysh. London: Sweet & Maxwell, 1974. 314pp.

1581. Schuster, N., and M.J. Bloch.   "Mechanical Copying, Copyright Law,
      and the Teacher," 10 Publishing, Entertainment, Advertising and
      Allied Fields Law Quarterly 307-337 (1970). (Reprinted from 17
      Cleveland-Marshall Law Review, 1968.)

1582. Squires, J.   "Copyright and Compilations in the Computer Era," 24
      Bulletin of the Copyright Society 18-46 (1976).

1583. "Symposium: Copyright and Educational Media," 1 Performing Arts Re-
      view 1-90 (1977).

1584. United Nations Educational, Scientific and Cultural Organization.
      Copyright Laws and Treaties of the World. Paris: UNESCO, 1956- .
      (loose-leaf).

1585. U.S. Congress, Senate, Committee on the Judiciary.   Copyright Law
      Revision: Index of Hearings. Washington, DC: U.S. Government
      Printing Office, 1968. 151pp.

1586. U.S. Congress, Senate, Committee on the Judiciary.   Copyright Law
      Revision: Studies Prepared for Subcommittee on Patents, Trade-
      marks, and Copyrights, 12 volumes. Washington, DC: U.S. Govern-
      ment Printing Office, 1960-61. (Reprinted as Copyright Society
      of the U.S.A. Studies on Copyright, Arthur Fisher Memorial Edi-
      tion, 2 volumes. South Hackensack, NJ: Rothman, 1963.)

1587. U.S. National Commission on New Technological Uses of Copyrighted
      Works (CONTU).   Transcript, CONTU Meetings 1-5, one volume.
      Springfield, VA: National Technical Information Service, 1975.

1588. Williams & Wilkins Co., Baltimore, plaintiff.   The Williams & Wilkins
      Case: The Williams & Wilkins Company v. the United States, compiled
      by M.G. McCormick. New York: Science Associates/International,
      1974- . (Landmark case on library photocopying as possible copy-
      right infringement.)

K.3.c   TRADE SECRETS

1589. Adelman, M.J., and R.P. Jaress.   "Inventions and the Law of Trade
       Secrets after Lear v. Adkins," 2 Patent Law Review 163-180
       (1970).

1590. Bender, D.   "Trade Secret Protection of Software," 38 George Wash-
       ington Law Review 909-957 (1970).

1591. Brosnahan, C.S., ed.   Attorney's Guide to Trade Secrets.   Berkeley,
       CA: California Continuing Education of the Bar, 1971.   202pp.

1592. Doerfer, G.L.   "The Limits on Trade Secret Law Imposed by Federal
       Patent and Antitrust Supremacy," 80 Harvard Law Review 1432-1462
       (1967).

1593. Ellis, R.   Trade Secrets.   Mount Kisco, NY: Baker, Voorhis, 1953.
       525pp.

1594. "Industrial Espionage: Piracy of Secret Scientific and Technical In-
       formation," 14 University of California Los Angeles Law Review
       911-934 (1967).

1595. Lowell, C.H.   "Corporate Privacy: A Remedy for the Victim of Indus-
       trial Espionage," 4 Patent Law Review 407-449 (1972).   (Reprinted
       from Duke Law Journal 391-433 (1971).)

1596. Practising Law Institute.   Protecting and Profiting from Trade Sec-
       rets.   R.M. Milgrim, Chairman.   New York: Practising Law Institute,
       1975.   280pp.

1597. Seidel, A.H., and R.L. Panitch.   What the General Practitioner
       Should Know about Trade Secrets and Employment Agreements.   Phila-
       delphia: Joint Committee on Continuing Legal Education of the Amer-
       ican Law Institute and the American Bar Association, 1973.   150pp.

1598. Stedman, J.C.   "Trade Secrets: Protection, Remedies, and Limita-
       tions," 6 Institute on Patent Law. Proceedings 15-36 (1969).

1599. Turner, A.E.   Law of Trade Secrets.   London: Sweet & Maxwell, 1962.
       519pp.

1600. Wade, W.   Industrial Espionage and the Mis-Use of Trade Secrets.
       Ardmore, PA: Advance House, 1964.   134pp.

1601. Wise, A.N.   Trade Secrets and Know-How throughout the World.   New
       York: Clark Boardman, 1974-   .   (loose-leaf).

K.4 DISTRIBUTION OF IDEAS AND INFORMATION, INCLUDING COMMUNICATIONS

1602. Berkner, L.V. Science and Foreign Relations: International Flow of Scientific and Technological Information. Washington, DC: Department of State, International Science Policy Survey Group, 1950. 170pp.

1603. Berman, P.J., and A.G. Oettinger. "Changing Functions and Facilities: The Politics of Information Resources," 28 Federal Communications Bar Journal 227-273 (1975).

1604. Berner, R.O. Constraints on the Regulatory Process: A Case Study of Regulation Cable Television. Cambridge, MA: Ballinger, 1976. 107pp.

1605. Brown, E.R., III. "Direct Broadcast Satellites and Freedom of Speech," 4 California Western International Law Journal 374-393 (1974).

1606. Colino, R.R. "Intelsat: Doing Business in Outer Space," 6 Columbia Journal of Transnational Law 17-60 (1967).

1607. "The Control of Program Content in International Telecommunications," 13 Columbia Journal of Transnational Law 1-113 (1974).

1608. Ende, A.H. "Intelsat: Evolution or Revolution?" 4 Law and Policy in International Business 529-556 (1972).

1609. Gibson, G.H. Public Broadcasting: The Role of the Federal Government, 1912-76. New York: Praeger, 1977. 236pp.

1610. Gold, M.E. "Direct Broadcast Satellites: Implications for Less-Developed Countries and for World Order," 12 Virginia Journal of International Law 66-90 (1971).

1611. Gotlieb, A.E., and C.M. Dalfen. "Direct Satellite Broadcasting: A Case Study in the Development of the Law of Space Communications," 7 Canadian Yearbook of International Law 33-60 (1969).

1612. Gotlieb, A.E., C.M. Dalfen, and K. Katz. "The Transborder Transfer of Information by Communications and Computer Systems: Issues and Approaches to Guiding Principles," 68 American Journal of International Law 227-257 (1974).

1613. Hagelin, T.M. "The First Amendment Stake in New Technology: The Broadcast-Cable Controversy," 44 University of Cincinnati Law Review 427-524 (1975).

1614. International Telecommunication Union. Report on Telecommunication and the Peaceful Uses of Outer Space. Geneva: The Union, 1973. 134pp.

1615. Jones, E.B. Earth Satellite Telecommunication Systems and International Law. Austin, TX: University of Texas, 1970. 167pp.

1616. Levin, H.J. "Organization and Control of Communications Satel-
       lites," 113 University of Pennsylvania Law Review 315-357 (1965).

1617. Machlup. F. The Production and Distribution of Knowledge in the
       United States. Princeton, NJ: Princeton University Press, 1962.
       416pp.

1618. McWhinney, E.W. The International Law of Communications. Leyden:
       Sijthoff, 1971. 170pp.

1619. Patel, S.F. "Transfer of Technology and Third UNCTAD," 7 Journal
       of World Trade Law 226-239 (1973).

1620. Practising Law Institute. Current Developments in CATV 1974. G.L.
       Christensen, Chairman. New York: Practising Law Institute, 1974.
       551pp.

1621. Rourke, F.E. Secrecy and Publicity: Dilemmas of Democracy. Balti-
       more, MD: Johns Hopkins Press, 1961. 236pp.

1622. Schwartz, H. "Comsat, the Carriers, and the Earth Stations: Some
       Problems with 'Melding Variegated Interests,'" 76 Yale Law Jour-
       nal 441-484 (1967).

1623. "Space Radiocommunications and Techniques," 38 Telecommunication
       Journal 234-429 (1971). (Summary of the articles prepared on the
       occasion of the opening of the second World Administrative Radio
       Conference for Space Telecommunications.)

1624. "Telecommunications," 5 Stanford Journal of International Studies
       (1970).

1625. Trooboff, P.D. "INTELSAT: Approaches to the Renegotiation," 9 Har-
       vard International Law Journal 1-84 (1968).

1626. United Nations Industrial Development Organization. Guidelines for
       the Acquisition of Foreign Technology in Developing Countries.
       New York: United Nations, 1973. 55pp.

1627. U.S. Congress, House, Committee on Foreign Affairs. Foreign Policy
       Implications of Satellite Communications: Hearings. Washington,
       DC: U.S. Government Printing Office, 1970. 212pp.

1628. U.S. Congress, House, Committee on Interstate and Foreign Commerce.
       Cable Television: Promise versus Regulatory Performance. Washing-
       ton, DC: U.S. Government Printing Office, 1976. 110pp.

1629. U.S. Domestic Council, Committee on the Right of Privacy. National
       Information Policy: Report to the President of the United States.
       Washington, DC: U.S. Government Printing Office, for National Com-
       mission on Libraries and Information Science, 1976. 233pp.

1630. U.S. Library of Congress, Science Policy Research Division. Science,
       Technology, and American Diplomacy: U.S. Scientists Abroad: An Ex-
       amination of Major Programs for Nongovernmental Scientific Ex-
       change. Washington, DC: U.S. Government Printing Office, 1974.
       163pp.

1631. U.S. National Aeronautics and Space Administration. Scientific and
       Technical Proceedings of the Conference on the Law of Space and
       of Satellite Communications. Washington, DC: U.S. Government
       Printing Office, 1964. 205pp.

1632. U.S. President's Science Advisory Committee. Science, Government,
       and Information: The Responsibilities of the Technical Community
       and the Government in the Transfer of Information. Washington,
       DC: U.S. Government Printing Office, 1963. 52pp. ("The Weinberg
       Report.")

1633. Wallenstein, G.D. International Telecommunications Agreements.
       Dobbs Ferry, NY: Oceana, 1977- . (loose-leaf).

1634. Wiggins, J.R. Freedom or Secrecy. New York: Oxford University
       Press, 1964. 289pp.

1635. Woodbridge, R.C. "Recent Trends in Technology Interchanges: The
       Case For and Against Pooling," 54 Journal of the Patent Office
       Society 507-537 (1972).

SUPPLEMENT
(COVERING MATERIALS PUBLISHED THROUGH MID-YEAR 1979)

The criteria used for inclusion in this Supplement are even more stringent than those described on page vi. Space limitations have dictated the exclusion of most periodical articles and many monographs. The "Current Sources" sections in the main text, and new additions in this Supplement, contain references to indexes and other references that can guide readers to further material. This Supplement covers materials published through the first half of 1979.

to A.   GENERAL DISCUSSION OF LAW AND SCIENCE:

1636.   Cranberg, L.,   "Law--Scientific and Juridical," 56 American
        Scientist 244-253 (1968).

1637.   Field, T.G.   "Science, Law and Public Policy: Meeting the
        Need in Legal Education," 13 New England Law Review 214-232
        (1977).

to A.1   GENERAL DISCUSSION OF LAW AND SCIENCE, CURRENT SOURCES:

1638.   Legal Bibliography Index.
        1978-   annual.
        Baton Rouge, LA: Legal Bibliography Index.
        A bibliography of bibliographies by Win-Shin S. Chiang and
        L.E. Dickson; includes such subjects as Energy, Human
        Experimentation, and Space Law.

to B.   LAW AND SOCIAL SCIENCE, INCLUDING EMPIRICAL RESEARCH ON THE LAW:

1639.   Calabresi, G.,   and P.C. Bobbitt. Tragic Choices.
        New York: Norton, 1978. 252pp. (The Fels lecture on public
        policy analysis, including treatment of several bioethical
        issues.)

1640.   Johnson, H.M., ed.   Social System and Legal Process: Theory,
        Comparative Perspectives, and Special Studies. San Francisco,
        CA: Jossey-Bass, 1978. 352pp.

1641.   Kalisch, B.J.   Child Abuse and Neglect: An Annotated
        Bibliography. Westport, CT: Greenwood, 1978. 535pp.
        (Chapter 7, "Legal Issues.")

1642.   Mednick, S.A.,   and S.G. Shoham, eds.   New Paths in
        Criminology: Interdisciplinary and Intercultural Explorations.
        Lexington, MA: Lexington Books, 1979. 235pp.

1643.   Moore, S.F.   Law as Process: An Anthropological Approach.
        London: Routledge & Kegan Paul, 1978. 270pp.

1644.   Nonet, P.,   and P. Selznick.   Law and Society in Transition:
        Toward Responsive Law. New York: Octagon, 1978. 122pp.

1645. Pospisil, L.J.   The Ethnology of Law, 2nd edition. Menlo
      Park, CA: Cummings, 1978. 136pp.

1646. Reasons, C.E., and R.M. Rich, eds.   The Sociology of Law:
      A Conflict Perspective. Toronto, Ont.: Butterworths, 1978.
      475pp.

1647. Schmid, A.A.   Property, Power, and Public Choice: An Inquiry
      into Law and Economics. New York: Praeger, 1978. 316pp.

1648. Segalman, R.   Conflicting Rights: Social Legislation and Policy,
      2 volumes. Washington, DC: University Press of America,
      1977-78. (Volume 2: The Deviant, the Society and the Law.)

1649. Tapp, J.L., and F.J. Levine, eds.   Law, Justice and the
      Individual in Society: Psychological and Legal Issues.
      New York: Holt, Rinehart and Winston, 1977. 446pp. (Published
      for the Society for the Psychological Study of Social Issues.)

1650. Timasheff, N.S.   An Introduction to the Sociology of Law.
      Westport, CT: Greenwood, 1977. 418pp. (Reprint of the 1939
      edition.)

1651. Wolff, R.P.   Understanding Rawls: A Reconstruction and Critique
      of 'A Theory of Justice'. Princeton, NJ: Princeton University
      Press, 1977. 224pp.

1652. Wright, B., and V. Fox.   Criminal Justice and the Social Sciences.
      Philadelphia: Saunders, 1978. 419pp.

to B.1 LAW AND SOCIAL SCIENCE, CURRENT SOURCES:

1653. Research in Law and Economics.
          v.1-   1979-   annual.
      Greenwich, CT: Jai Press.

1654. Research in Law and Sociology.
          v.1-   1978-   annual.
      Greenwich, CT: Jai Press.

to C. LAW AS SCIENCE: SCIENTIFIC METHODS, LOGIC, AND LEGAL REASONING:

1655. Marvell, T.B.   Appellate Courts and Lawyers: Information
      Gathering in the Adversary System. Westport, CT: Greenwood,
      1978. 391pp.

to C.2 JURISPRUDENCE AND LEGAL REASONING:

1656. Carter, L.H.   Reason in Law. Boston: Little, Brown, 1979. 258pp.

1657. Dias, R.W.M.   A Bibliography of Jurisprudence, 3rd edition.
      London: Butterworths, 1979. 453pp.

1658. Moore, R. <u>Legal Norms and Legal Science: A Critical Study of Kelsen's 'Pure Theory of Law'</u>. Honolulu: University Press of Hawaii, 1978. 234pp.

to C.3 SCIENTIFIC METHOD AND LOGIC:

1659. Tammelo, I. <u>Modern Logic in the Service of Law</u>. New York: Springer, 1978. 175pp.

to C.4 LINGUISTICS AND SEMANTICS:

1660. Bergeron, V., D.C. Burke, <u>et al</u>. <u>Words, Computers and Communications in Law (Lexicographie, bilinguisme juridique et ordinateur)</u>, 2nd edition. Ottawa: Les Editions de l'Université d'Ottawa, 1977. 332pp.

to C.6 QUANTITATIVE ANALYSIS AND PREDICTION:

1661. Finkelstein, M.O. <u>Quantitative Methods in Law: Studies in the Application of Mathematical Probability and Statistics to Legal Problems</u>. New York: Free Press, 1978. 318pp.

to D. SCIENCE AND THE ADJUDICATORY FUNCTION OF LAW:

1662. McCall, G.J. <u>Observing the Law: Field Methods in the Study of Crime and the Criminal Justice System</u>. New York: Free Press, 1978. 259pp.

to D.2 LEGAL EVIDENCE:

1663. Cohen, L.J. <u>The Probable and the Provable</u>. Oxford: Clarendon Press, 1977. 363pp.

to D.4 SCIENTIFIC EVIDENCE:

1664. Center for Health Services Research. University of Southern California, Los Angeles. <u>Paternity Case Processing Handbook</u>. Washington, DC: U.S. Government Printing Office, 1978. 123pp.

1665. Moenssens, A.A., and F.E. Inbau. <u>Scientific Evidence in Criminal Cases</u>, 2nd edition. Mineola, NY: Foundation Press, 1978. 697pp.

to D.4.b VOICEPRINTS:

1666. National Research Council, Committee on Evaluation of Sound Spectrograms. <u>On the Theory and Practice of Voice Identification</u>. Washington, DC: National Academy of Sciences, 1979. 161pp.

1667. Tosi, O. Voice Identification: Theory and Legal Applications.
      Baltimore, MD: University Park Press, 1979. 182pp.

to D.4.c LIE DETECTION:

1668. Ansley, N., and F. Horvath, eds. Truth and Science: A Biblio-
      graphy, one volume. Linthicum Heights, MD: American Polygraph
      Association, 1977.

to D.5 SCIENCE IN AID OF LAW ENFORCEMENT:

1669. Bertillon, A. Instructions for Taking Descriptions for the
      Identification of Criminals, and Others, translated by G.
      Muller. New York: AMS, 1977. 94pp. (Reprint of the 1889
      edition.)

1670. Greenberg, D.F. Mathematical Criminology. New Brunswick, NJ:
      Rutgers University Press, 1979. 448pp.

1671. Nudelman, S., J.C. Richmond, and C.M. Freeman, eds. Optics in
      Security and Law Enforcement: Seminar. Bellingham, WA:
      Society of Photo-optical Instrumentation Engineers, 1977. 154pp.

1672. Sheleff, L. The Bystander: Behavior, Law, Ethics. Lexington, MA:
      Lexington Books, 1978. 223pp.

1673. Standish, S.M., and P.G. Stimson, eds. Symposium on Forensic
      Dentistry: Legal Obligations and Methods of Identification for
      the Practitioner. Philadelphia: Saunders, 1977. 196pp.

to E. THE LAW OF COMPUTERS AND LEGAL USES OF COMPUTERS:

1674. Bender, D. Computer Law: Evidence and Procedure, 1 volume.
      New York: Matthew Bender, 1978-   . (loose-leaf).

1675. Bequai, A. Computer Crime. Lexington, MA: Lexington Books,
      1978. 207pp.

1676. Seipel, P. Computing Law: Perspectives on a New Legal Discipline.
      Stockholm: Liber Forlag, 1977. 375pp.

1677. Tapper, C.F.H. Computer Law. New York: Longman, 1978. 190pp.

1678. Teaching Law with Computers: A Collection of Essays, by R. Burris,
      R.E. Keeton, C.P. Landis, and R. Park. Boulder, CO: Westview
      Press for EDUCOM, 1979. 150pp.

to E.1 THE LAW OF COMPUTERS AND LEGAL USES OF COMPUTERS, CURRENT SOURCES:

1679. Computer/Law Journal.
      v.1-   1978-   quarterly.
      Los Angeles: Center for Computer/Law.

to E.2   COMPUTERS & OTHER TECHNOLOGY IN LEGISLATIVE AND
         JUDICIAL ADMINISTRATION:

1680. U.S. Library of Congress, Science Policy Research Division.
       State Legislature Use of Information Technology, by R.L.
       Chartrand and J. Bortnick. Westport, CT: Greenwood, 1978.
       308pp.

to E.3   COMPUTERIZED LEGAL RESEARCH:

1681. SEARCH Group, Inc.   Automated Legal Research: A Study for Criminal
       Justice Agencies. Sacramento, CA: SEARCH Group, 1978. 112pp.

to F.   LEGAL PROBLEMS OF PRIVACY:

1682. Smith, R.E.   Compilation of State and Federal Privacy
       Laws, 1978/79 Edition. Washington, DC: Privacy Journal, 1978.
       166pp. (Update of entry no. 479.)

1683. U.S. Privacy Protection Study Commission.   Personal Privacy in an
       Information Society. Washington, DC: U.S. Government Printing
       Office, 1977. 654pp.

to F.1   EAVESDROPPING AND WIRETAPPING:

1684. Fishman, C.S.   Wiretapping and Eavesdropping. Rochester, NY:
       Lawyers Co-operative Publishing Company, 1978. 587pp.

to F.2   PERSONAL RECORDS:

1685. Association for Computing Machinery, Los Angeles Chapter, Ombudsman
       Committee on Privacy.   Privacy, Security, and the Information
       Processing Industry. New York: ACM, 1976. 187pp.

1686. Hayt, E.   Medicolegal Aspects of Hospital Records, 2nd edition.
       Berwyn, IL: Physicians' Record Company, 1977. 519pp.
       (Update of entry no. 509.)

1687. National Commission on Confidentiality of Health Records.   Health
       Records and Confidentiality: An Annotated Bibliography.
       Washington, DC: The Commission, 1979. 112pp.

1688. U.S. Law Enforcement Assistance Administration, National Criminal
       Justice Information and Statistics Service.   Privacy and
       Security of Criminal History Information: Compendium of State
       Legislation. Washington, DC: U.S. Government Printing Office,
       1978. 858pp.

to G. MEDICINE AND LAW:

1689. American Bar Association, Commission on Medical Professional
       Liability. Report. Chicago, IL: ABA, 1977. 161pp.

1690. Aspen Systems Corporation, Health Law Center. Problems in Hospital
       Law, 3rd edition, by D.G. Warren. Germantown, MD: Aspen, 1978.
       339pp.

1691. Bandman, E.L., and B. Bandman, eds. Bioethics and Human
       Rights: A Reader for Health Professionals. Boston: Little,
       Brown, 1978. 386pp.

1692. Cardozo, B.N. What Medicine Can Do for Law. New York: Harper,
       1930. 55pp. (Discourse before the New York Academy of
       Medicine.

1693. Encyclopedia of Bioethics, 4 volumes. W.T. Reich, ed.   New
       York: Free Press, 1978. (Includes legal aspects of most issues
       covered.)

1694. Hemelt, M.D., and M.E. Mackert. Dynamics of Law in Nursing
       and Health Care. Reston, VA: Reston Publishing Company, 1978.
       250pp.

1695. Holder. A.R. Medical Malpractice Law, 2nd edition. New York:
       Wiley, 1978. 562pp. (Update of entry no. 557.)

1696. Institute of Medicine, Division of Legal, Ethical, and Educational
       Aspects of Health. Beyond Malpractice: Compensation for
       Medical Injuries: A Policy Analysis. Washington, DC: National
       Academy of Sciences, 1978. 88pp.

1697. Law, S.A., and S. Polan. Pain and Profit: The Politics of
       Malpractice. New York: Harper & Row, 1978. 305pp.

1698. Murchison, I., T.S. Nichols, and R. Hanson.   Legal Accountability
       in the Nursing Process. St. Louis, MO: Mosby, 1978. 157pp.

1699. National Conference on Legal Implications of Emergency Medical
       Care, New Orleans, 1979. Proceedings, one volume. Sponsored
       by the American Society of Law and Medicine and the American
       Bar Association Committee on Medicine and Law. Boston: American
       Society of Law and Medicine, 1979.

1700. Nemec, J. Highlights in Medicolegal Relations, revised and
       enlarged edition. National Library of Medicine. Washington,
       DC: U.S. Government Printing Office, 1976. 116pp.

1701. Warren, D.G.   A Legal Guide for Rural Health Programs.
       Cambridge, MA: Ballinger, 1979. 197pp.

to G.1   MEDICINE AND LAW, CURRENT SOURCES:

1702.   Patient Rights Digest.
            v.1-   1977-   5 numbers a year.
            Montgomery, AL: Center for the Study of Civil Liberties & Civil
            Rights.

1703.   Specialty Law Digest--Health Care Law.
            v.1-   1979-   monthly, plus annual digest-index compila-
            tion. New Brighton, MN: Specialty Digest Publications.

to G.2   ISSUES OF LIFE AND DEATH:

1704.   Grisez, G.G., and J.M. Boyle.   Life and Death with Liberty and
            Justice: A Contribution to the Euthanasia Debate.   Notre Dame,
            IN: University of Notre Dame Press, 1979. 521pp.

1705.   Thomas, J.E., ed.   Matters of Life and Death: Crises in Bio-
            Medical Ethics. Toronto: S. Stevens, 1978. 378pp.

to G.3.b   BIRTH AND POPULATION CONTROL, INCLUDING STERILIZATION:

1706.   United Nations Fund for Population Activities.   Survey of Laws on
            Fertility Control, final revision by Jan Stepan. New York, 1979.
            98pp.   Part 1: Voluntary Sterilization. Part 2: Termination of
            Pregnancy. (Summaries of the law in 135 countries.)

to G.3.c   ABORTION:

1707.   Gorby, J.D., and R.E. Jonas.   "West German Abortion Decision:
            A Contrast to Roe v. Wade," 9 John Marshall Journal of
            Practice and Procedure 551-684 (1976). (Includes a transla-
            tion of the German Federal Constitutional Court decision.)

1708.   Mohr, J.C.   Abortion in America: The Origins and Evolution of
            National Policy, 1800-1900. New York: Oxford University
            Press, 1978. 331pp.

to G.4   DEVELOPMENTS IN PSYCHIATRY, PSYCHOLOGY, AND TREATMENT OF
            MENTAL ILLNESS:

1709.   Aker, J.B., A.C. Walsh, and J.R. Beam.   Mental Capacity: Medical
            and Legal Aspects of the Aging. Colorado Springs, CO:
            Shepard's, 1977. 372pp.

1710.   Barton, W.E., and C.J. Sanborn, eds.   Law and the Mental Health
            Professions: Friction at the Interface. New York: International
            Universities Press, 1978. 330pp.

1711. Daniel McNaughton: His Trial and the Aftermath, edited by D.J. West
       and A. Walk. Ashford, Kent, England: Headley, Gaskell Books, for
       the British Journal of Psychiatry, 1977. 185pp. (Studies on
       the landmark 19th-century English case dealing with insanity and
       criminal responsibility.)

1712. Ennis, E.J., and R.D. Emery. The Rights of Mental Patients:
       The Revised Edition of the Basic ACLU Guide to a Mental Patient's
       Rights. New York: Avon, 1978. 220pp. (ACLU Handbook.)

1713. Fingarette, H., and A.F. Hasse. Mental Disabilities and Crimi-
       nal Responsibility. Berkeley, CA: University of California
       Press, 1979. 329pp.

1714. Friedman, P.R. The Rights of the Mentally Retarded: The Basic
       ACLU Guide for the Mentally Retarded Person's Rights.
       New York: Avon, 1976. 186pp. (American Civil Liberties Union
       Handbook.)

1715. Hogan, D.B. Regulation of Psychotherapists, 3 volumes.
       Cambridge, MA: Ballinger, 1978. Vol 1: A Study in the Philo-
       sophy and Practice of Professional Regulation; Vol. 2: A Hand-
       book of State Licensure Laws; Vol 3: A Review of Malpractice
       Suits in the U.S.

1716. Morozov, G.V. and I.M. Kalashnik, eds. Forensic Psychiatry: A
       Translation of a Text Approved by the RSFSR Ministry of Higher
       and Secondary Specialized Education. White Plains, NY: Inter-
       national Arts and Sciences Press, 1970. 499pp.

1717. Psychiatrists and the Legal Process: Diagnosis and Debate, edited
       by R.J. Bonnie. New York: Insight Communications, 1977.
       350pp. (Collection of articles published in Psychiatric
       Annals, 1973-77; includes contributions by W.J. Curran,
       D.L. Farnsworth, and A.A. Stone.)

1718. Rubin, J. Economics, Mental Health, and the Law. Lexington, MA:
       Heath, 1978. 178pp.

1719. Thornberry, T.P., and J.E. Jacoby. The Criminally Insane: A
       Community Follow-Up of Mentally Ill Offenders. Chicago:
       University of Chicago Press, 1979. 292pp.

1720. U.S. President's Commission on Mental Helath. Report to the
       President, 4 volumes. Washington, DC: U.S. Government
       Printing Office, 1978.

1721. Watson, A.S. Psychiatry for Lawyers, 2nd edition. New York:
       International Universities Press, 1978. 466pp.

1722. Wilson, J.P. The Rights of Adolescents in the Mental Health
       System. Lexington, MA: Lexington Books, 1978. 321pp.

to G.5   BEHAVIOR MODIFICATION AND PSYCHOSURGERY:

1723. Hippchen, L.J., ed.   Ecologic-Biochemical Approaches to
       Treatment of Delinquents and Criminals. New York: Van Nostrand
       Reinhold, 1978. 396pp.

to G.6   MEDICAL AND PSYCHOLOGICAL EXPERIMENTATION:

1724. Gallant, D.M., and R. Force, eds.   Legal and Ethical Issues
       in Human Research and Treatment: Psychopharmacologic Consi-
       derations. New York: SP Medical and Scientific Books, distri-
       buted by Halsted, 1978. 186pp.

to H.   LEGAL CONTROL OF HAZARDS TO PUBLIC HEALTH AND SAFETY:

1725. Ashford, N.A.   Crisis in the Workplace: Occupational Disease
       and Injury: A Report to the Ford Foundation. Cambridge, MA:
       MIT Press, 1976. 588pp.

1726. Reams, B.D., and J.R. Ferguson, compilers and editors.
       Federal Consumer Protection: Laws, Rules and Regulations, 1 volume.
       Dobbs Ferry, NY: Oceana, 1979-   (loose-leaf).

1727. Rothstein, M.A.   Occupational Safety and Health Law. St. Paul,
       MN: West, 1978. 594pp.

1728. Shapo, M.S.   A Nation of Guinea Pigs: The Unknown Risks of
       Chemical Technology. New York: Free Press, 1979. 300pp.

1729. Toxic Substances Sourcebook: The Professional's Guide to the
       Information Sources, Key Literature and Laws of a Critical
       New Field, edited by S. Ross and M. Pronin. New York:
       Environment Information Center, 1978. 560pp.

1730. Vaughn, R.C.   Legal Aspects of Engineering, 3rd edition.
       Dubuque, IA: Kendall/Hunt, 1977. 279pp.

to H.2   PRODUCT SAFETY AND LIABILITY:

1731. National Research Council, Bureau of Biomedical Sciences Review
       Committee, Committee on Toxicology. A Review of the Role
       of the Health Sciences in the Consumer Product Safety
       Commission. Washington, DC: National Academy of Sciences, 1977.

1732. World Congress on Product Liability, 1st, London, 1977.
       Proceedings and Program Materials, 2 volumes. Charlottes-
       ville, VA: The Research Group International, 1977.

to H.3 FOOD PURITY AND QUALITY

1733. National Academy of Sciences. Food Safety Policy: Scientific
       and Societal Considerations, 2 volumes. Washington, DC:
       Assembly of Life Sciences, National Research Council, and
       Institute of Medicine, National Academy of Sciences, 1979.

to H.5 NARCOTICS AND ADDICTION:

1734. Weissman, J.C. Drug Abuse: The Law and Treatment Alternatives.
       Cincinnati, OH: Anderson, 1978. 339pp.

to H.6 AUTOMOBILE AND TRAFFIC HAZARDS:

1735. Manne, H.G., and R.L. Miller, eds. Auto Safety Regulation:
       The Cure or the Problem? Glen Ridge, NJ: T. Horton, 1976.
       144pp.

to H.7 NUCLEAR HAZARDS:

1736. International Nuclear Law Association. Congresses.
       Nuclear Inter Jura '73 (Karlsruhe, 1973), 513pp. and
       Nuclear Inter Jura '75 (Aix-en-Provence, 1975), 279pp.

to I.   NATURAL RESOURCES AND ENVIRONMENTAL CONTROLS, NATIONAL AND
        INTERNATIONAL:

1737. Baker, M.S., J.S. Kaming, and R.E. Morrison. Environmental
       Impact Statements: A Guide to Preparation and Review.
       New York: Practising Law Institute, 1977. 334pp.

1738. Environmental Law Handbook, 5th edition, by J. Gordon Arbuckle,
       et al. Washington, DC: Government Institutes, 1978. 560pp.

1739. Erçman, S. European Environmental Law: Legal and Economic
       Appraisal. Bern: Bubenberg, 1977. 508pp.

1740. "Health Hazards in the Environment: The Interface of Science and
       Law," 8 Environmental Law 645-868 (1978(.

1741. Legal Protection of the Environment in Developing Countries:
       Colloquium of the International Association of Legal Science,
       edited by I. Carrillo Prieto and R. Nocedal. Mexico:
       Universidad Nacional Autónoma de México, Instituto de Inves-
       tigaciones Jurídicas, 1976. 463pp.

1742. Organization for Economic Cooperation and Development. Legal
       Aspects of Transfrontier Pollution. Paris: OECD, 1977. 487pp.

1743. Stewart, R.B., and J.E. Krier. Environmental Law and Policy:
       Readings, Materials and Notes, 2nd edition. Indianapolis, IN:
       Bobbs-Merrill, 1978. 1026pp.

1744. Toxic Torts: Tort Action for Cancer and Lung Disease Due to Environmental Pollution. P.D. Rheingold, N.J. Landau, and M.M. Canavan. Washington, DC: Association of Trial Lawyers of America, 1977. 448pp.

1745. Worsham, J.P. The National Environmental Policy Act and Related Materials: A Selected Bibliography. Monticello, IL: Vance, 1978. 24pp.

to I.1 NATURAL RESOURCES AND ENVIRONMENTAL CONTROLS, CURRENT SOURCES:

1746. Solar Law Reporter.
   v.1- 1979- bimonthly.
   Golden, CO: Solar Energy Research Institute for the U.S.
   Department of Energy.
   Includes "Solar Energy Legal Bibliography."

to I.5 ENERGY:

1747. Kraemer, S.F. Solar Law: Present and Future, with Proposed Forms. Colorado Springs, CO: Shepard's, 1978. 364pp.

1748. Thomas, W.A., A.S. Miller, and R.L. Robbins. Overcoming Legal Uncertainties about the Use of Solar Energy Systems. Chicago, IL: American Bar Foundation, 1978. 80pp.

to I.6 WEATHER MODIFICATION:

1749. Davis, R.J., and L.O. Grant. Weather Modification: Technology and Law. Boulder, CO: Westview Press for the American Association for the Advancement of Science, 1978. 124pp.

1750. Hemel, E.I., and C.G. Holderness. An Environmentalist's Primer on Weather Modification. Stanford, CA: Stanford Environmental Law Society, 1977. 106pp.

to J.1 SCIENCE AND INTERNATIONAL LAW, CURRENT SOURCES:

1751. Ocean Yearbook.
   v.1- 1978- annual.
   Chicago, IL: University of Chicago Press.
   Edited by E.M. Borgese and N. Ginsburg.

1752. The United Nations Disarmament Yearbook.
   v.1- 1976- annual.
   New York: United Nations Centre for Disarmanent.

to J.2 AVIATION LAW:

1753. Speiser, S.M. and C.F. Krause. Aviation Tort Law, 3 volumes.
       Rochester, NY: Lawyers Co-operative Publishing Company,
       1978-   .

to J.3 OUTER SPACE:

1754. Manual on Space Law, compiled and edited by N. Jasentuliyana
       and R.S.K. Lee. Dobbs Ferry, NY: Oceana, 1979. 2 volumes.

to J.4 SEA AND SEA RESOURCES:

1755. Baram, M.S., D.Rice, and W. Lee. Marine Mining of the Continen-
       tal Shelf: Legal, Technical and Environmental Considerations.
       Cambridge, MA: Ballinger, 1978. 301pp.

1756. Galey, M.E. Marine Environmental Affairs Bibliography.
       Kingston, RI: Law of the Sea Institute, University of Rhode
       Island, 1977. 131pp.

1757. Odidi Okidi, C. Regional Control of Ocean Pollution: Legal and
       Institutional Problems and Prospects. Alphen aan den Rijn:
       Sijthoff & Nordhoff, 1978. 283pp.

1758. United Nations Conference on the Law of the Sea, 3rd, New York and
       Caracas, 1973-   . Official Records. New York: United
       Nations, 1975-   .

to·J.5 ARMS CONTROL AND DISARMAMENT:

1759. Diplomatic Conference on the Reaffirmation and Development of
       International Humanitarian Law Applicable in Armed Conflicts,
       1st-4th, Geneva, 1974-1977. Official Records, 17 volumes.
       Bern: Federal Political Department, 1978.

1760· United Nations, Dag Hammarskjöld Library. Disarmament: A Select
       Bibliography, 1973-1977. New York: United Nations, 1978.
       139pp. (Continues entry no. 1389.)

to J.5.a CHEMICAL AND BIOLOGICAL WARFARE:

1761. Meselson, M., ed. Chemical Weapons and Chemical Arms Control.
       New York: Carnegie Endowment for International Peace, 1978.
       128pp. (From a conference at the American Academy of Arts
       and Sciences, Boston.)

to K. GOVERNMENT, LAW, AND SCIENTIFIC RESEARCH:

1762. Hill, C.T. Federal Regulation and Chemical Innovation, ACS Symposium Series 109. Washington, DC: American Chemical Society, 1979. (See N.A. Ashford and G.R. Heaton, "The Effects of Health and Environmental Regulation on Technological Change in the Chemical Industry: Theory and Evidence".)

1763. Houdek, F.G. The Freedom of Information Act: A Comprehensive Bibliography of Law Related Materials. Austin, TX: Tarlton Law Library, University of Texas School of Law, 1978. 46pp.

1764. Metric System Guide. v.1-   1974-   . Neenah, WI: J.J. Keller. Loose-leaf volumes. Vol. 2: Legislation and Regulatory Activities.

1765. Sofaer, A.D. "The Science Court: Unscientific and Unsound," 9 Environmental Law 1-27 (1978).

1766. "Symposium: Biotechnology and the Law: Recombinant DNA and the Control of Scientific Research," 51 Southern California Law Review 969-1554 (1978). Twenty-one articles, including "The Scientists's Right to Research: A Constitutional Analysis" by J.A. Robertson, "A Purposive Analysis of Constitutional Standards of Judicial Review and a Practical Assessment of the Constitutionality of Regulating Recombinant DNA Research" by R.G. Spece, Jr., and "Health Hazards Associated with Recombinant DNA Technology: Should Congress Impose Liability Without Fault?" by J.M. Friedman.

1767. U.S. Law Enforcement Assistance Administration, National Criminal Justice Information and Statistics Service. Confidentiality of Research and Statistical Data: A Compendium of State Legislation. Washington, DC: U.S. Government Printing Office, 1978. 128pp.

1768. U.S. Library of Congress, Science Policy Research Division. Federal Management of Scientific and Technical Information. R.L. Chartrand and R.A. Chalk. Washington, DC: U.S. Government Government Printing Office, 1975. 104pp.

1769. Wax, M.L., and J. Cassell, eds. Federal Regulations: Ethical Issues and Social Research. Boulder, Co: Westview Press, 1979. (AAAS Selected Symposium Series, No. 36.)

to K.2 TAXATION AND RESEARCH:

1770. Postlewaite, P.F. "Deductibility of Expenses for Conventions and Educational Seminars," 2 Review of Taxation of Individuals 203-240 (1978).

1771. Taxing the Brain Drain, two volumes, edited by J.M. Bhagwati and M. Partington. Amsterdam: North-Holland; New York: American Elsevier, 1976.

to K.3.a PATENTS:

1772. Chisum, D.S.   Patents : A Treatise on the Law of Patentability,
      Validity and Infringement, 5 volumes.
      New York: Bender, 1978-   (loose-leaf).

1773. Walton, A.M., and H.I.L. Laddie.   Patent Law of Europe and the
      United Kingdom, 1 volume. London: Butterworths,
      1978-   (loose-leaf).

to K.3.b COPYRIGHT:

1774. Dietz, A.   Copyright Law in the European Community: A Comparative
      Investigation of National Copyright Legislation.   Alphen aan
      den Rijn: Sijthoff & Noordhoff, 1978. 312pp.

1775. Henry, N., ed.   Copyright, Congress and Technology: The Public
      Record, 4 volumes. Phoenix, AZ: Oryx, 1978-   . Vol. 4:
      CONTU: The Future of Information Technology.

1776. Saltman, R.G.   Copyright in Computer-Readable Works: Policy
      Impacts of Technological Change, 1 volume. National Bureau
      of Standards. Washington, DC: U.S. Government Printing Office,
      1977.

1777. Seltzer, L.E.   Exemptions and Fair Use in Copyright: The
      Exclusive Rights Tensions in the 1976 Copyright Act. Cambridge,
      MA: Harvard University Press, 1978. 199pp.

1778. U.S. National Commission on New Technological Uses of Copyrighted
      Works.   Final Report. Washington, DC: CONTU, 1978. 201,144pp.

to K.4 DISTRIBUTION OF IDEAS AND INFORMATION, INCLUDING COMMUNICATIONS:

1779. Adkinson, B.W.   Two Centuries of Federal Information.
      Stroudsburg, PA: Dowden, Hutchinson & Ross, 1978. 235pp.
      (Government gathering of scientific and technical information.)

1780. Ginsburg, D.H.   Regulation of Broadcasting: Law and Policy
      Towards Radio, Television and Cable Communications. St. Paul,
      MN: West, 1979. 741pp.

INDEX

Environmental Law Institute, 1051, 1187
Environmental Mutagen Society, 948
Epilepsy Foundation of America, 543
Epstein, S.S., 948
Epstein, W., 1369
Erçman, Seviç, 1739
Ernst, Morris L., 19, 20
Ervin, S.J., 480
Erwin, Richard E., 1011
Estep, Samuel, 1207
European Atomic Energy Community
   (EURATOM), 1188
European Conference of Directors of
   Criminological Research Institutes,
   999
European Space Research Organization,
   1288
Evan, W.M., 77, 162
Evers, R.C., 1421

Fairley, William B., 282, 336
Falk, R.A., 1237
Farnsworth, D.L., 1717
Farrell, R.T., 769
Farrington, Benjamin, (pp. viii, ix)
Fasan, E., 1289
Fawcett, J.E.S., 1290
Feld, B.T., 1358, 1380
Feldman, W.M., (p. xvi)
Feldstein, P.J., 544
Feliciano, F.P., 1238
Fellner, B.A., 871
Ferguson, J. Ray, 1726
Ferster, E.Z., 756
Field, Thomas G., 1637
Finch, Henry, (p. viii)
Finch, J.R., 1012
Findley, R.W., 1163
Finegold, W.J., 681
Fingarette, Herbert, 949, 1713
Finkelstein, Louis, (p. xiv)
Finkelstein, Michael O., 282, 336, 1661
Fischer, G., 1408
Fisher, Edward C., 1013
Fisher, Roger, 1232
Fishman, Clifford S., 1684
Fleming, J.G., 328
Fletcher, Joseph Francis, 670, 740
Floyd, M.K., 615
Flynn, P.P., 1268
Foley, H.A., 770
Food and Drug Law Institute, 926
Force, Robert, 1724
Ford Foundation, 950, 1725
Forensic Sciences Foundation, 381
Forman, Howard I., 1523, 1536
Forte, W.E., 914
Foust, L.L., 778
Fox, R.M., 545
Fox, Vernon, 1652
Franck, T.M., 1246

Frank, Jerome, 78, 293
Frankena, William K., 664
Frederick II (King of Prussia),
   (p. xiv)
Freed, R. N.,337, 411, 546
Freedman, D., 942
Freedman, Warren, 79, 547
Freeman, Charles M., 1671
Fremouw, W.J., 792
Frenkel, D.A., 837
Freud, Sigmund, (p. xi)
Freund, P.A., 838
Fried, Charles, 188, 189, 839
Friedman, James, 302
Friedman, Jane M., 741, 840, 1766
Friedman, L.M., 81, 82, 83, 84
Friedman, P.R., 1714
Friedmann, W.G., 85, 190
Fuller, Lon L., 51, 86, 191, 192, 193,
   194
Fysh, M., 1580

Galey, Margaret E., 1756
Galileo (Galileo Galilei), (pp. viii, x
   xi)
Gallant, Donald M., 1724
Gamble, J.K., Jr., 1330
Garner, J.F., 1135
Gebhard, Paul H., 672
Gee, D.J., 397
Gelfand, L., 538
Gellhorn, Walter, (p. xii), 1431
George, B.J., Jr., 323
George Washington University, Program o
   Policy Studies in Science and
   Technology, 1189
Gerard, A., 909, 915
Gerety, T., 468
Gershenson, Daniel E., (p. ix)
Gibson, George H., 1609
Gilchrist, B., 433
Gilchrist, I., 841
Gillam, C.W., 1014
Gilmer, W., Jr., 548
Gilpin, Robert, 1432
Ginger, Raymond S., (p. xi)
Ginsburg, Douglas, 1779
Ginsburg, Norman, 1751
Glantz, L.H., 833
Gluckman, M., 87
Glueck, Eleanor, 256
Glueck, Sheldon, 256, 771
Golann, S., 792
Gold, Martin B., 963
Gold, Martin E., 1610
Goldberg, A.L., 981
Goldberg, E.M., 466
Goldie, L.F.E., 1054
Golding, M.P., 195, 742
Goldsmith, L.S., 594
Goldstein, Irving, 549

Hodson, F.C., 29
Hoebel, E.A., 96, 108
Hoffman, D., 470
Hoffman, P.B., 778
Hofstadter, Samuel H., 472
Hogan, Daniel B., 1715
Hohfeld, Wesley N., 173, 197
Holder, A.R., 556, 557, 1695
Holderness, Clifford G., 1750
Holmes, Grace W., 434
Holmes, Oliver W., 11, 97
Honoré, A.M., 288
Hood, V., 1294
Hoorn, J.V., Jr., 1495
Hopkins, B.R., 1496, 1497
Horan, D.J., 844
Horowitz, D.L., 98
Horowitz, George, 472
Horowitz, Joseph, 198
Horowitz, Lester, 1528
Horvath, F., 1668
Horwitz, M.J., 99
Hotchen, J.S., 953
Houdek, Frank G., 1763
House of Representatives, U.S.
    (See U.S. Congress)
Houts, Marshall, 312, 538, 558, 559
Howe, Mark DeW., 97
Howell, Herbert A., 1565
Huang, Te-Hsien, 1566, 1567
Hughes, G.B.J., 199
Hughes, K.B., 338
Hugo, M., 427
Huisken, R., 1357
Humber, J.M., 560
Hunter, B.T., 916
Hursh, Robert D., 897
Hutchins, Robert M., 295, 1242
Huxley, Julian S., (p. xi), 14
Hydeman, Lee M., 1022, 1027
Hyland, W.F., 653

Ihering (See Jhering)
Inbau, Fred E., 369, 370, 373, 384, 612,
    1665
Indiana University, Institute for Sex
    Research, 672
Institute of Continuing Legal Education
    (See Michigan, University of)
Institute of Medicine, 1733
_____, Division of
    Legal, Ethical, and Educational
    Aspects of Health, 1696
Institute for Defense Analyses (IDA),
    385
Interamerican Conference on Legal
    Medicine and Forensic Science, 562
Inter-Governmental Maritime Consulta-
    tive Organization, 1325
International Atomic Energy Agency,
    1028, 1192, 1409

International Civil Aviation Organiza-
    tion, 1270
International Nuclear Law Association,
    1736
International Peace Academy, 1326
International Telecommunication Union,
    1614
International Union for Conservation of
    Nature and Natural Resources, 1069
Irvine, L.M., 779

Jackson, C.O., 873
Jacobstein, Joseph Myron, 1153
Jacoby, H.D., 1139
Jacoby, J.E., 1719
Jaffe, L.L., 201, 1063
Jakobovits, Immanuel, (p. xiv)
Jaksetic, E., 565
James, Fleming, Jr., 289
James, H.J., 120
James, Patricia A., 445
James, S., 1559
Janda, K., 427, 449
Janicke, P.M., 1535
Jaress, R.P., 1589
Jarvik, L.G., 747
Jasentuliyana, Nandasiri, 1754
Jaszi, P.A., 961
Jehoram (See Cohen Jehoram)
Jenks, C. Wilfred, 1295
Jensen, O.C., 202
Jessup, Philip C., 1296
Jhering, R. von, 203
Johnson, A., 76
Johnson, B., 1064
Johnson, Harry M., 1640
Johnston, D.F., 1568
Johnston, D.M., 1333
Joint Committee of the ABA and the AMA
    on Narcotic Drugs, 955
Jonas, R.E., 1707
Jones, C.O., 1140
Jones, Edgar A., 413
Jones, Erin B., 1615
Jones, Harry W., (p. v), 13, 151, 424
Jones, J.K., 1442
Jones, W.R., 360
Jurewitz, J.L., 1180
Juris, G., 1066

Kadish, Sanford H., 664
Kalashnik, I.M., 1716
Kalisch, Beatrice J., 1641
Kalisch, J.R., 538
Kalven, Harry, Jr., 14, 56, 163
Kaming, Joseph S., 1737
Kamisar, Yale, 501
Kantrowitz, Arthur, 1434
Kaplan, J., 992
Kaplan, M.A., 1372

152

Warren, David G., 576, 1690, 1701
Warren, Earl, 462
Warren, Samuel D.. 483
Wasmuth, Carl E., 613
Wassenbergh, H.A., 1281
Wasserstrom, R.A., 237
Watson, A., 157
Watson, Andrew S., 1721
Wax, Murray L., 1769
Weber, Max, 158
Wecht, C.H., 593, 614
Wegner, G., 583
Weihofen, Henry, 774, 816, 817
Weiler, L.D., 1381
Weiner, A.S., 357
Weinstein, Jerry L., 1032
Weisband, E., 1246
Weissman, James C., 1734
Wellford, Harrison, 911
Wells, K.M., 406
Wells, L.T., Jr., 1205
Wentz, W.B., 1422
Wepman, Joseph M., 321
Werne, B., 306
Wessel, Milton R., 433, 484
West, D.J., 142, 1710
West, Ranyard, 1242
Westin, Alan F., 485, 486, 519, 520
Weston, P.B., 406
Wexler, D.B., 819
White, Andrew D., (p. x)
White, I.L., 1317, 1318
White, James B., 248
Whitebread, C.H., Jr., 988
Whiting, B., 148
Whitlock, F.A., 820, 979
Whitman, T.L., 46
Wick, W.A., 316
Wiggins, James Russell, 1634
Wigmore, J.H., 283
Wiles, P., 142
Wilhelm, Paul L., 377
Willey, D., 1408
Williams, Edward Bennett, 501
Williams, Glanville L., 669, 678
Williams, Harold, 577, 578
Williams, M.P., 1233
Williams & Wilkins Co., 1588
Willy, F.J., 521
Wilson, C.E., 1318
Wilson, J.B., 668
Wilson, John Pasley, 862, 1722
Wilson, Paul E., 356
Winner, R., 1352
Wise, Aaron N., 1601
Wojcichowsky, S., 735
Wolff, Christian, 1247
Wolff, Robert P., 1651
Wolfman, Bernard, 13, 1503
Wood, D.J., 346
Wood, L.D., 1215
Woodbridge, R.C., 1635

Woodhead, W.W., 1324
World Health Organization (WHO), 736, 629
World Intellectual Property Organization (WIPO), 1526, 1527
Worsham, John P., 1745
Worthley, J.A., 464
Wright, Burton, 1652
Wright, C., 1432
Wright, G.P., 1160
Wright, R.R., 1282
Wulff, T., 1365
Wurfel, S.W., 1343, 1344

Yntema, Hessel E., 216
Young, J.B., 487

Zander, Michael, 160
Zarafonetis, C.J.D., 954
Zavala, A., 407
Zeisel, Hans, 14, 141, 161, 162, 163
Zelermyer, William, 488
Zhukov, G.P., 1320
Ziegel, J.S., 164
Zillman, D.N., 1217
Ziskin, J., 325